D1069006

THE RUSSIAN REVOLUTION AND THE
SOVIET STATE 1917–1921

THE
RUSSIAN REVOLUTION
AND THE
SOVIET STATE 1917–1921

Documents

Selected and edited by
MARTIN McCAULEY

First published 1975 by
THE MACMILLAN PRESS LTD
London and Basingstoke

Published in the U.S.A. 1975 by
HARPER & ROW PUBLISHERS, INC.
BARNES & NOBLE IMPORT DIVISION

ISBN 0–06–494678–9

Printed in Great Britain

For
Marta and John

Contents

List of Maps

These maps are taken from *Russian History Atlas* by Martin Gilbert (London 1972), pp. 84, 86–97, 100, 102–4, 106.

Preface

The revolution of October 1917 in Russia is one of the turning points of contemporary history. Its significance and influence can be felt in most countries of the world today. That a Communist party should seize power in an industrially underdeveloped country was a surprise; that it should hold on to power was a shock to most observers outside Russia. Indeed few of those living and politically active in Russia in 1917 seem to have realised the way the political tide was flowing, and many were unprepared for the harsh realities of the post-October Russia.

The October revolution stirred the radical and revolutionary wing of the Marxist movement. Never again would the cautious, unprovocative, legalistic, parliamentary approach of the German Social Democratic Party exert great influence on the course of working class politics as it had done in the pre-1914 days. War and revolution accorded the accolade of success to Lenin's interpretation of Marx's writings. The extreme left had triumphed. They had carried through the first successful radical revolution in modern times which had not succumbed to a counter-revolution. The world would never be the same again. Moderates would find it difficult henceforth to win respect and authority.

Rosa Luxemburg saw the dangers of presenting the Bolshevik revolution as a model for the world to follow. She understood the disadvantages and temptations of the dictatorship of a small group instead of the dictatorship of a whole class, the working class. Her voice was soon silenced in Germany and her strictures fell on deaf ears since no other country staged a successful revolution for a generation.

It is perhaps in the developing world that the Bolshevik revolution has produced its greatest impact. Leninism, or twentieth-century Marxism, as the Soviets say, has provided a theoretical framework for radical revolutionary activity in lands which have not yet experienced advanced industrialisation. No longer is it considered necessary to wait for the development of industry before a Communist-inspired party can seize power. Take power first, then industrialise, is the message. The Mensheviks rejected this interpretation of Marx and perished in Russia.

This book is not a comprehensive history of the period. Many documents, which are easily available elsewhere, have not been included. Some documents are published for the first time, others for the first time in English.

I am particularly grateful to Nicholas Brown, Olga Crisp, Charles Drage, David Kirby, William Ryan and Janusz Tomiak, of the School of Slavonic Studies, University of London, to Marika Boshyk, of St Antony's College, University of Oxford, and to Barry Hollingsworth of the University of Manchester, for their valuable help in providing material, checking my translations and providing translations from languages which I do not know.

A special word of gratitude is due to those publishers who have permitted me to reprint extracts from their works; the list appears on page xv.

Finally I am deeply indebted to Chan Oi-han, Joan Cahill and Barbara Komoniewska for their skill and patience in transforming my almost illegible handwriting into typescript.

Martin McCauley

All dates before the October revolution (25 October) are according to the Julian calendar (Old Style). All dates after 25 October/ 7 November are according to the Gregorian calendar (New Style). To arrive at a date (New Style) before 25 October, add thirteen days.

Acknowledgements

The editor and publishers wish gratefully to acknowledge permission given by the following to reproduce documents in this volume:

Edward Arnold and Everett Jacobs: 7/10b
Bonnier Magazine Group: 9/3
Edicom: 5/6, 5/8, 5/9, 5/10, 5/13, 5/14, 5/15a, 5/21a, 5/22, 5/25a,b, 6/12, 6/13e, 6/15b, 7/6
Garnstone Press: 4/8
Izdatelstvo Politicheskoi Literatury (Moscow): 6/14a,b,c,d,e
Lawrence & Wishart: 5/2, 5/4a, 5/5, 6/2, 6/6, 6/9, 6/10, 7/3, 7/4, 7/10a, 7/17
Novoye Russkoye Slovo: 2/11c
Pathfinder Press Inc.: 10/1, 10/2
Penguin Books and Alec Nove: 7/18
Prentice-Hall Inc.: 3/2c
Werner Söderström: 9/4
Soviet Studies and David Collins: 4/10
Thames & Hudson and VEB Verlag der Kunst, Dresden: 8/2a,b,c,d
A. P. Watt & Son: 9/2
Weidenfeld & Nicolson and Martin Gilbert for the maps on pp. 76–111
Z. A. B. Zeman: 2/17a, 5/1

The private papers of Sir Bernard Pares are in the Library of the School of Slavonic and East European Studies, University of London.

1 The Revolution of February 1917

Modern war imposes a terrible burden on society. If victory is feasible then a nation may hold together. Faced with almost certain defeat a society is more likely than not to disintegrate. Two great empires, one in Russia, the other in Austria–Hungary, found the demands of modern war too much for them. The Russians succumbed first and had it not been for German support, Austria–Hungary would have retired before 1918. Germany, to the surprise of many, proved unequal to the task and was also engulfed by defeat and revolution. The revolution in February 1917 in Russia swept away the old order; the same occurred in Austria and Germany less than two years later.

War, therefore, was one of the principal reasons for revolution in Russia. The Tsarist régime could not adjust itself rapidly enough to the demands of a war of attrition. Its losses, in terms of human life, were fearful. Nevertheless the great upheaval came as a surprise to almost everyone. The imperial government had blundered through before, it would do so again, seemed to be in most people's minds. Even those who were venting their wrath on the autocracy, most notably Lenin in Switzerland, were surprised at the turn of events.

The lack of opposition to the revolution illustrates the weakness of the Tsar and his entourage. The monarch's own personal indecisiveness contributed greatly to this.

Two institutions stepped into the power vacuum. A provisional government was established to tide Russia over until a constituent assembly could agree on a constitution and legally establish a government (1/9). The soviet of workers' and soldiers' deputies, based on the experiences of 1905–7, spoke for those who did not feel they were represented in the new government. No one proposed a government of national unity. Social Democrats, Men-

sheviks and Bolsheviks alike, felt that since the revolution of
February was a bourgeois one, they could not participate in the
government. The soviet would support the government, if its
decisions met with its approval, but would not accept any responsibility for them (1/8). This implied dual power. This was to
prove fatal to moderate opinion, both in the government and in
the soviet before long.

1/1   BACKGROUND STATISTICS

(a) POPULATION OF RUSSIA 1885–1913*

Territory	1885	1897	1913
50 provinces of European Russia	81,725,200	93,442,900	121,780,000
Caucasus	7,284,500	9,289,400	12,717,200
Siberia	4,313,700	5,758,800	9,894,500
Steppe Krai (Ural, Turgai, Akmolinsk and Semipalatinsk *oblasts*)	1,588,500	2,465,700	3,929,500
Central Asia	3,738,600	5,281,000	7,106,000
Russia (excluding Poland and Finland)	98,650,500	116,237,800	155,422,200†

  * From A. G. Rashin, *Naselenie Rossii za 100 let* (Moscow 1956) p. 26
  † Mathematical inaccuracy in original.

(b) GROWTH OF POPULATION IN ST PETERSBURG 1881–1917*

15 Dec	1881	928,000
12 Dec	1890	1,033,600
28 Jan	1897	1,264,700
15 Dec	1900	1,439,600
15 Dec	1910	1,905,600
mid-Dec	1914	2,217,500
mid-Dec	1917	2,300,000

  * From ibid., p. 112.

(c) GROWTH OF POPULATION IN MOSCOW 1882–1917

1882	753,500
1897	1,038,600
1902	1,174,700
1907	1,345,700
1912	1,617,700
1 Jan 1914	1,762,700
Sep 1917	1,854,400

 * From ibid., p. 115.

(d) RUSSIAN WAGE EARNERS IN 1917*

Type of work	Total	% of total
(1) Workers in manufacturing, metallurgy and mining, of which	3,643, 300	18.4
Mining and metallurgical	810,000	—
Workers in state-owned factories and artillery establishments	385,700	—
Workers in naval establishments	57,700	—
Workers in army repair shops and in other enterprises at the front	134,800	—
(2) Workers employed at home and in rural and urban workshops	3,500,000†	17.6
(3) Unskilled and casual labourers	1,500,000	7.5
(4) Building workers	1,500,000	7.5
(5) Railway workers and employees, of which	1,265,700	6.3
On lines in use	1,001,500	—
On lines under construction	202,300	—
Railway workshop workers	61,900	—
(6) Water transport workers and employees	500,000	2.5
(7) Postal and telegraph workers	91,000	0.5
(8) Agricultural workers	5,000,000	24.9
(9) Workers and employees in commercial establishments and in the catering trade	865,000	4.2
(10) Domestic servants, cleaners, etc.	2,100,000	10.6
	19,965,000	100.0

 * From L. S. Gaponenko, 'Rabochii Klass Rossii nakanune velikogo Oktyabrya', *Istoricheskie Zapiski*, Vol. 73 (Moscow 1963), p. 51 and O. Crisp, *Private Correspondence*.

 † Underestimate; estimates normally fluctuate between 5 and 10 millions.

Note: In assessing the number of wage earners attention should be paid to the fact that in some jobs seasonal work was normal, e.g. 2, 3, 4, 6 and 8.

(e) DISTRIBUTION OF FACTORIES AND LABOUR, 1 JANUARY 1917*

The following table, compiled by the Ministry of Trade and Industry, provides information on the distribution of factories and labour subject to the factory inspectorate on 1 January 1917.

Raion	Enterprises	Workers	% of total workers
Petrograd	1,617	345,438	16.·4
Moscow	4,055	1,000,114	47.6
Kiev	2,329	269,998	12.9
Kharkov–Ekaterinoslav	1,224	188,421	9.0
Volga	1,177	114,250	5.4
Caspian	711	63,776	3.1
Rostov	520	51,241	2.5
Urals	438	45,063	2.2
Transcaucasian	361	15,691	0.9
Total	12,432	2,093,881 †	100.0
Siberia	Not available		
Turkestan	Not available		

 * From Gaponenko, 'Rabochii Klass Rossii', p. 86.
 † Mathematical inaccuracy in original.

(f) COMPOSITION OF WORKERS IN ENTERPRISES UNDER THE
  SUPERVISION OF THE FACTORY INSPECTORATE BY 1917*

	Number	% of total
Workers, of which	2,093,862	100.0
Adult males	1,083,906	51.6
Adult females	717,134	33.7
Total	1,801,040	85.3
15 to 17-year-old males	141,849	6.7
females	101,017	4.9
Total	242,866	11.6
12 to 15-year-old boys	28,873	1.3
girls	21,088	1.1
Total	49,961	2.4

 * From ibid., p. 61.

The following table is the most detailed available on the number of enterprises and workers employed in the defence industry. It was compiled by the Special Conference on Defence and relates to the period 1 January to 1 May 1917.

(g) THE DEFENCE INDUSTRY IN 1917*

Raion	Enterprises	%	Workers	%
Moscow	1,228	23.3	845,198	13.4
Petrograd	670	12.7	304,134	15.6
Urals	477	9.0	289,650	14.9
Ekaterinoslav	275	5.2	136,718	7.0
Nizhny-Novgorod	305	5.8	85,264	4.3
Odessa	504	9.5	69,857	3.6
Rostov-on-Don	293	5.5	59,602	3.1
Siberian	933	17.8	42,806	2.2
Kharkov	201	3.8	38,897	1.7
Caucasian	204	8.8	30,638	1.6
Revel	41	0.8	28,277	1.5
Kiev	147	2.8	21,889	1.1
Total	5,278	100.0	1,952,930	100.0

* From ibid., pp. 70, 76.

There were 379,227 workers employed in Petrograd and Petrograd *raion* on 1 January 1917. The labour force of the metallurgical industry grew fastest during the war.

(h) FOREIGN CAPITAL IN MAJOR RUSSIAN INDUSTRIES 1893–1915*

(in million rubles†)

	Total	1893 Foreign	%	Total	1900 Foreign	%	Total	1915 Foreign	%
Mining									
Metallurgy	100.9	61.0	61	472.2	343.8	72	} 1700	740.8	} 63
Engineering									
Machinery	32.7	16.4	50	177.3	125.6	71		322.7	
Glass	9.1	0.2	2	59.1	26.6	45	129.9	185.7	14
Timber	8.1	0.2	2	17.8	7.8	44	74.4	24.3	32
Chemicals	17.1	9.4	55	93.8	29.3	31	173.2	70.8	41
Food Processing	94.8	8.0	8	158.3	11.4	7	447.8	34.6	8
Leather Processing	6.6	3.1	47	16.5	5.9	35	54.2	14.5	26
Paper	14.3	1.1	7	31.8	6.1	20	93.2	19.9	20
Textiles	225.9	37.0	26	373.7	71.4	20	729.2	115.0	21
Total	509.5	136.4	27	1,401.5	627.9	45	3,402.0	1,401.3	41

* From L. Ya. Eventov, *Inostrannye kapitaly v russkoi promyshelnnosti* (Moscow 1931), pp. 22–3.
† 10 rubles = £1.

(i) INVESTMENT IN JOINT STOCK COMPANIES (DEBENTURE CAPITAL NOT INCLUDED)*

Year: 1 Jan	Total capital	Foreign capital	Foreign as % of total
	(In million rubles)		
1881	331	53	16
1893	502	146	29
1900	1,508	640	42
1914	3,224	1,431	44

(Based on I. F. Gindin, *Russkie Kommercheskie Banki* (Moscow 1948) p. 448 and L. E. Shepelev, 'Aktsionernoe Uchreditelstvo v Rossii', in Akademiya Nauk, *Iz Istorii Imperializma v Rossii*, (Moscow/Leningrad 1959), pp. 134–82, especially pp. 152–3).

    * From O. Crisp, *Private Correspondence*.

(j) RUSSIA'S PUBLIC DEBT HELD ABROAD*

	Total on 1 July 1914 (in million rubles)	Estimated held abroad (in million rubles)	% held abroad	% of foreign holding in France
(1) Direct government debt	8,811	4,229	47.9	63.9
(2) Guaranteed debt†	4,317	1,726.8	40.0	59.4
(3) Municipal debt	563	420	74.6	52.2
In addition joint stock capital	5,124	2,242.9†	43.8	30·0

    * From ibid.

    † Mainly bonds of railway companies, the interest of which was guaranteed by the state.

    † Vainshtein added reserve capital, share capital in railways and foreign capital in private business (not in joint stock companies). His total was 2,849 million rubles.

(k) LITERACY RATES AMONG FACTORY WORKERS IN 1897 AND 1918*

(Percentages)

Trade	Average 1897	Total 1918	Men 1897	Men 1918	Women 1897	Women 1918
Mining &	31.8 ⎱ 70.0		33.5		12.2	
Metallurgy	38.2 ⎰		39.3	74.0	12.5	42.6
Metalworking	66.2	76.5	66.8	81.4	32.1	50.0
Machines, instruments †						
& apparatus	82.9	83.6	85.1	86.7	57.9	59.0
Processing of timber	58.4	69.6	59.6	84.3	28.6	46.6
Chemicals	49.7	70.0	55.8	78.7	30.3	54.7
Food & drink	49.7	66.0	52.6	75.0	28.9	48.3
Printing & allied trades		94.7	87.4	96.6	44.2	89.4
Textiles	38.9		53.9		12.2	
cotton		52.2		76.4		37.9
woollens		52.2		68.2		37.1
linen		55.5		78.3		40.3
Overall Average	50.3	64.0	57.8	79.2	21.3	44.2

* From ibid.

† It is not clear whether the group 'Machines, instruments, etc.' applies to the same group of trades at both dates; in 1897 it applied specifically to precision instruments, watches, etc. and it is possible that machine construction as such was included under metal working. (Based on A. G. Rashin, *Formirovanie Rabochego Klassa Rossii* (Moscow 1958), pp. 593–601.)

The above table is based on a third of the labour force in 1918. It probably underestimated the rural element who were literate. On the other hand, women represented a larger proportion of the labour force than was normally the case (31 per cent by 1913 as against 40 per cent in 1918).

1/2 THE CRITICAL FOOD SITUATION*

War broke out at the beginning of the harvest of 1914. The harvest yielded 3,509 million puds of cereals.† This was slightly less than the 1909–13 average but about a quarter less than the

* From O. Crisp and M. McCauley, *Private Correspondence*.

† The total quoted here and in subsequent years covers production in fifty-seven provinces of European and Asiatic Russia. Excluded are Russian Poland, Turkestan, Transcaucasia, the *guberniyas* of Kovno, Courland, Vilno, Grodno, Volhynia, Podoliya, Yakutsk, Kamchatka, Sakhalin and the Kuban. Only Russian Poland, Podoliya and Volhynia *guberniyas* and the Kuban make any serious difference.

record 1913 crop. Since exports in 1913–14 at 663 million puds were less than average, grain reserves in Russia at the outbreak of war totalled about 500 million puds.

Grain production in 1915 reached 4,006 million puds or 10 per cent above the 1909–13 average. Thus in the first two years of the war gross production was slightly above the 1909–14 average. However in 1916 and in 1917 production fell. In 1916 it was down to 3,319 million puds and in 1917 to 3,185 million puds. However since only about 100 million puds were exported during the war instead of an average 700 million puds before the war, the shortfall in the harvests was almost entirely made up.

The war created a great new consumer, in the form of a huge army.

NUMBER AND PERCENTAGE OF MEN MOBILIZED

	1914	1915	1916	Mid-1917
Number of men mobilized (millions)	6.5	11.2	14.2	15.1
Percentage of males of working age	14.9	25.2	35.7	36.7

Army rations normally included meat, butter and sugar. The peasant could seldom afford such items. Thus the impact of army demand was akin to an increase in urban demand. Such was the demand of the army for cereals such as buckwheat and millet that the civilian population was confronted with shortages, notwithstanding the fact that little was exported.

The army also required huge quantities of cereals, mainly oats, for its horses.

During the first two years of the war the army covered its cereal requirements comfortably but in 1916 and in 1917 it was seriously in deficit. The army bread ration was cut from 2.7 lb. to 2.3 lb. per day in December 1916 and to 1.8 lb. per day in March 1917.

The gross production of cereals during the period 1914–17 was such that there should have been no serious shortages throughout Russia. There were fewer peasants in the countryside due to mobilization. However the dislocation resulting from the war and the evacuation of civilians from conflict zones imposed an intolerable burden on communications. The disorganization of transport broke the country up into several isolated areas. The link between the food surplus areas of the south and southeast and the food deficit areas of the centre, north and northwest was broken.

Shortages occurred mainly in large cities, more so in Petrograd than in Moscow. Peasants who moved to Moscow normally kept some contact with their native village. Those who moved to Petrograd were in a different situation. The capital city was much farther away from the populous central agricultural region and this made it more difficult to maintain contact. Peasants were on average better off during the war because of the dry régime and the allowances paid for those in the armed forces. Money hoarding was not as attractive as before 1914 due to the suspension of convertibility into gold. Manufactured goods were expensive and hence not so attractive. The breakdown of communication often made it impossible to secure the necessary agricultural implements, etc. The peasants built up stocks of grain. These came in very useful during War Communism when food was in very short supply.

Shortages, inflated prices and general discontent were common occurrences. It was cold comfort to be informed by the government that adequate supplies were available and on their way. Communications, or the lack of them, played an important role in creating the circumstances which produced the February revolution in Petrograd.

1/3 UNOFFICIAL MEETING OF THE MEMBERS OF THE STATE DUMA, 27 FEBRUARY 1917*

All members of the Duma were present. Rodzyanko and the elders were at the table. The others were crowding around. Disturbed, agitated, as if pressing cordially together . . . Even people who had been enemies for years felt that here was something which was equally dangerous, threatening, repulsive to them all . . . This something was the street, the crowd in the street . . . Its breathing, which had come close, could be felt. From the street came That, about which very few were thinking then but

* From V. V. Shulgin, *Dni* (Belgrade 1925), pp. 158–62.

many probably sensed it unconsciously. Therefore they were pale with secretly contracting hearts. Death passed along the street, surrounded by a crowd of many thousands.

Rodzyanko proposed what came about. And he put the question: 'What is to be done?' to this quivering human mass milling around the table of the elders, pressed into the *Polutsirkulnaya* frame of the room.

In reply, here, there, on the right, on the left excited people wished to speak and something was proposed . . . What?

I do not know. I don't remember. Something. It appears that someone proposed that the State Duma should declare itself the government. If it did so it would not dissolve, it would not be subject to the ukaz. Declare itself the Constituent Assembly. This could not get support. It appears that Milyukov replied. In any case Milyukov spoke, recommending caution, recommending that too hasty decisions should not be taken, especially when we did not yet know what would happen and as is said, the old order has fallen, that it existed no more, when we on the whole did not understand the situation and do not know how serious, how resolute the incipient popular movement is . . .

Someone spoke and demanded that the Duma declare on which side it was: with the old order or with the people? With those people who were coming here and would be here soon and to whom an answer had to be given.

At that moment there was a commotion at the door, there was some kind of loud conversation, then the crowd parted and an officer rushed into the room.

He interrupted the session and stated in a loud resonant voice:

'Members of the Duma, I need to be defended. I am the commander of the guard, your guard, which took the State Duma. Some soldiers have broken in . . . My aide has been seriously injured. They wanted to kill me. I was just able to save myself. What is this? Help me!'

This caused even more alarm among the excited human mass. It appears that Rodzyanko told him that he was safe and could calm himself.

Kerensky began to speak at this moment.

'What has happened confirms that we must not lose any time. I am receiving reports constantly that the army is in revolt. They are going on to the streets. I am going to the regiments! It is necessary to know what I am to say to them. May I tell them that the State Duma is with them, that it is taking on itself responsibility and that it is leading the movement?'

I don't remember if Kerensky received an answer or not. It appears not. But he grew into a man of 'importance' at that very moment. He spoke decisively, powerfully and cogently. Words and gestures were precise, distinct, his eyes were blazing.

1/4 TELEGRAM OF 27 FEBRUARY 1917 FROM RODZYANKO, PRESIDENT OF THE STATE DUMA, TO THE TSAR*

The session of the State Duma has been suspended until April by Your Majesty's Ukaz. The last bulwark of order has been eliminated. The Government is absolutely powerless to suppress disorders. Nothing can be hoped from the troops of the garrison. The reserve battalions of the guard regiments are in rebellion. Officers are being killed. Having joined the crowds and the popular movement, they are proceeding to the Ministry of the Interior and the State Duma. Civil war has started and is spreading rapidly. Order the immediate calling of a new government according to the principles reported by me to Your Majesty in my telegram of yesterday. Cancel Your Imperial Ukaz, and order the reconvening of the legislative chambers. Make these measures known without delay through an Imperial manifesto. Your Majesty, do not delay. If the movement spreads to the army, the Germans will triumph, and the ruin of Russia, and with her the Dynasty, will become inevitable. In the name of all Russia I beg Your Majesty to fulfil the foregoing. The hour which will decide the fate of Yourself and of the motherland has come. Tomorrow it may already be too late.

RODZYANKO
President of the State Duma

* From *Krasnii Arkhiv* (Moscow–Leningrad 1927), Vol. 21, pp. 6–7.

1/5 TELEGRAM OF 28 FEBRUARY 1917 FROM
GENERAL ALEKSEEV, CHIEF OF STAFF OF THE
SUPREME COMMANDER TO ALL THE
COMMANDERS IN CHIEF*

. . . On February 27 about midday, the President of the State
Duma reported that the troops were going over to the side of the
population and killing their officers.

General Khabalov around midday on the 27th reported to
His Majesty that one company of the Pavlovsky Regiment's
reserve battalion had declared on February 26 that it would not
fire on the people. The Commander of a battalion of this regiment
was wounded by the crowd. On February 27 training detachments of the Volynsky Regiment refused to proceed against the
rebels, and its commander shot himself. Then this detachment
together with a company of the same regiment proceeded to the
quarters of other reserve battalions, and men from these units
began to join them . . .

On the 27th, after 7 p.m. The Minister of War reported that
the situation in Petrograd had become very serious. The few
units which have remained faithful to their duty cannot suppress
the rebellion, and troop units have gradually joined the rebels.
Fires have started. Petrograd has been placed under martial
law . . .

On February 28 at 1 a.m. His Majesty received a telegram
from General Khabalov stating that he could not restore order
in the capital. The majority of the units have betrayed their duty
and many have passed over to the side of the rebels. The troops
which have remained faithful to their duty, after fighting the
whole day, have suffered many casualties.

Towards evening the rebels seized the greater part of the capital,
and the small units, which have remained faithful to their oath,
have been rallied in the vicinity of the Winter Palace.

On February 28 at 2 a.m. the Minister of War reported that
the rebels had occupied the Mariinsky Palace and that the
members of the revolutionary government were there. On
February 28, at 8.25 a.m., General Khabalov reported that the
number of those who had remained faithful had dropped to 600

* From *Arkhiv Russkoi Revolyutsii* (Berlin 1922), Vol. 3, pp. 250–1.

infantrymen and 500 cavalrymen with 15 machine guns and 12 guns having only 80 cartridges and that the situation was extremely difficult ...

We have just received a telegram from the Minister of War, stating that the rebels have seized the most important buildings in all parts of the city. Due to fatigue and propaganda the troops have laid down their arms, passed to the side of the rebels, or become neutral. In the streets disorderly shooting is going on all the time; all traffic has stopped; officers and soldiers who appear in the streets are being disarmed.

The ministers are all safe, but apparently the work of the Ministry has stopped.

According to private information, the President of the State Council Shcheglovitov, has been arrested. In the State Duma, a council of party leaders has been formed to establish contact for the revolutionary government with institutions and individuals. Supplementary elections to the Petrograd Soviet of Workers' and Soldiers' Deputies from the workers and the rebel troops have been announced.

We have just received a telegram from General Khabalov which shows that actually he cannot any longer influence events. Communicating to you the foregoing, I should add that we, the active army, all have the sacred duty before the Tsar and the motherland to remain true to our duty and to our oath, and to maintain railway traffic and the flow of food. 1813. ALEKSEEV. February 28.

1/6 NICHOLAS II ABDICATES*

To the Chief of Staff

In the days of great struggle with an external foe, who has been striving for almost three years to enslave our native land, it has been God's will to visit upon Russia a new grievous trial. The internal disturbances which have begun among the people threaten to have a calamitous effect on the future conduct of a hard-fought war. The destiny of Russia, the honour of our heroic army, the welfare of the people, the whole future of our beloved fatherland

* From N. de Basily, *Diplomat of Imperial Russia 1903–1917 Memoirs* (Stanford, California 1973), pp. 187–8.

demand that the war be carried to a victorious conclusion no matter what the cost. The cruel foe is straining his last resources and the time is already close at hand when our valiant army, together with our glorious allies, will be able to crush the foe completely. In these decisive days in the life of Russia, We have deemed it Our duty in conscience to help Our people to draw closer together and to unite all the forces of the nation for a speedier attainment of victory, and, in agreement with the State Duma, We have judged it right to abdicate the Throne of the Russian State and to lay down the Supreme Power. Not wishing to be parted from Our beloved Son, We hand over Our succession to Our Brother, the Grand Duke Mikhail Alexandrovich, and bless Him on his accession to the Throne of the Russian State. We enjoin Our Brother to conduct the affairs of the state in complete and inviolable union with the representatives of the people in the legislative bodies on the principles to be established by them, and to take an inviolable oath to this effect. In the name of the dearly beloved native land, We call upon all true sons of the Fatherland to fulfil their sacred duty to It by their obedience to the Tsar at this time of national trial and to help Him, together with the people's representatives, to lead the Russian State onto the path of victory, prosperity, and glory. May the Lord God help Russia!

Nicholas

Pskov, March 2, 1917, 3:00 p.m.

Minister of the Imperial Court, Chief-Aide-de-Camp Count Fredericks

1/7 GRAND DUKE MIKHAIL REFUSES THE THRONE*

During the conference on the morning of March 3 [A. F. Kerensky's] opinion that it was necessary to convince the Grand Duke to abdicate had a decisive influence. N. V. Nekrasov had already prepared a draft for the abdication. The opposite view, that of conserving a constitutional monarchy until the Constituent

* From P. N. Milyukov, *Istoriya vtoroi Russkoi Revolyutsii* (Sofia 1921), Vol. 1, pp. 53–5.

Assembly had met, was held only by P. N. Milyukov. After many exchanges, it was decided that both sides should put their opposite points of view to the Grand Duke and should leave the decision to the Grand Duke without entering into further discussions. About midday Prince G. E. Lvov, P. N. Milyukov, A. F. Kerensky and other members of the government and M. V. Rodzyanko. V. V. Shulgin and other members of the Temporary Committee assembled at the home of the Grand Duke on Millionaya Street. The need to abdicate was argued at length by M. V. Rodzyanko, and then by A. F. Kerensky. After them, P. N. Milyukov developed his point of view that a strong authority, which was essential for the strengthening of the new order, required the support of a symbol of power, to which the masses were accustomed. He said that the Provisional Government alone, without a monarch, represented 'an unseaworthy boat' which might sink in an ocean of popular unrest; in this case, the country would be in danger of losing all consciousness of a state system and of falling into complete anarchy, before the meeting of the Constituent Assembly; alone, the Provisional Government would not live long enough to see it, etc. Despite what had been previously agreed, this speech was followed by other speeches of a polemical nature. Then P. N. Milyukov asked to speak a second time, and, despite the heated objections of A. F. Kerensky, his request was granted. In his second speech he stressed that, although those who were saying that the acceptance of power would jeopardise the personal safety of the Grand Duke and of the ministers themselves were right, this risk should be taken in the interests of the motherland, for only thus could the persons involved be freed from their responsibility for the future. Besides, outside Petrograd there was every possibility of gathering together the military force necessary for the protection of the Grand Duke. Only A. I. Guchkov supported P. N. Milyukov. Both sides declared that in the event of a decision contrary to their views, they would not object and would support the Government, although they would not take part in it.

After the speeches, the Grand Duke, who had remained silent all the time, asked for some time to think the matter over. Going to another room, he invited M. V. Rodzyanko to follow him so as to talk with him alone. When he returned to the deputies waiting for him, he said quite firmly that his final decision was the same as that of the President of the State Duma. Then A. F. Kerensky made a pathetic declaration: 'Your Highness, you are a noble man!' He added that henceforth he would always state this. Kerensky's pathos was out of tune with the decision being taken. Not love and grief for Russia but only personal fear was behind it.

1/8 ATTITUDE OF THE EXECUTIVE COMMITTEE OF THE PETROGRAD SOVIET ON THE QUESTION OF PARTICIPATION IN THE PROVISIONAL GOVERNMENT*

Before the meeting, there was an informal conference with the deputies of the soldiers who had become members of the Soviet. They were informed about what had been done on 1 March. While this conference was in session, news was received of trouble in the Life Guard Regiment. Ten men from those present were sent at once to the different regiments to calm them and explain Order No. 1 to them.

A speech by N. S. Chkheidze ended the conference. He greeted the revolutionary army in the name of the working class and of the people who had revolted.

In the regular order of business, the report of the Executive Committee on its negotiations with the Temporary Committee of the State Duma was submitted, on the subject of the formation of a provisional government and the attitude of the Executive Committee of the Soviet Workers' and Soldiers' Deputies towards such a government. The Executive Committee refused to participate in the Provisional Government and made the following demands:

1. Complete and immediate amnesty for all charged with political and religious crimes, terroristic acts, military uprisings, etc.
2. Political freedom in all its forms: freedom of speech, press, unions, meetings, and strikes; this freedom to apply equally to the army.
3. The organisation of the army on the basis of self-government. The Duma Committee believed that it was impossible, during

* From *Izvestiya*, 3 March 1917.

wartime, to introduce a system that had not been tried out by any other army in the world. After considerable discussion, the Duma Committee had agreed that while on duty the soldier should be subject to strict military discipline, but when off duty he should have the same rights afforded other Russian citizens.

4.   The organisation of a civilian militia to enforce order; this militia to be subject to the local authorities, elected on the basis of universal, equal, direct, and secret suffrage.

5.   The abolition of all class, nationality, and religious restrictions.

6.   The garrison of Petrograd not to be removed from the city and not to be disarmed.

All the above were accepted unanimously by the Duma Committee.

The proposition to establish a democratic republic immediately, was rejected on the grounds that the form of government for the Russian Empire was a matter for the Constituent Assembly, and that the Provisional Government would call such a body in the very near future.

A. F. Kerensky was offered the office of Minister of Justice, and N. S. Chkheidze that of Minister of Labour, but the Executive Committee did not give them its permission to accept these offices.

The Executive Committee recommended that the Soviet of Workers' Deputies should take note of the intended declaration of the newly formed Government to appeal to the inhabitants to organise, to establish order, and to support the Provisional Government in so far as it followed the directives laid out above.

Following the report of the Executive Committee, Kerensky, in a powerful and ardent speech, appealed to the Soviet, as a whole, to approve his action in accepting the duties of Minister of Justice in the Provisional revolutionary Government. Kerensky's speech was received with thunderous applause, which turned into a long ovation.

In the debate that followed, two points of view were brought out: one against contact with the Duma Committee and demanding a provisional government of the Soviet of Soldiers' and Workers' Deputies; and the other in favour of having a representative of the Soviet of Deputies in the Provisional Government . . .

After vigorous discussion, all the recommendations of the report of the Executive Committee were approved, with the following corrections:

1. The Provisional Government should proceed to carry out the indicated measures, despite the fact that the country is in a state of war.
2. The Manifesto of the Provisional Government should be signed both by the Government and by M. Rodzyanko.
3. A paragraph should be included in the programme of the Provisional Government giving cultural and national self-determination to all nationalities.
4. A committee of representatives from the Soviet of Soldiers' and Workers' Deputies should be formed to supervise the acts of the Provisional Government.

All the corrections were accepted by an overwhelming majority. The session lasted about seven hours. The next session was set for 6 p.m. on 3 March.

1/9   THE FIRST PROVISIONAL GOVERNMENT*

The Temporary Committee of the members of the State Duma, with the help and the support of the army and the inhabitants of the capital, has now attained such a large measure of success over the dark forces of the old régime that it is possible for the Committee to undertake the organisation of a more stable executive power.

With this end in mind, the Temporary Committee of the State Duma has appointed the following persons as ministers of the first cabinet representing the public; their past political and public activities assure them the confidence of the country:

Minister-President and Minister of the Interior
Prince G. E. Lvov (Non-Party)
Minister of Foreign Affairs   P. N. Milyukov (Kadet)
Minister of War and Navy   A. I. Guchkov (Octobrist)
Minister of Transport   N. V. Nekrasov (Kadet)
Minister of Trade and Industry   A. I. Konovalov (Kadet)
Minister of Finance   M. I. Tereshchenko (Non-Party)

* From *Izvestiya*, 3 March 1917.

Minister of Education	A. A. Manuilov (Kadet)
Ober-Procurator of the Holy Synod	V. N. Lvov (Centrist)
Minister of Agriculture	A. I. Shingarev (Kadet)
Minister of Justice	A. F. Kerensky (SR)

The actual work of the cabinet will be guided by the following principles:

1. An immediate and complete amnesty in all cases of a political and religious nature, including terrorist acts, military revolts and agrarian offences, etc.

2. Freedom of speech, press, and assembly, and the right to form unions and to strike and the extension of political freedom to persons serving in the armed forces limited only by the demands of military and technical circumstances.

3. The abolition of all restrictions based on class, religion, and nationality.

4. The immediate arrangements for the calling on the Constituent Assembly on the basis of universal, equal and direct suffrage and secret ballot, which will determine the form of government and the constitution of the country.

5. The substitution of a people's militia for the police, with elective officers responsible to the organs of local self-government.

6. Elections to the organs of local self-government are to be held on the basis of universal, equal and direct suffrage and secret ballot.

7. Those military units which took part in the revolutionary movement shall be neither disarmed nor withdrawn from Petrograd.

8. While preserving strict military discipline on duty and during military service, the soldiers are to be freed from all restrictions in the exercise of those civil rights which all other citizens enjoy.

The Provisional Government wishes to add that it has no intention whatsoever of taking advantage of the military situation to delay in any way the carrying through of the reforms and the measures outlined above.

2 Russia Between Two Revolutions: Political Aspects of the Period February to October 1917

Much was expected of the first Provisional Government. Soldiers awaited an end to the war; peasants hoped for more land; workers looked forward to an amelioration of working conditions and an improvement in their living standards; the politically articulate wanted freedom of association, a free press, etc.; the subject nationalities dreamed of self-determination and autonomy, the Allies aimed at encouraging Russia to stay in the war until victory was secure; in short, everyone expected a better life now that the Tsar and his autocratic rule had been toppled. Under peacetime conditions a Russian government would have found it difficult to measure up to expectations. War, hunger and, most important of all, the fact that it was only provisional, temporary, combined to confront the government with an almost insuperable task. The Petrograd Soviet regarded itself as much more democratic than the government. It was. The Soviet had been elected by popular vote, whereas the Provisional Government had elected itself. The latter's invariable reply, when confronted with a difficult problem was to state that such a problem could only be resolved by the Constituent Assembly, when it met. The fact that the Constituent Assembly never met before the October revolution despite the repeated assurances of the government that it would, was another nail in the government's coffin. Its room for manoeuvre was limited. It had always to be mindful of the Soviet, which was willing to support the government if it agreed with the legislation passed but unwilling in the beginning to join the government and accept responsibility for running the country. Order

No. 1 (2/1) illustrates the situation. The order was not intended for front-line troops, only for those in Petrograd, but the impact was felt throughout the army.

After the removal of the Tsarist central authority, local authority had to be reformed as well. The government nominated zemstva *chairmen as local commissars and the district commissar was to reorganise the police into a militia. Many peasants and intellectuals resented this and called for elections. This decree orginated in the Ministry of the Interior but was never made public.*

The desire for peace was very strong in the Soviet and is mirrored in the appeal to all the peoples of the world (2/2).

The ambivalent attitude of the Soviet is well demonstrated during the first all-Russian conference of Soviets (2/3). The people were informed that their first loyalty was to the Soviet and not to the government.

The government's desire to honour the war obligations of the previous régime contradicted the Soviet's strongly felt longing for an end to hostilities. The first major confrontation between the two organs of power was provoked by the Milyukov note (2/15b). The resignation of the Foreign Minister and the dissolution of the first government indicated the dual nature of power in Russia. This was reflected in the setting up of the first coalition government. The Soviet agreed that some of its members should accept portfolios. The new government persisted in pursuing the war aims of its predecessor and went as far as launching an offensive in June (2/7). The débâcle which resulted brought down the government.

The February revolution took the Social Democrats by surprise. Both Bolsheviks and Mensheviks were cautious in their support of the first Provisional Government. The situation was changed dramatically by the return of Lenin to Petrograd. He denounced the government immediately and foresaw the passing of power to the proletariat and the poor strata of the peasantry (2/17b). Looking forward to a republic of soviets was something quite new in Marxist thought. The Bolsheviks did not wish to work with the majority socialists (Mensheviks and Socialist Revolutionaries) in the Soviet but aimed at supplanting their influence. A major clash between the Soviet and the Bolsheviks occurred in June over a demonstration called by the Bolsheviks without the knowledge of the Soviet (2/6). The Bolsheviks backed down but the support they received surprised their opponents. The defeat of the army in June resulted in demonstrations in Petrograd and the Bolsheviks called for 'all power to the Soviets'. Were the Bolsheviks aiming to seize power, as some believed? The Soviet published an appeal not to go on to the streets armed to protest against the disbandment of regiments which had disgraced themselves at the front (2/8a). The situation changed dramatically when news circulated that the government had evidence linking the Bolsheviks with the Germans. The Bolsheviks were accused of accepting subventions from the imperial German government. This appears to be borne out in a German document (5/1).

Something approaching despair overtook Lenin after the failure of the July Days (2/19). He had to hide in Finland, Pravda *was closed down, and some Bolsheviks were under arrest. Kerensky headed the second coalition government. Just what he and Kornilov were negotiating about remains unclear in his version but the result was confusion and misunderstanding. Ukraintsev however is very clear in his account (2/11c). Kornilov launched his attack on Petrograd and Kerensky called on the Soviet to help in repelling him (2/11a). The events widened the credibility gap between government and people even further.*

The Kornilov revolt rapidly transformed the fortunes of the Bolsheviks. The military revolutionary committee set up in the Petrograd Soviet shortly after the revolt was an organ which, under Bolshevik control, could act as the armed wing of the coming revolution.

As Bolshevik influence increased, it was only a matter of time before they achieved a majority in the Petrograd and Moscow Soviets. A third coalition government was set up in September (2/14). It was as unsuccessful as its predecessors at solving the problems of war and land hunger. A Constituent Assembly could have taken far-reaching decisions but it was never convened.

The provisional governments failed for many reasons. War and the land question were inextricably linked. If land were given to the peasants, soldiers (peasants in uniform) would desert and return to their village to secure their share. The politicians had very little experience of government and administration. When the government did act it had to do so in a legal, democratic manner. It had to prove it was superior to Tsarist rule. It had to share power with the Soviet. Only a Constituent Assembly could have legitimised the government's rule. *One of the main reasons for its failure was that it was confronted with a politician of the highest order, Lenin. He was a master of political tactics and propaganda, utterly believed in the correctness of his views, and he also had fortune on his side. His political opponents made most of the mistakes he would have wished them to make. He understood how to capitalise on their errors.*

2/1   ORDER NO. 1*

To the garrison of the Petrograd Military District, to all soldiers of the guard, army, artillery and fleet for immediate and exact execution, and to all the workers of Petrograd for their information.

The Soviet of Workers' and Soldiers' Deputies has decreed:

(1) Committees are to be elected immediately in all companies, battalions, regiments, parks, batteries, squadrons, and individual units of the different forms of military directorates, and in all naval vessels, from the elected representatives of the rank and file of the above-mentioned units.

(2) All troop units which have not yet elected their representatives to the Soviet of Workers' Deputies are to elect one representative per company. Such representatives are to appear, with written confirmation, at the State Duma building at 10 a.m. on 2 March.

(3) In all political actions, troop units are subordinate to the Soviet of Workers' and Soldiers' Deputies, and to the committees thereof.

(4) The orders of the Military commission of the State Duma are to be obeyed, *with the exception of those instances in which they contradict the orders and decrees†* of the Soviet Workers' and Soldiers' Deputies.

(5) All types of arms, such as rifles, machine guns, armoured

* From *Izvestiya*, 2 March 1917.

† Order No. 1 was also printed in *Pravda* on 9 March. The passage in italics reads: 'only in such instances when they do not contradict the orders and decrees of the Soviet'.

cars, and others, must be put at the disposal of company and battalion committees, and under their control, and are not, in any
case, to be issued to officers, even upon demand.

(6) On duty and in the performance of service responsibilities,
soldiers must observe the strictest military discipline, but when off
duty, in their political, civil and private lives, soldiers shall enjoy
fully and completely the same rights as all citizens.

In particular, standing at attention and compulsory saluting
when off duty are abolished.

(7) In the same way, addressing officers by honorary titles
('Your Excellency', 'Your honour', etc.) is abolished and is replaced
by the following form of address: 'Mr General', Mr Colonel', etc.

Addressing soldiers rudely by anyone of higher rank, and in particular, addressing soldiers by *ty** is prohibited, and any breach of
this provision, as well as any misunderstandings between officers
and soldiers, are to be reported by the latter to the company
committees.

This order is to be read to all companies, battalions, regiments,
ships' crews, batteries and other combatant and non-combatant
units.

Petrograd Soviet of Workers' and Soldiers' Deputies.

2/2   SOVIET APPEAL TO ALL THE PEOPLES OF THE
      WORLD†

14 March 1917

Comrade proletarians and toilers of all countries:

We, Russian workers and soldiers, united in the Petrograd
Soviet of Workers' and Soldiers' Deputies, send you cordial greetings and inform you of a great event. Russian democracy has overthrown the age-old despotism of the Tsar and has entered your
family (of nations) as an equal member, and as a powerful force
in the struggle for our common liberation. Our victory is a great
one for universal freedom and democracy. There was not a greater
pillar of reaction in the world than the 'Gendarme of Europe'.

* Second person singular.
† From *Izvestiya*, 15 March 1917.

May the earth lie as a heavy stone on his grave! Long live freedom! Long live the international solidarity of the proletariat, and its struggle for final victory!

Our work is not yet finished; the shades of the old order have not yet disappeared, and not a few enemies are collecting their forces against the Russian revolution. Nevertheless our achievements so far have been enormous. The peoples of Russia will express their will in a Constituent Assembly, which will be convened very soon on the basis of universal, equal, direct, and secret suffrage. And it may already be predicted with confidence that a democratic republic will triumph in Russia. The Russian people possesses full political freedom. They can now assert their mighty power in the internal self-government of the country and in its foreign policy.

And, appealing to all the people who are being destroyed and ruined in the monstrous war, we say that the time has come to begin a decisive struggle against the acquisitive ambitions of the governments of all countries; the time has come for the people to take into their own hands the decision of war and peace.

Conscious of its revolutionary power, Russian democracy announces that it will oppose the policy of conquest of its ruling classes by every means, and it calls the people of Europe to common, decisive action in favour of peace.

We also appeal to our brother proletarians of the Austro–German coalition, and, above all, to the German proletariat. From the first days of the war, they assured you that by taking up arms against autocratic Russia, you were defending the culture of Europe from Asiatic despotism. Many of you saw in this a justification of the support you gave to the war. Now even this justification has disappeared; democratic Russia cannot be a threat to freedom and civilisation.

We shall defend resolutely our own liberty against all reactionary attempts both from within and without. The Russian Revolution will not retreat before the bayonets of conquerors, and will not allow itself to be crushed by foreign military force.

But we appeal to you: Throw off the yoke of your semi-autocratic rule, as the Russian people have cast off the Tsar's autocracy; refuse to serve as an instrument of conquest and violence in the hands of kings, *pomeshchiks*, and bankers – and then by our united efforts, we shall stop the dreadful butchery that is a stain on humanity and is darkening the great days of the birth of Russian freedom.

Toilers of all countries: extending our hands as brothers across the mountains of our brothers' corpses, across the rivers of innocent blood and tears, across the smoking ruins of cities and villages, across the ruined treasures of civilisation, we appeal to you to restore and strengthen international unity. In this is the pledge of our future victories and of the complete liberation of humanity.

Proletarians of all countries, unite!

PETROGRAD SOVIET OF WORKERS' AND SOLDIERS' DEPUTIES

2/3   RESOLUTION OF SUPPORT FOR THE PROVISIONAL GOVERNMENT BY THE ALL-RUSSIAN CONFERENCE OF SOVIETS*

5 April 1917

1. In agreement with the Petrograd Soviet of Workers' and Soldiers' Deputies, the Provisional Government, formed in the course of the revolution, published a declaration containing a programme of governmental work.

2. The All-Russian Conference of the Soviets of Workers' and Soldiers' Deputies recognises that this programme includes the basic political demands of Russian democracy and that so far the Provisional Government has, on the whole and in general, been fulfilling the obligations which it assumed.

3. Conference appeals to the whole revolutionary democracy of Russia to rally around the Soviets of Workers' and Soldiers' Deputies as organisational centres of the forces of democracy, created by the revolution. These soviets, united with other progressive forces, are capable of countering attempts at a Tsarist and bourgeois counter-revolution, and of consolidating and increasing the gains of the revolution.

4. Conference recognises the necessity of gradually gaining political control and influence over the Provisional Government and its local organs so as to persuade it to conduct the most energetic struggle against counter-revolutionary forces, to take

* From *Izvestiya*, 6 April 1917.

the most resolute steps towards a complete democratisation of all walks of Russian life, and to make preparations for universal peace without annexations and indemnities based on the self-determination of nations.

5. Conference appeals to democracy to support the Provisional Government without assuming responsibility for all the work of the government, as long as the government steadfastly confirms and expands the gains of the revolution and so long as its foreign policy is based on the renunciation of ambitions of territorial expansion.

6. At the same time, Conference appeals to the revolutionary democracy of Russia to be prepared, while organising and rallying its forces around the Soviets of Workers' and Soldiers' Deputies, to vitiate all efforts by the government to escape the control exercised by democracy, or to evade the fulfilment of the obligations it has assumed.

2/4 FIRST COALITION GOVERNMENT OF 5 MAY 1917*

The composition of the government is as follows:

Minister-President and Minister of the Interior
Prince G. E. Lvov (Non-Party)

Minister of War and Navy	A. F. Kerensky (SR)
Minister of Justice	P. N. Pereverzev (SR)
Minister of Foreign Affairs	M. I. Tereshchenko (Non-Party)
Minister of Transport	N. V. Nekrasov (Kadet)
Minister of Trade and Industry	A. I. Konovalov (Kadet)
Minister of Education	A. A. Manuilov (Kadet)
Minister of Finance	A. I. Shingarev (Kadet)
Minister of Agriculture	V. M. Chernov (SR)
Minister of Labour	M. I. Skobelev (Menshevik)
Minister of Posts and Telegraph	I. G. Tseretelli (Menshevik)
Minister of Food	A. V. Peshekhonov (Popular Socialist)
Minister of Welfare	Prince D. I. Shakhovskoi (Kadet)
Ober-Procurator of the Holy Synod	V. N. Lvov (Centrist)
State Controller	I. V. Godnev (Octobrist)

* From *Rech* 6 May 1917.

2/5 THE SITUATION IN THE TOWNS, MARCH–MAY 1917*

The general impression of the mood in various places is this: a fine, exhilarating holiday, followed by dreary workdays.

The town dweller, who impetuously rushed on to the streets at the first opportunity, soon came to the conclusion that nothing catastrophic had happened; and having satisfied himself that the revolution was over and freedom won, he returned to his home without showing any wish to participate actively in establishing the new order.

On the surface life flows peacefully in its usual channels: the factories are working, trade is being carried on, dealers are returning to their affairs, there are no noticeable acts of disorder – but there is no certainty what tomorrow will bring. People feel that it is safe to stay at home; and this fear of personal assault has been intensified of late by frequent lootings of wine shops. The mood in the *uezd* towns does not inspire really happy feelings; the prevailing notes are those of anxiety and fatigue. The inhabitants show little interest in reorganisation; they are sinking more and more into inertia, from which, however, they might be aroused by energetic people, quite irrespective of the doctrines preached.

The villages show a far healthier spirit: the fear and vacillation, which are so obvious among the town dwellers, are absent here; there is no reason to suspect a sudden and cowardly jump backwards. The inhabitant of the town is timorous and likes being frightened. On the whole he is noted for his intense conservatism; and though he was called upon to forgive much to the old authorities, he will certainly not forgive the new administration for any errors it might commit. He is accustomed to bow down only to power; the slightest weakening of the new authority or the spread of any abuses of the revolution causes him to look regretfully backward and to reproach the new and the untried. If the peasant can be made to move only under the pressure of heavy trials, the town dweller panics at the thought of losing some of his comforts.

To the peasant the new order means land. He has grasped this idea clearly and firmly. The land is everything to him. The town dweller, who does not, on the whole, set very great store by liberty,

* From *Krasnii Arkhiv* (Moscow–Leningrad 1926), Vol. 25, pp. 58–9.

regards the new order with favour only when it falls into his lap like manna, without causing him any inconvenience or tension or threatening him with the loss of his tranquillity and safety. This applies to the petty bourgeoisie in the towns, not to the industrial workers, who value freedom for its own sake.

The town dweller is frightened by demonstrations of extremist parties most of all. And in the meanwhile, as though aware of this unspoken support, the right wing elements, which had cowered in their hiding places during the first enthusiastic days of deliverance, slowly reappear. They make use of the town dweller's discontent and his fear of the extremes of revolutionary activity.

2/6 SOVIET PROHIBITS DEMONSTRATIONS*

DON'T LISTEN TO THE APPEALS OF THE PROVOCATEURS!

Comrade soldiers and workers,

The Bolshevik Party is calling on you to go on to the streets.

This appeal is being prepared without the knowledge of the Soviet of Workers' and Soldiers' Deputies, without the knowledge of the Soviet of Peasants' Deputies and all the socialist parties. It is being made precisely at the alarming moment when the All-Russian Congress called on the comrade workers of the Viborg district to remember that any demonstration at present may damage the cause of the revolution.

Comrades, on behalf of millions of workers, peasants, and soldiers in the rear and at the front, we say to you:

DO NOT DO WHAT YOU ARE BEING ASKED TO DO.

At this alarming moment you are being called on to the streets in order to make demands for the overthrow of the Provisional Government, the support of which the All-Russian Congress has just recognised to be essential. Those who are calling on you cannot know that your peaceful demonstration may give rise to bloody disorders. Knowing your loyalty to the revolutionary cause, we say to you:

You are being called out to demonstrate in support of the revolution.

* From *Izvestiya*, 10 June 1917.

But we know that concealed counter-revolutionaries want to profit from your demonstration.

We know that counter-revolutionaries are awaiting eagerly the moment when fratricidal strife in the ranks of revolutionary democracy will give them the opportunity of crushing the revolution.

———

Comrades:

On behalf of all the Soviets of Workers' and Soldiers' Deputies, on behalf of the Soviet of Peasants' Deputies, the active armies and the socialist parties, we say to you:

THERE MUST NOT BE A SINGLE COMPANY, A SINGLE REGIMENT, A SINGLE GROUP OF WORKERS IN THE STREETS.

THERE MUST NOT BE A SINGLE DEMONSTRATION TODAY.

A GREAT STRUGGLE STILL LIES AHEAD OF US.

When a counter-revolutionary danger really threatens the freedom of Russia, we shall appeal to you.

Disorganising demonstrations, however, will bring about the downfall of the revolution.

CONSERVE YOUR STRENGTH, REMAIN IN UNISON WITH THE WHOLE OF REVOLUTIONARY RUSSIA.

———

The All-Russian Congress of the Soviets of Workers' and Soldiers' Deputies has resolved:

All street demonstrations are to be banned for three days (10, 11 and 12 June).

A violation of this resolution is a blow against the revolution.

Whoever calls for the violation of this resolution is an enemy of the revolution.

———

RESOLUTION OF THE SOLDIERS' SECTION OF THE SOVIET OF WORKERS' AND SOLDIERS' DEPUTIES.

Having discussed the 'peaceful demonstration' called for 10 June, under the slogan of the struggle against counter-revolution, the Soldiers' Section of the Soviet of Workers' and Soldiers' Deputies has resolved that:

1. The solidarity and organisation of democracy is its only support and defence against all counter-revolutionary acts.
2. The Soviet of Workers' and Soldiers' Deputies is the leading organ in democracy's struggle against counter-revolution.
3. The demonstration of 10 June, called without the knowledge or consent of the Soviet of Workers' and Soldiers' Deputies and the All-Russian Congress, is a disorganising action.
4. Under circumstances of exceedingly strained relations, this demonstration may give rise to street fighting and provoke a civil war.

Therefore, the Soldiers' Section of the Soviet of Workers' and Soldiers' Deputies considers it necessary to take the most resolute measures to prevent the demonstration of 10 June taking place.

2/7 THE JUNE OFFENSIVE*

Russia, having thrown off the chains of slavery, has firmly resolved to defend, at all costs, its rights, honour, and freedom. Believing in the brotherhood of mankind, Russian democracy appealed most earnestly to all the belligerent countries to stop the war and conclude a peace honourable to all. In answer to our fraternal appeal, the enemy has called on us to play the traitor. Austria and Germany have offered us a separate peace and tried to hoodwink us by fraternisation, while they threw all their forces against our allies, with the idea that after destroying them, they would turn on us. Now that he is convinced that Russia is not going to be fooled, the enemy threatens us and is concentrating his forces on our front.

Warriors, our country is in danger! Liberty and revolution are threatened. The time has come for the army to do its duty. Your Supreme Commander [General Brusilov], beloved through victory, is convinced that each day of delay merely helps the enemy, and that only by an immediate and determined blow can we disrupt his plans. Therefore, in full realisation of my great responsibility

* From *Izvestiya*, 20 June 1917.

to the country, and in the name of its free people and its Provisional Government, I call upon the armies, strengthened by the vigour and spirit of the revolution, to take the offensive.

Let not the enemy celebrate prematurely his victory over us! Let all nations know that when we talk of peace, it is not because we are weak! Let all know that liberty has increased our might.

Officers and soldiers! Know that all Russia gives you its blessing on your undertaking, in the name of liberty, the glorious future of the country, and an enduring and honourable peace.

Forward!

Kerensky, Minister of War and Navy
16 June 1917

2/8   THE JULY DAYS

(a) THE SOVIET APPEAL*

Comrade soldiers and workers:

Contrary to the clearly expressed will of *all* socialist parties, without exception, some unknown persons are calling on you to go out armed on to streets. In this way you are being asked to protest against the disbandment of regiments which have discredited themselves at the front by criminally violating their duty to the revolution.

We, the authorised representatives of the revolutionary democracy of the whole of Russia, issue this statement to you:

The disbandment of the regiments at the front was carried out at the insistence of the army and organisations at the front and in compliance with the order of our Minister of War, Comrade A. F. Kerensky, who was elected by us.

An action taken in defence of the disbanded regiments is an action against our brothers who are shedding their blood at the front.

We remind comrade soldiers that no military unit has the right to go out armed without a call for such action by the Commander, who acts in complete accord with us.

Anyone who violates this resolution during the troubled days

* From *Izvestiya*, 4 July 1917.

that Russia is passing through will be denounced by us as a traitor and enemy of the revolution.

All available resources at our disposal will be used to carry out the present resolution.

BUREAU OF THE ALL-RUSSIAN CENTRAL EXECUTIVE COMMITTEE OF THE SOVIETS OF WORKERS' AND SOLDIERS' DEPUTIES

BUREAU OF THE ALL-RUSSIAN EXECUTIVE COMMITTEE OF THE SOVIETS OF PEASANTS' DEPUTIES

(b) THE BOLSHEVIK PROCLAMATION OF THE NIGHT OF 5 JULY 1917*

COMRADES! On Monday you came out on the streets. On Tuesday you decided to continue the demonstration. We called you to a peaceful demonstration yesterday. The object of this demonstration was to show to all the toiling and exploited masses the strength of our slogans, their weight, their significance and their necessity for the liberation of the peoples from war, hunger and ruin.

The object of the demonstration was achieved. The slogans of the vanguard of the working class and of the army were imposingly and worthily proclaimed. The scattered firing of the counter-revolutionaries on the demonstrators could not disturb the general character of the demonstration.

Comrades! for the present political crisis, our aim has been accomplished. We have therefore decided to end the demonstration. Let each and every one peacefully and in an organised manner bring the strike and the demonstration to a close.

Let us await the further development of the crisis. Let us continue to prepare our forces. Life is with us, the course of events shows the correctness of our slogans.

Central Committee, R.S.-D.L.P.
Petrograd Committee, R.S.-D.L.P.
Interborough Committee, R.S.-D.L.P.
Military Organisation of the Central Committee, R.S.-D.L.P.
Commission of the Workers' Section of the Soviet of Workers' and Soldiers' Deputies.

* From Lenin, *Toward the Seizure of Power* (London n.d.), Book 2, p. 300.

2/9 THE SECOND COALITION GOVERNMENT OF 24 JULY 1917*

The membership of the government is as follows:

Minister-President and Minister of War and Navy
A. F. Kerensky (SR)

Deputy Minister-President and Minister of Finance
N. V. Nekrasov (Kadet)

Minister of Foreign Affairs	M. I. Tereshchenko (Non-Party)
Minister of Labour	M. I. Skobelev (Menshevik)
Minister of Food	A. V. Peshekhonov (Popular Socialist)
Minister of Agriculture	V. M. Chernov (SR)
Minister of Education	S. F. Oldenburg (Non-Party)
Minister of Justice	A. S. Zarudny (Popular Socialist)
Minister of Welfare	I. N. Efremov (Progressive)
Minister of Transport	P. P. Yurenev (Kadet)
Minister of Trade and Industry	S. N. Prokopovich (Menshevik)
Minister of Posts and Telegraph	A. M. Nikitin (Menshevik)
State Controller	F. F. Kokoshkin (Kadet)
Ober-Procurator of the Holy Synod	A. V. Kartashev (Kadet)
Minister of the Interior	N. D. Avksentev (SR)

2/10 DAVID SOSKICE'S REMINISCENCES†

One day about the end of July (1917), I was sitting in the Editorial Offices of *Narodnaya Volya* (the People's Will) the organ of the right wing of the SR Party. During my conversation with the editor the door of the room opened and the attendant admitted a man in khaki of about 40 years of age, of middle size, clean shaved, with small eyes, keen and piercing as needles, with a dry face and wiry thin figure.

'Boris Viktorovich Savinkov', said the editor, introducing the newcomer to me.

I looked at him with great curiosity. Savinkov the famous revolutionist, who some twelve years ago took part in the attempts against Plehve and the Grand Duke Sergius; who was subse-

---

* From *Izvestiya*, 25 July 1917.
† From Private Papers.

quently arrested and condemned to death, and, on the very eve of his execution when all hope was at an end, was suddenly let out of the prison by a sympathising guard, and set at liberty. He escaped to Paris, lived there for some time in safety; but his indomitable courage and hatred of Tsardom caused him to return to Russia, and for two years he became the organiser of new terroristic acts, which failed however, thanks to the treachery of Azev . . .

'This is the latest news if you want to know. Brusilov is dismissed. Kornilov is appointed to the Chief Command in his place'.

This was news indeed. No one in Petrograd was aware of it. I began to question Savinkov and from his explanations I understood he had been instrumental in the important change and had succeeded in impressing Kerensky with the belief that Brusilov was dangerous as a possible leader of a counter-revolution; while Kornilov was a true democrat and staunch republican as well as a great general, and that therefore his appointment would inspire the army with fresh enthusiasm and the spirit of cohesion.

'When are you returning to the Front?' I asked.

'I don't know whether I shall return', he replied. 'I may receive a post here'.

A few days later indeed, Savinkov was appointed acting War Minister, to the general satisfaction, as everyone expected great things from him. He would reorganise the army and restore discipline, and fill the troops with a new fighting spirit.

Shortly after that I accepted the post of Kerensky's Private Secretary, and on my very first day in the Winter Palace I met Savinkov again. It was nearing the middle of August. The Bolsheviks were just beginning to reappear and to raise their voices again after the arrests and repression following their rebellion of July 3–5. A report was published in the Petrograd Press giving the details of a secret Congress they had been holding somewhere in Petrograd. Inflammatory speeches against the war, the Provisional Government and the Imperialistic plots of the Allies had been poured forth during this Conference and the Press was asking why the Government tolerated such proceedings.

On that day just before commencing my new duties I called upon Mme. Breshkovsky in the Winter Palace and found Savinkov with her. He was going to ask Kerensky for authorisation to suppress the Conference; and he begged the venerable lady to go with him to use her influence with Kerensky in the matter.

Babushka agreed, as she always did to personally assist in everything she considered right. So we all three proceeded to Kerensky's reception room below . . .

At last Savinkov reported the matter of the Bolshevik Conference. When he had finished Kerensky said nothing. I learnt afterwards by experience that this was his way of declining to accede to a demand.

Babushka then rose from her place, approached Kerensky, and, in earnest words, begged him to forbid the Bolshevik Conference and arrest the leaders.

Kerensky listened to her with deep attention. It was clear that he carefully weighed every word she uttered. At last he said:

'Babushka, I cannot suppress the Conference. I don't even know where they meet. Besides, how can I arrest people relying exclusively upon newspaper information from any source. And even had I such information I should first be obliged to consult Avksentev (Minister of the Interior) and obtain his consent to any arrest by administrative order. Such is the law'.

Kerensky's argument seemed to be irresistible. But Babushka was not a lawyer. She was always guided by common sense and she felt intensely with all her being that the need was supreme and that if the Bolsheviks were not suppressed with or without law they would contaminate the whole army and disorganise the country; and that her great dream of a Russian free democracy to which she had given her whole life would be dispelled.

But suddenly without answering his arguments the grey haired woman bowed to the ground before Kerensky and repeated several times in solemn imploring tones:

'I beg thee, Alexander Fedorovich, suppress the Conference, suppress the Bolsheviks. I beg thee do this, or else they will bring ruin on our country and the revolution'.

It was truly a dramatic scene. To see the grandmother of the Russian revolution who had passed thirty eight years of her life in prison and in Siberia in her struggle for liberty, to see that highly cultured and noble woman bowing to the ground in the ancient orthodox manner before the young Kerensky, and implore him, the champion of liberty, to suppress and imprison the Bolsheviks by Administrative order against law was a thing I shall never forget.

I looked at Kerensky. His pale face grew still whiter. His eyes reflected the terrible struggle that was proceeding within him. He was silent for long, and at last he said in a low voice:

'How can I do it?'

'Do it, A. F., I beseech thee' and again Babushka bowed to the ground.

Kerensky could stand it no longer. He sprang to his feet and seized the telephone.

'I must learn first where the Conference meets', he said, 'and consult Avksentev', and rang up the Ministry of the Interior.

But Avksentev was not in his office and the matter had to be adjourned for the time. I fancy to Kerensky's great relief.

[David Soskice (1866–1941) was drawn into the revolutionary movement in Russia in the early 1880s and after several spells in prison fled abroad in 1893. He moved to England in the late 1890s and later was active in the Society of Friends of Russian Freedom. He returned to Russia briefly as the St Petersburg correspondent of *The Tribune* after the 1905 revolution, and in 1917 went out again as a correspondent of the *Manchester Guardian*, joining Kerensky's secretariat in the summer of that year. At one time sympathetic to the Marxists, he subsequently joined the Socialist Revolutionaries. He returned to England after the October Revolution.]

2/11   THE KORNILOV REVOLT

(a) KERENSKY'S TELEGRAM TO ALL THE COUNTRY*

I hereby announce:

On August 26 General Kornilov sent Vladimir Lvov, a member of the State Duma, with a demand for the surrender by the Provisional Government of all civil and military power, so that he may form, according to his wishes, a *new government* to administer the country. Deputy Lvov's authority to make me such a proposal was confirmed subsequently by General Kornilov in his

* From *Vestnik Vremennago Pravitelstva*, 29 August 1917.

conversation with me by direct wire. Realising that such demands, addressed to the Provisional Government through me, revealed the longing of certain circles in Russian society to take advantage of the serious situation the state finds itself in to set up a régime opposed to the gains of the revolution, the Provisional Government finds it necessary to:

Authorise me, for the salvation of our motherland, of freedom, and of our republican order, to take prompt and decisive action to counter any attempt to limit Supreme Power in the state and the rights which the citizens have gained as a result of the revolution.

I am taking all necessary measures to protect the liberty and order of the country, and the population will be informed in due course of the measures adopted.

At the same time I hereby order:

1.   General Kornilov to surrender his post of Supreme Commander to General Klembovsky, the Commander in Chief of the Northern Front, which guards the way to Petrograd; and General Klembovsky to assume temporarily the post of Supreme Commander while remaining at Pskov.

2.   The city and *uezd* of Petrograd to be placed under martial law, extending to it the regulations for regions under martial law.

I call upon all citizens to remain completely calm and to maintain order, which is so indispensable for the salvation of the country. I call upon all ranks of the army and the navy to continue calmly and with self-sacrifice their duty of defending the country against the external enemy.

> A. F. Kerensky, Minister-President, Minister of War
> and the Navy
> 27 August 1917

(b) KORNILOV'S RESPONSE TO THE TELEGRAM*

The first part of the Minister-President's telegram No. 4163 is a complete lie. It was not I who sent Vladimir Lvov, Member of the State Duma, to the Provisional Government, but he came to me as the envoy of the Minister-President. Aleksei Aladin, Member

* From E. I. Martynov, *Kornilov* (Leningrad 1927), pp. 110–11.

of the State Duma, is a witness to this. A *great provocation* has thus taken place which puts the fate of the motherland in doubt.

People of Russia! Our great motherland is dying. The hour of her death is near. Obliged to speak openly, I, General Kornilov, declare that under the pressure of the Bolshevik majority in the soviets, the Provisional Government is acting in complete accord with the plans of the German General Staff, and simultaneously with the imminent landing of the enemy forces at Riga, it is destroying the army and is undermining the very foundations of the country.

The heavy sense of the inevitable ruin of our country forces me to call upon all the Russian people in these terrible times to come to the aid of the dying motherland. All in whose breast a Russian heart is beating, who believe in God, in the Church, pray to the Lord for the greatest miracle, the saving of our motherland!

I, General Kornilov, son of a Cossack peasant, declare to everyone that I want nothing for myself, save the preservation of a Great Russia, and I swear that my goal for the people is the convocation of a Constituent Assembly which will come about as a result of victory over the enemy. They will there decide their fate and choose their new form of government. But it is quite impossible for me to betray Russia into the hands of her ancient enemy, the German race, and to turn the Russian people into slaves of the Germans. I prefer to die on the battlefield of honour rather than see disgrace and dishonour descend on Russia.

People of Russia, the life of your motherland is in your hands!
27 August 1917.

General Kornilov

(c) N. UKRAINTSEV'S OBSERVATIONS*

Observations by a member of the Extraordinary Commission of Inquiry

It was very late when we arrived at General Kornilov's. He was still living in the Governor's house. He received us immediately in a vast, almost empty study. The General was expecting us of course and was either completely calm or was keeping complete

* From *Novoye Russkoye Slovo* (New York), 28 October 1956.

control of himself. We, or to be exact, Shablovsky, said that since it was so late we would restrict ourselves, during this first meeting, to listening to a brief explanation of the events in question from him. And indeed he then gave a fairly coherent, concise, logical and convincing account, much of it quite familiar to us: the disintegration of the army, the malicious and unscrupulous agitation of the Soviets against the war and the powerlessness of the government which was trying to continue it, but which was either incapable or unwilling to protect the army from Bolshevik disruption. Then Kornilov catalogued all the measures which the high command, responsible for waging the war, had proposed to the government in order to rebuild the army and which that command had adopted itself independently to that end.

Finally, Kornilov came to the most important part, a part so unexpected that it literally staggered us. He informed us that in the interests of maintaining order in the capital he had reached an agreement with Kerensky to move a large military force to Petrograd so that disturbances, if they occurred, could be suppressed immediately. It was quite clear from Kornilov's account that the Soviets (the Soviets of Workers' and Soldiers' Deputies) were regarded as the main source of the possible disturbances and that by suppression of disturbances was understood the suppression of none other than the Soviets and, moreover, that this was so understood not only in Stavka but also by Kerensky himself.

To confirm this latter point Kornilov took from a drawer in his desk a tape with a record of his conversation by direct wire with Kerensky. Unfortunately I have forgotten when the conversation took place. Each of us read the tape and, I must confess, we were completely dumbfounded. As the tape revealed, the main theme of the conversation was the dispatch of the cavalry force to Petrograd for the purpose which Kornilov had stated and a purpose which Kerensky's answers did nothing to contradict.

In informing us of the agreement with Kerensky to send troops he did not hide the fact that there were differences of opinion between them on the makeup of the force (the 'Wild Division') and also on the appointment of the commander (General Krymov).

When Shablovsky had read the taped conversation he cut short Kornilov's further explanations and told him that, in view of the seriousness of the charges made against him by the government, the Commission had no alternative but to place him under arrest. Kornilov nodded his head in assent and when the order for his arrest had been drawn up he signed it without protest.

We returned to the station, told General Alekseev to carry out the necessary measures involved in arresting Kornilov, sent Kerensky a telegram and returned to our carriage.

We read and re-read the tape trying to find in it something which would contradict General Kornilov's statement. In fact, a certain lack of preciseness in some expressions could have given rise to doubt, but this could be easily explained away by the necessity of General Kornilov to be rather secretive as the conversation was not conducted directly, but through an intermediary, namely, the military telegraphist. There was the same lack of precision in Kerensky's expressions, obviously for the same reason. Taking this into account, the fact remained that we had in our hands a tape which provided incontrovertible material evidence that the cavalry corps was advancing on Petrograd with the knowledge and permission, if not of the whole government, then of its head, and that the whole case against General Kornilov had therefore collapsed. What in Petrograd had appeared as a crime of the supreme commander was transformed into a legal act and we, the Commission, found ourselves in a wholly absurd position. Doubts about our position went so far that in the circumstances we did not know whether we had the right to carry out the instructions regarding the arrest of the generals accused by the government. Nor could we imagine what the investigation we were carrying out would lead to. We were so uncertain of our position that we even discussed returning to Petrograd and laying down our responsibilities. If we did not do this it was primarily because we realised that to have done so would have caused a political scandal of tremendous proportions that would have destroyed once and for all the very precarious balance of political forces in the country, and the Bolsheviks clearly would have benefited . . .

As regards the testimony of all the witnesses we questioned, I must say that not one of them told us anything which we had not heard from General Kornilov himself, whom we questioned on several occasions. He was very forthright in his evidence, totally disregarding the possibility that it might be used against him. He spoke like a supreme commander in extraordinary times, when military measures alone are inadequate for waging war, let alone winning it. He believed the government to be weak and incapable of helping the army. He attributed its weakness to the conditions of dual power. He regarded some members of the government as not far short of being traitors. These circumstances had forced him into politics. He was seeking contact with people in public life and was trying to increase his prestige and authority, because without prestige and authority one could not command a disintegrating army. He regarded the Petrograd Soviet as enemy number one. Although the July uprising in Petrograd organized by the Soviets had been put down, the character of the Soviets remained the same, therefore he felt obliged to take precautionary measures. Hence he ordered the formation of officer groups which, if the occasion arose, would have the task of quelling an uprising. After the Moscow Conference he decided to strengthen these groups and to do so he ordered some officers who still imposed military discipline to be recalled from the front in order to train them in grenade throwing and send them from Stavka to Petrograd . . .

We regarded our investigation almost complete when we had heard Lvov's evidence. Only one more witness remained to be questioned, A. F. Kerensky. We wanted to find out from him the answers to the following questions, without which there remained too much scope for surmise, conjecture and suspicion: (1) Was there an agreement to send a cavalry corps to Petrograd, when exactly was it reached and with what aim in mind; if this agreement was an invention of General Kornilov's, why then did not he, Kerensky, point this out in the telegraph (direct line) conversation. What objection did he have to General Krymov and did his desire to see General Krymov replaced take the form of an objection or of a clearly expressed order to General Kornilov; (2) Did he give Lvov instructions to visit Kornilov at Mogilev, and for precisely what purpose and what did Lvov say in his report about the visit; (3) Did discussions take place among members of the government on the possibility or desirability of establishing a dictatorship, did he, Kerensky, participate in such discussions, what was his own attitude to the question and, if such discussions did take place, then whom, did he, Kerensky, express himself in favour of as dictator?

Kerensky was questioned in the second half of October . . . Shablovsky as a sign of respect stood up while putting his questions. Tumanova, an elderly Duma stenographer whom we had invited to attend, took notes.

Kerensky's first replies were delivered in such a sharp manner and in such a raised voice that Shablovsky lost his nerve. Glancing at the list of questions he changed both the wording and the whole sense of the questions to such a degree that I failed completely to recognize my own work. The answers to these amended questions only obscured what we wanted to clarify. Raupakh was the first to lose patience. He stood up and asked for a more precise answer. Lieber did the same. Then Kerensky finally lost his self-control. He jumped up and began literally to bellow at us. Shablovsky and the rest of us exchanged glances in silence and Shablovsky firmly called an adjournment. At that point Tumanova stood up and, turning to Kerensky, said to him in a loud voice: 'I am ashamed of you, Aleksandr Fedorovich. I am ashamed that you should have permitted yourself to behave in such a way towards the Commission which was only doing its duty . . .'

This was the last act of our Commission . . .

There is no proof that Kornilov had a definite plan for using force not only against the Soviet, but against the legitimate government as well. Krymov's advance was directed against the Soviet.

In his letter to this newspaper Kerensky claims that any idea of a 'pact' is pure invention. He had opportunity enough to scotch this idea by taking advantage of his right and of his obligation as a witness before the Commission of Inquiry to give an accurate and detailed statement. The Commission could surely rely on the fact that he would do so. Instead of this, he squandered an opportunity to clarify a question not only of state importance, but one which concerned him personally very closely. Did this happen unconsciously?

2/12 FORMATION OF THE COUNCIL OF FIVE, 1 SEPTEMBER 1917*

At its meeting on 1 September the Provisional Government decided that until the final formation of the cabinet, and in view of the present extraordinary circumstances, the government of

* From *Izvestiya*, 3 September 1917.

the country should be entrusted directly to the Minister-President, A. F. Kerensky; the Minister of Foreign Affairs, M. I. Tereshchenko; the Minister of War, Major General Verkhovsky; the Minister of the Navy, Admiral Verderevsky; and the Minister of Posts and Telegraph, A. M. Nikitin.

2/13   PROCLAMATION OF A REPUBLIC*

The rebellion of General Kornilov has been suppressed, but the turmoil which it has brought into the army and to the country is great. Again the danger threatening the country and its freedom is grave. Believing it necessary to terminate the outward vagueness of the form of government, and mindful of the wholehearted and enthusiastic acceptance of the republican idea that was shown at the Moscow State Conference, the Provisional Government declares that the political form under which the Russian State is governed is a republican form, and it proclaims the Russian Republic.

The urgent necessity of taking immediate and decisive measures to restore the impaired order of the State has induced the Provisional Government to transfer the fullness of its power of government to five of its members, headed by the Minister-President.

The Provisional Government regards its main task to be the restoration of order in the State and the fighting power of the army. Convinced that only a rallying of all the vital forces of the country can lead the country out of the difficult situation in which it now finds itself, the Provisional Government will strive to enlarge its membership by taking in the representatives of all those elements who place the lasting and common interests of our country above the transitory and private interests of separate classes or parties. The Provisional Government has no doubt that it will bring this about in the course of the next few days.

A. F. KERENSKY,
Minister-President

ZARUDNY
Minister of Justice

1 September 1917.

* From *Izvestiya*, 3 September 1917.

2/14   THE THIRD COALITION GOVERNMENT OF 25 SEPTEMBER 1917*

The membership of the government is as follows:

Minister-President	A. F. Kerensky (SR)
Minister of War	A. I. Verkhovsky (Non-Party)
Minister of the Navy	D. V. Verderevsky (Non-Party)
Minister of the Interior, and Posts and Telegraph	
	A. M. Nikitin (Menshevik)
Minister of Foreign Affairs	M. I. Tereshchenko (Non-Party)
Minister of Food	S. N. Prokopovich (Menshevik)
Minister of Finance	M. V. Bernatsky (Non-Party)
Minister of Education	S. S. Salazkin (Non-Party)
Minister of Transport	A. V. Liverovsky (Non-Party)
Minister of Trade and Industry	A. I. Konovalov (Kadet)
Minister of Welfare	N. M. Kishkin (Kadet)
Minister of Justice	P. N. Malyantovich (Menshevik)
Minister of Labour	K. A. Gvozdev (Menshevik)
Minister of Agriculture	S. L. Maslov (SR)
Minister of Confessions	A. V. Kartashev (Kadet)
State Controller	S. A. Smirnov (Kadet)
Chairman of the Economic Council	
	S. N. Tretyakov (Non-Party)

2/15   FOREIGN AFFAIRS

(a) MILYUKOV PROTESTS AGAINST EXCLUSION OF RUSSIA FROM CONFERENCES†

13/26 April 1917

In my conversation with the ambassadors about the recent meetings of the statesmen of France, Great Britain, and Italy in Folkestone and at St. Jean, I expressed to them my great surprise that the Russian Government had not been informed beforehand of these conferences or the topics for discussion, and was told only

* From *Rech*, 26 September 1917.
† From E. A. Adamov, *Razdel Aziatskoi Rossii po sekretnym dokumentam v Ministerstve Inostrannykh Del* (Moscow 1924), p. 322.

afterwards of the decisions reached. On the other hand, not only current affairs, but also matters of great political significance, in which, as in the question of Asia Minor, Russia is directly interested, were discussed at the aforementioned conferences.

Apparently, negotiations of equal importance between the governments of France, Great Britain, and the United States are soon to take place in Washington, in which, as has already been announced and revealed in the press, it is the intention to discuss world politics.

The fact that we are not taking part in these negotiations and are even unacquainted about the subject matter of the forthcoming conferences may produce a very unfavourable impression on public opinion here and even give rise to undesirable rumours of strife and discord among the Allies.

Please talk with the Minister of Foreign Affairs in a confidential and friendly manner on the matters mentioned above and telegraph the results.

MILYUKOV

(b) MILYUKOV'S NOTE OF 18 APRIL*

On 18 April, the Minister of Foreign Affairs instructed the Russian representatives with the Allied Powers to transmit the following note to the Governments to which they are accredited:

'On 27 March of the present year, the Provisional Government issued a declaration to the citizens, containing the views of the Government of free Russia regarding the aims of the present war. The Minister of Foreign Affairs has instructed me to communicate to you the contents of the document referred to, and to make at the same time the following comments:

'Our enemies have been striving of late to sow discord among the Allies, disseminating absurd reports alleging that Russia is ready to conclude a separate peace with the Central Powers. The text of the attached document will most effectively refute such falsehoods. You will note from the same that the general principles enunciated by the Provisional Government are in entire agreement with those lofty ideas which have been constantly expressed, up to the very last moment, by eminent statesmen in the Allied countries, and which were given especially vivid expression in the

* From *Rech*, 20 April 1917.

declaration of the president of our new Ally, the great republic across the Atlantic.

'The Government under the old régime was, of course, incapable of grasping and sharing these ideas of the liberating character of the war, the establishment of a firm basis for the amicable existence of the nations, of self-determination for oppressed peoples, and so forth. Emancipated Russia, however, can now speak in a language that will be comprehensible to the leading democracies of our own time, and she now hastens to add her voice to those of her Allies. Imbued with this new spirit of a free democracy, the declaration of the Provisional Government cannot, of course, afford the least excuse for the assumption that the revolution has entailed any slackening on the part of Russia in the common struggle of the Allies. Quite to the contrary, the aspiration of the entire nation to carry the world war to a decisive victory has grown more powerful, thanks to our understanding of our common responsibility, shared by each and every one. This striving has become still more active, since it is concentrated upon the task which touches all and is urgent – the task of driving out the enemy who has invaded our country. It is obvious, as stated in the communicated document, that the Provisional Government, while safeguarding the rights of our own country, will, in every way, observe the obligations assumed towards our Allies.

'Continuing to cherish the firm conviction of the victorious issue of the present war, in full accord with our Allies, the Provisional Government feels also absolutely certain that the problems which have been raised by this war will be solved in a spirit that will afford a firm basis for lasting peace, and that the leading democracies, inspired by identical desires, will find the means to obtain those guarantees and sanctions which are indispensable for the prevention of sanguinary conflicts in the future.'

(c) THE SOVIET CALLS FOR AN INTERNATIONAL SOCIALIST
   CONFERENCE, 25 APRIL*

At the session of the Executive Committee on April 25, the following resolution was adopted:

   1. The Executive Committee of the Soviet of Workers' and

* From *Izvestiya*, 27 April 1917.

Soldiers' Deputies takes upon itself the initiative of calling an International Socialist Conference.

2. All parties and factions of the proletariat International [that are ready to accept the platform which was adopted by the Soviet on March 14 in its Call to the People of the World] should be invited.

3. The Executive Committee considers an essential condition of the conference, the possibility for all socialist parties and factions without exception to come to the place of meeting. The Executive Committee calls this to the mind of the governments and most categorically demands from the majority factions an open and energetic insistence that their governments should allow the minority delegates to come to the conference.

4. The place of the conference should be in a neutral country.

5. To prepare for the conference and to lay out a programme, a special body, 'The Commission for the Calling of the Conference,' is being organized, in connection with the Executive Committee. This commission is made up of members of the Executive Committee, and representatives of parties who are members of the International and, at the same time, members of the Executive Committee.

6. A call should be issued at once to all peoples, and in particular to the socialists of these countries and with the delegation at Stockholm for the purpose of making preparations for the conference.

7. A special delegation of the Executive Committee should be sent to neutral and Allied countries to establish contact with socialists in these countries and with the delegation at Stockholm so as to make preparations for the conference.

2/16   THE NATIONALITIES

LENIN ON THE NATIONAL QUESTION, 29 APRIL 1917*

Beginning in 1903, when our party adopted its programme, we have met each time desperate resistance from the Poles. If you study the protocols of the Second Congress, you will see that even

* From V. I. Lenin, *Sochineniya* (Moscow–Leningrad 1927), Vol. 20, pp. 275–8.

then they were putting forward the same arguments which we are now confronted with, and Polish social democrats left that Congress, finding that the acknowledgement of the right of national self-determination was unacceptable to them ...

Polish policy is a completely national one, as a result of long Russian oppression and the whole Polish nation is saturated through and through with the thought of vengeance on the Moscow gentlemen. No one has ever oppressed the Poles as the Russians have. The Russian people served under the tsars as the executioner of Polish freedom. There is no people which had such a terrible hatred of Russia as the Poles. This has given rise to a strange phenomenon. Poland is hindering the socialist movement because of the Polish bourgeoisie. Let the whole world be consumed in fire as long as Poland is free ...

Why must we, Great Russians, who are oppressing a greater number of nations than any other people, refuse to acknowledge the right of separation to Poland, the Ukraine and Finland? ...

Polish social democrats state that just because they find the alliance with Russian workers advantageous they oppose the secession of Poland. This they are completely free to do. But people do not wish to understand that in order to strengthen internationalism one does not need to repeat the very same words, and so in Russia one should support the freedom of secession of oppressed nations whereas in Poland one should emphasise the freedom of accession. The freedom of accession presupposes the freedom of secession. We Russians must emphasise the right of secession and in Poland they should emphasise the right of accession ...

The Finns only want autonomy at present. We are for giving Finland complete freedom when it increases their trust in Russian democracy. When this is put into practice they will not secede then ... The proletariat cannot resort to violence because it must not interfere with the freedom of peoples ...

The question of war is quite a different thing. We shall not refrain from waging a revolutionary war if it is necessary. We are not pacifists ...

When we have Milyukov and he sends Rodichev to Finland and he negotiates shamelessly with the Finnish people there we say: no, people of Russia, do not dare to violate Finland. A people which oppresses other peoples cannot be free itself. In the Borgberg resolution we stated: withdraw the troops and permit the nation to decide the question on its own. Suppose the Soviet takes power tomorrow that would not be the 'method of socialist revolution', we shall say then: Germany, withdraw your troops from Poland, Russia, withdraw your troops from Armenia. Anything else would be deceit.

Comrade Dzerzhinsky tells us about his oppressed Poland that all are chauvinists there. But why won't one of the Poles say a single word about what is to happen to Finland, what is to happen to the Ukraine? Since 1903 we have been arguing so much about this that it is becoming difficult to talk about it. Choose any way you like . . . Whoever does not accept this point of view is an annexationist, a chauvinist. We want the fraternal union of all peoples. If there were a Ukrainian republic and a Russian republic, there would be more contacts and more trust between them. If Ukrainians see that we have a republic of soviets, they will not secede, but if we have Milyukov's republic, then they will secede . . .

But every Russian socialist who does not recognise the freedom of Finland and the Ukraine is sliding towards chauvinism . . .

2/17 LENIN

(a) CONDITIONS FOR PASSAGE THROUGH GERMANY*

The Minister in Berne to the Chancellor

Report No. 970

AS 1317   5 April 1917

I have the honour to present the enclosed draft of the conditions for the passage of Russian *émigrés* from Switzerland to Stockholm, given me by Herr Platten.

ROMBERG

Enclosure:

Basis for discussions concerning the return of *émigrés* to Russia

1. I, Fritz Platten, will conduct the carriage carrying political *émigrés* wishing to travel to Russia, through Germany, bearing full responsibility and personal liability at all times.

* From Z. A. B. Zeman, *Germany and the Revolution in Russia 1915–1918* (London 1958), pp. 38–9.

2. All communication with German organisations will be undertaken exclusively by Platten, without whose permission absolutely nobody may enter the carriage, which will be locked at all times.

The carriage will be granted extra-territorial rights.

3. No control of passports or persons may be carried out either on entering or on leaving Germany.

4. Persons will be allowed to travel in the carriage absolutely regardless of their political opinions or their attitude towards the question of the desirability of war or peace.

5. Platten will buy tickets at the normal tariffs for those travelling.

6. As far as possible the journey shall be made without stops and in a through train. The *émigrés* may not be ordered to leave the carriage, nor may they do so on their own initiative. The journey may not be interrupted except in case of technical necessity.

7. Permission to make the journey is granted on the basis of an exchange of those travelling for Germans and Austrians imprisoned or interned in Russia.

8. The negotiator and those travelling undertake to exert themselves, publicly and especially among the workers, to see that this condition is fulfilled.

9. The time of departure from the Swiss frontier for the Swedish frontier, which should be as soon as possible, shall be agreed immediately.

Berne – Zürich, 4 April 1917

FRITZ PLATTEN

(b) THE APRIL THESES*

The tasks of the Proletariat in the present Revolution
I arrived in Petrograd on the night of April 3 and I could therefore, of course, deliver a report at a meeting on April 4 on the tasks of the revolutionary proletariat only upon my own responsibility, and with reservations as to insufficient preparation.

The only thing I could do to facilitate matters for myself and for *honest* opponents was to prepare *written* theses. I read them, and gave the text to Comrade Tseretelli. I read them very slowly,

* From Lenin, *Selected Works* (Moscow–Leningrad 1935), Vol. 6, pp. 21–4.

twice: first at a meeting of Bolsheviks, then at a meeting of Bolsheviks and Mensheviks.

I publish these personal theses with only the briefest explanatory comments. The comments were developed in far greater detail in the report.

Theses

(1) In our attitude towards the war not the slightest concession must be made to 'revolutionary defencism', for even under the new government of Lvov and Co. the war on Russia's part unquestionably remains a predatory imperialist war owing to the capitalist nature of that government.

The class conscious proletariat can consent to a revolutionary war, which would really justify revolutionary defencism, only on condition: (a) that the power of government pass to the proletariat and the poor sections of the peasantry bordering on the proletariat; (b) that all annexations be renounced in deed as well as in words; (c) that a complete and real break be made with all capitalist interests.

In view of the undoubted honesty of the mass of the rank-and-file believers in revolutionary defencism, who accept the war as a necessity only and not as a means of conquest; in view of the fact that they are being deceived by the bourgeoisie, it is necessary thoroughly, persistently and patiently to explain their error to them, to explain the indissoluble connection between capital and the imperialist war, and to prove that *it is impossible* to end the war by a truly democratic, non-coercive peace without the overthrow of capital.

The widespread propaganda of this view among the army on active service must be organised.

Fraternisation.

(2) The specific feature of the present situation in Russia is that it represents a *transition* from the first stage of the revolution – which, owing to the insufficient class consciousness and organisation of the proletariat, led to the assumption of power by the bourgeoisie – *to the second stage,* which must place power in the hands of the proletariat and the poor strata of the peasantry.

This transition is characterised, on the one hand, by a maximum of freedom (Russia is *now* the freest of all the belligerent countries in the world); on the other, by the absence of violence in relation to the masses, and, finally, by the naïve confidence of the masses in the government of capitalists, the worst enemies of peace and socialism.

This specific situation demands on our part an ability to adapt ourselves to the specific requirements of Party work among unprecedentedly large masses of proletarians who have just awakened to political life.

(3) No support must be given to the Provisional Government; the utter falsity of all its promises must be exposed, particularly of those relating to the renunciation of annexations. Exposure, and not the unpardonable illusion-breeding 'demand' that this government, a government of capitalists, should *cease* to be an imperialist government.

(4) The fact must be recognised that in most of the Soviets of Workers' Deputies our Party is in a minority, and so far in a small minority, as against *a bloc of all* the petty-bourgeois opportunist elements, who have yielded to the influence of the bourgeoisie and are the conveyors of its influence to the proletariat, from the Narodni-Socialists and the Socialist-Revolutionaries down to the Organisation Committee (Chkheidze, Tsereltelli, etc.), Steklov, etc., etc.

It must be explained to the masses that the Soviet of Workers' Deputies is the *only possible* form of revolutionary government and that therefore our task is, as long as *this* government submits to the influence of the bourgeoisie, to present a patient, systematic, and persistent *explanation* of its errors and tactics, an explanation especially adapted to the practical needs of the masses.

As long as we are in the minority we carry on the work of criticising and exposing errors and at the same time advocate the necessity of transferring the entire power of state to the Soviets of Workers' Deputies, so that the masses may by experience overcome their mistakes.

(5) Not a parliamentary republic – to return to a parliamentary republic from the Soviets of Workers' Deputies would be a retrograde step – but a republic of Soviets of Workers', Agricultural Labourers' and Peasants' Deputies throughout the country, from top to bottom.

Abolition of the police, the army and the bureaucracy.

The salaries of all officials, who are to be elected and be subject to recall at any time, not to exceed the average wage of a competent worker.

(6) The agrarian programme must be centred around the Soviets of Agricultural Labourers' Deputies.

Confiscation of all landed estates.

Nationalisation of *all* lands in the country, the disposal of such lands to be in the charge of the local Soviets of Agricultural Labourers' and Peasants' Deputies. The organisation of separate Soviets of Deputies of the Poor Peasants. The creation of model farms on each of the large estates (varying from 100 to 300 dessyatinas, in accordance with local and other conditions, at the discretion of the local institutions) under the control of the Agricultural Labourers' Deputies and for the public account.

(7) The immediate amalgamation of all banks in the country into a single national bank, control over which shall be exercised by the Soviet of Workers' Deputies.

(8) Our *immediate* task shall be not the 'introduction of socialism', but to bring social production and distribution of products at once only under the *control* of the Soviet of Workers' Deputies.

(9) Party tasks:

    (a) Immediate summoning of a Party congress.

    (b) Alteration of the Party programme, mainly:

        1. On the question of imperialism and the imperialist war;

        2. On the question of our attitude towards the state and our demand for a 'commune state.'

        3. Amendment of our antiquated minimum programme;

    (c) A new name for the Party.

(10) A new International.

(c) KAMENEV DISSENTS*

In yesterday's issue of *Pravda* Comrade Lenin published his 'theses'. They represent the *personal* opinion of Comrade Lenin and by publishing them Comrade Lenin did something which is the duty of every outstanding public man – to submit to the judgment of the revolutionary democracy of Russia his under-

* From 'Our Differences', by L. Kamenev, *Pravda*, 8 April 1917, as reproduced in Lenin, *The Revolution of 1917*, Book 2 (London n.d.), pp. 380–1.

standing of current events. Comrade Lenin did it in a very concise form, but he did it *thoroughly*. Having begun with a characterisation of the World War, he came to the conclusion that it is necessary to create a new Communist Party. In his report he naturally had to criticise not only the policy of the leaders of the Soviet of Workers' and Soldiers' Deputies, but also the policy of *Pravda* as it appeared at the time of the Soviet Congress and expressed itself in the activities of the Bolshevik delegates at the congress. This policy of *Pravda* was clearly formulated in the resolutions on the same Provisional Government and on the war, formulated and made public at the same congress after they were prepared by the Bureau of the Central Committee and approved by the Bolshevik delegates at the congress.

Pending new decisions of the Central Committee and of the All-Russian conference of our party, those resolutions remain our platform which we will defend both against the demoralising influence of 'Revolutionary defencism' and against Comrade Lenin's criticism.

As regards Comrade Lenin's general line, it appears to us unacceptable inasmuch as it proceeds from the assumption that the bourgeois-democratic revolution *has been completed* and it builds on the immediate transformation of this revolution into a Socialist revolution. The tactics that follow from such analysis are greatly at variance with the tactics defended by the representatives of *Pravda* at the All-Russian Congress both against the official leaders of the Soviet and against the Mensheviks who dragged the Soviet to the Right.

In a broad discussion we hope to carry our point of view as the only possible one for revolutionary Social-Democracy in so far as it wishes to be and must remain to the very end the one and only party of the revolutionary masses of the proletariat without turning into a group of Communist propagandists.

Pravda, No. 27, 8 April 1917.

2/18   WHO INSTIGATED THE FEBRUARY REVOLUTION?

(A)*

The collapse of the Romanov autocracy in February 1917 was one of the most leaderless, spontaneous, anonymous revolutions of all time. While almost every thoughtful observer in Russia in the winter of 1916–17 foresaw the likelihood of the crash of the existing régime no one, even among the revolutionary leaders, realized that the strikes and bread riots which broke out in Petrograd on February 23 would culminate in the mutiny of the garrison and the overthrow of the government four days later.

(B)*

The February revolution of 1917 which overthrew the Romanov dynasty was the spontaneous outbreak of a multitude exasperated by the privations of the war and by manifest inequality in the distribution of burdens. It was welcomed and utilized by a broad stratum of the bourgeoisie and of the official class, which had lost confidence in the autocratic system of government and especially in the persons of the Tsar and of his advisers; it was from this section of the population that the first Provisional Government was drawn. The revolutionary parties played no direct part in the making of the revolution. They did not expect it, and were at first somewhat nonplussed by it. The creation at the moment of the revolution of a Petrograd Soviet of Workers' Deputies was a spontaneous act of groups of workers without central direction. It was a revival of the Petersburg Soviet which had played a brief but glorious role in the revolution of 1905, and was, like its predecessor, a non-party organization elected by factory workers, Social-Revolutionaries, Mensheviks and Bolsheviks being all represented in it. It did not at first aspire to governmental power, partly because its leaders took the hitherto accepted view that Russia was ripe only for a bourgeois and not yet for a

* From W. H. Chamberlin, *The Russian Revolution 1917–1921* (New York 1952), Vol. 1, p. 73.

† From E. H. Carr, *The Bolshevik Revolution 1917–1923* (London 1966), Vol. 1, p. 81.

socialist revolution, and partly because it had no sense of its own competence or preparedness to govern.

(c)*

As for the third 'conspiratorial' theory of the Petrograd rising, we have lent this throughout our unreserved support, more particularly in the chapter on German intervention. The belief that German agents were behind it is as old as the events themselves – indeed older, for the Russian government had suspected and indeed known of the German wartime influence on the labour movement in Russia long before the Petrograd rising. But only in the last ten years or so have certain revelations tended to corroborate these suspicions. We know now for certain that from the very beginning of the war the German government consistently pursued in Russia a *Revolutionierungspolitik*, an essential element of which was the support of an economic strike movement capable, so it was hoped, of gradually escalating into a political revolution. The chief theoretician of this policy, Alexander Helphand, thought the country ripe for revolution as early as 1916. We know for certain that the German government expended considerable sums on fostering the strike movement up to the spring of 1916. For most of 1916 and the beginning of 1917, we lack evidence of direct instigation of labour unrest in Russia by the German agencies. It would, however, be foolish to ignore the existence of such agencies as a factor contributing to the revolution of 1917, which took precisely the form predicted by Helphand as early as the spring of 1915. It seems reasonable either to suggest that the successful popular rising of February 1917 was organised by the same agents as instigated the abortive 'trial run' the previous February or to assume that it was a direct sequel to the movement begun in 1916.

A political revolution entailing the fall of the Tsarist régime was the maximum the Germans could hope for in organising and backing Russian labour unrest during the war. The disruption of the war effort brought about by frequent and prolonged strikes was regarded by them as sufficient justification in itself for the support they gave Helphand and similar agents. The revolution

* From G. Katkov, *Russia 1917 The February Revolution* (London 1967), pp. 422–3.

came as a windfall much hoped for by some, but hardly expected by any, and necessitated a radical revision of German policy. The problem was now not so much to weaken Russia as an opponent as to effect a separate peace. Again on Helphand's suggestion, the Germans decided the best way to achieve this result would be to bring to power the Bolshevik Party, which alone among major political groups in the new Russia was prepared to conclude an immediate armistice. The dislocation of production could also safely be left to the Bolsheviks, who would effect it as part of the class war. Military sabotage which Helphand always linked with his strike propaganda, continued to be organised by special German agents trained for work of this kind. But the tenuous and highly conspiratorial links connecting Helphand with the Russian strike movement could now be safely severed, and all record of them be erased. This explains why so little documentary evidence of these links exists.

(D)*

To the question, who led the February uprising? we can answer definitely enough: conscious and tempered workers educated in the main by the party of Lenin. But we must add here: this leadership proved sufficient to guarantee the victory of the uprising but it was not adequate to secure immediately the leading role in the revolution for the proletarian vanguard.

* From L. Trotsky, *Fevralskaya Revolyutsiya* (Berlin 1931), p. 180.

3 Russia Between Two Revolutions: Economic and Social Aspects of the Period February to October 1917

The task which faced the government after the revolution was formidable. Russia was suffering severely from the effects of almost three years of war. Industry was deteriorating. New equipment was very difficult to acquire. The transport network, especially the railways, was not equal to the demands placed on it. Essential fuel supplies and raw materials were not reaching their destinations.

The government passed some socially advanced labour legislation (for example 3/1). It permitted factory committees which made life very difficult for management. It tried its hands at planning. It decreed the state monopoly of grain purchases in March so as to ensure a supply of bread for the population. Peasants resented having to sell to the state. The notes they received in payment were rapidly devalued by inflation (3/6).

The militancy of factory committees contributed to the disruption of industry (3/3). There was little the government could do except appeal for calm.

The peasant's conviction that he had been cheated out of his fair portion during the emancipation in 1861 was still alive in 1917. His eyes were always on the landlord's land. The weakening of central authority emboldened him to seize some of the landlord's land.

The main peasant political party, the Socialist Revolutionaries, had adopted the transfer of landlord's land to the peasant as part of their programme. The SRs were influential in the Soviets and their leader, Victor Chernov, was Minister of Agriculture in the first and second coalition governments. The demands of the rural population were loud and clear (3/2b). Nevertheless no government could agree on how to solve the problem. No land reform, and it would have been a very complex subject to legislate upon, could have been enacted without an end to the war. The peasants in uniform at the front would have returned to their villages to ensure their fair shares. Also a government which contained liberals could hardly have been expected to give land to peasants without compensation for the previous owners.

Separatist tendencies, especially in the Ukraine and Trans-caucasia, added to the problems.

The food situation in one area on the eve of the October revolution is well illustrated (3/7).

3/1 WORKING CONDITIONS IN PETROGRAD: THE EIGHT-HOUR DAY, etc.*

An agreement has been reached between the Petrograd Soviet of Workers' and Soldiers' Deputies and the Petrograd Association of Manufacturers on the introduction of an eight hour working day in factories and works, factory committees and on the setting up of councils of arbitration.

I. The Eight Hour Working Day

1. Until the law standardising the working day is promulgated, the eight hour working day (eight hours of actual work), affecting all shifts, is introduced in all factories and works.

2. On Saturdays the working day is to last seven hours.

3. The reduction of working hours is not to affect the wages of workers.

4. Overtime is permitted only with the consent of factory committees.

II. Factory Committees

1. Factory committees (councils of elders), elected from among the workers of a given enterprise on the basis of universal, equal, and etc. suffrage, are to be established in all factories and works.

* From *Izvestiya*, 11 March 1917.

2. The duties of these committees are to be as follows: (i) to represent the workers in a given enterprise in their relations with government or public institutions; (ii) to advance opinions on questions relating to the social and economic life of workers in a given enterprise; (iii) to settle problems arising from disputes among workers in a given enterprise; (iv) to represent workers before the management in matters concerning labour–management relations.

III. Councils of Arbitration

1. Councils of arbitration are to be set up in all works and factories to settle all misunderstandings arising from labour–management relations.

Note: If necessary, councils of arbitration may be subdivided into sections and shops.

2. Councils of arbitration are to be composed of an equal number of elected representatives from the shop floor and from the management of the enterprise.

3. The procedure for electing the workers is to be decided by the factory committee.

4. Councils of arbitration are to meet when circumstances require it.

5. If no agreement is reached by workers and employers in the council of arbitration, the matter is then to be passed to and settled by the Central Council of Arbitration.

6. The Central Council of Arbitration is to be composed of an equal number of elected representatives from the Soviet of Workers' Deputies, on the one hand, and from the Association of Manufacturers, on the other.

IV. The removal of foremen and other administrative officials without recourse to a council of arbitration, and their subsequent removal (by physical force) are prohibited.

V. The matter of the status of employees must be determined straight away.

3/2   THE LAND QUESTION

(a) *Izvestiya* PROCLAIMS ALL LAND TO THE PEOPLE*

The revolution in Russia brought peasants the good news of the realisation of their old dream concerning the transfer of all land to the people.

There is no place for landowner tutelage in a free Russia. It is quite out of the question that peasants should start paying a ransom to their age-old oppressors to end bondage.

All land will be transferred to the people without redemption payments. The revolution will not allow any other solution of the land question.

The land question is the most important question affecting national life. This question affects the basic interests of tens of millions of our citizens. And that is why all the people must be asked to resolve this question. Deciding the land question without the participation of all the people would be like deciding the question without the master.

The Constituent Assembly expresses the will of all the people. This means that the right to the final decision on the land question rests with the Constituent Assembly.

Peasants must get ready to decide the land question before the Constituent Assembly meets. All data for deciding the question must be provided; land relations must be regulated; organisation must be efficient. This is the responsibility of the local peasant committees.

However, these committees would be gravely in error if they start seizing landowners' property to transform it into the property of the local peasant population. Such land seizures would result in an inequitable distribution of *pomeshchik* property among the peasants. Villages near rich estates would seize more than their share. Other villages would receive nothing. One section of the peasantry would begin to bear a grudge against the other. Village would rise against village, *volost* against *volost*. This would greatly harm the revolution since the strength of the revolution is the unity of the people any discord would be fatal to the revolution.

There is yet another danger in unauthorised land seizures.

* From *Izvestiya*, 2 May 1917.

These seizures may reduce the sown area and may decrease the quantity of grain in the country. No one can be sure that everyone will not take more land than he can cultivate. Russia will face a famine if the sown area is reduced as a result of land and stock seizures. We have no surplus grain now. Even so, the country is just able to produce enough grain . . .

All vacant and free land must be taken immediately and communally cultivated. Not a single piece of land may be wasted. The *guberniya* committees must ensure that the private livestock of the *pomeshchiks* is put to the best use in the interests of the people.

However, it must be remembered that the final decision on the land question belongs to the Constituent Assembly. It alone can solve the land question in all its ramifications and in all fairness.

Let the local peasant committees not interfere with the rights of the Constituent Assembly.

Seize the free land, brother peasants! Grow again grain for the country!

Wait for the Constituent Assembly to take the final decision!

(b) THE FIRST ALL-RUSSIAN CONGRESS OF PEASANTS' SOVIETS: RESOLUTION ON LAND QUESTION*

The All-Russian Congress of Peasants' Deputies announces to the entire Russian peasantry that henceforth not only the final solution of the agrarian problem in the Constituent Assembly, but all the preparatory work to be done by the local and central land committees passes into the hands of the working people themselves. For this reason, the first, most important, and most responsible task of the more progressive part of the peasantry is the organization of elections to the *volost* and *uezd zemstvos,* and the establishment of land committees in connection with these *zemstvos.* The work of these committees in the preparation of land reforms is to be based on the following principles: The transfer, without compensation, of all lands now belonging to the state, monasteries, churches, and private persons into the possession of the nation, for equitable and free use by agricultural workers.

Firmly believing in the growing strength, organization, and intelligence of the toiling peasantry, the All-Russian Congress of

* From *Rech,* 25 May 1917.

Peasants' Delegates is deeply convinced that private ownership of land with its forests, water power, and mineral resources will be abolished by the National Constituent Assembly, which will establish a fundamental law as regards the land, the conditions of its transfer to the workers, and its distribution for use.

The All-Russian Congress of Peasants' Deputies is also convinced that in all land committees, from that of the *volost* to the Central Committee, the working peasantry, taking advantage of the elective system, will see to it that all the preparatory work for the agrarian reform shall be carried out with the object of emancipating the land from the bonds of private property, without any compensation.

The All-Russian Congress of Peasants' Deputies expects the Provisional Government to assist, as far as it lies within its power, in the free expression of the working people's opinion on the important problem of reorganization, now confronting Russia, and to prevent all attempts at interference with this work by persons who put their personal and party interests above those of the country.

The All-Russian Congress of Peasants' Deputies urges the Provisional Government to issue an absolutely clear and unequivocal statement which will show that on this question the Provisional Government will allow nobody to oppose the people's will.

The All-Russian Congress of Peasants' Deputies resolves that:

The necessity of settling the food-supply crisis, and of a successful struggle with the economic disorder throughout the country, in this hour of an oppressive and exhausting world war, imperatively demands that all private and party interests yield to the higher interests of the whole people and the State.

In view of this, all land, without exception, must be given over to the land committees, which should have the power to issue regulations for cultivation, sowing, harvesting, making hay, etc.

Because of the drafting for war service of an enormous number of workers, and their extreme scarcity in the harvest season, it is necessary that all able-bodied workers, voluntary agricultural organizations, artels, and war prisoners be put at the disposal of the above land committees, and be distributed not to the advantage of individuals, but in the interests of all the toiling population.

Because of the lack and the worn condition of the agricultural machinery, most energetic measures are necessary for the requisitioning and putting to use on a public and a co-operative basis of all agricultural machines and tools which Russia can make available, and for inviting technical men to run them. Also, in view of the number of peasants' horses requisitioned and the extreme scarcity of live farm stock, it is necessary to utilize the live stock to be found outside of farms.

Making hay, harvesting, storing of grain, fishing, preparation of timber, firewood and other forest materials must be put under the control of the land committees and other authorised public organisations, in order to prevent individual hoarding of the greatly needed supplies or exploiting the natural resources of the land.

The fixing of land rents and payments, the fixing of wages for agricultural labour, and similar questions must be given over entirely to the local land committees. In disputed cases, the rent is to be kept in the local State treasury.

Until the putting into force of national reforms, the local land committees shall be allowed complete freedom of initiative and activity in all the above-mentioned land questions. With this in mind, all interference on the part of *guberniya* and *uezd* commissars must be removed. One-sided selection of staffs, from among the land-owning class, must also be done away with.

In order to preserve intact the amount of land available for the coming land reform, it is necessary [to pass a strict law] to be enforced by the land committees, prohibiting the buying, selling, bequeathing and mortgaging of land, until the Constituent Assembly.

The All-Russian Congress of Peasants' Deputies is of the opinion that only under such arrangements is it possible to prepare, for the land reform, without too many disturbances, lawless seizures, civil dissensions, and other illegal acts. Only under such arrangements is it possible to bring to life a new agrarian order, worthy of free Russia, able to unite in one fraternity, one State, all toilers of the land, without distinction of nationality, religion, and condition – Great Russians and Little Russians, Christians and Muslims, peasants and Cossacks, natives of Russia and of outlying regions. . . . Each of these groups will feel the beneficial results of the great reform, and will bless it.

The All-Russian Congress of Peasants' Deputies invites the whole peasantry to remain peaceful, but to work with determination and steadfastness for the realization in a legal manner of the cherished thoughts and hopes of the agricultural labourer, which have long since found expression in the motto, so dear to each peasant, 'Land and Liberty.'

The Congress decided in favour of the following special appeal to the population:

The All-Russian Congress of Peasants' Deputies appeals to the peasants and the whole wage-earning population of Russia to vote, at the elections to the Constituent Assembly, only for those candidates who pledge themselves to advocate the nationalization of the land, without reimbursement, and on principles of equality.

This was followed by a few remarks by Rivkin . . . who called attention to the bands of deserters, and pointed out that all the efforts to organize committees and soviets would be of no value, if they were to live in fear of these armed bands. It was necessary, he said, to form a committee of self-defence, and to arm the population; otherwise they could have no assurance that they would live long enough to see the Constituent Assembly.

3/3 THE ECONOMIC SITUATION

(a) KONOVALOV ON CHAOS*

Without false shame, openly and honestly we must recognise that we are confronted with a task which needs a solution urgently. A task which is absolutely unprecedented in its dimensions and difficulty. You know very well yourselves that both at the centre and in the provinces there are continually attempts to override the rights of some and to create privileges for others, attempts to deny the principles of liberty and law and to replace them with the principles of violence. These anti-national tendencies mask their real content under slogans which are hypnotising the masses and are leading Russia towards catastrophe very rapidly. We must frankly and honestly recognise that under the old order this catastrophe was never so vividly and clearly apparent as now;

* From *Vestnik Vremennago Pravitelstva*, 18 May 1917.

never during the whole war has our position at the front been as ominous as now; never has the enemy sensed his superiority over us to such an extent as now; and, finally, never have our allies been so alarmed by the possibility of losing completely everything that guarantees a successful end to the war. And, internally, have we ever been so near a catastrophe which would shatter our whole economic life and which we are now moving towards? The slogans which are now being unfurled among the workers, exciting the dark instincts of the mob, are being followed by devastation, anarchy and the destruction of public and national life. Influenced by the agitation of irresponsible individuals, the working masses are putting forward demands which would lead to the total destruction of enterprises, if accepted. The deliberate fanning of passions is being conducted systematically and relentlessly; demands are being constantly followed by new ones; their presentation becoming more intolerable and unacceptable. The normal working of industrial enterprises has been seriously interrupted and the energy of the nation must be marshalled to overcome the economic disintegration, to prevent economic ruin overtaking the country, and to defend adequately the country. When we overthrew the old régime we believed absolutely that freedom would bring about a great expansion of the productive forces of the country. Now it is not a question of thinking about developing productive forces, but of making every effort to protect the industry which existed in the difficult conditions of the old régime from total ruin. And if the confused minds do not see reason soon, if people do not realise that they are sawing off the branch they are sitting on, if the leaders of the Soviet of Workers' and Soldiers' Deputies do not manage to control the movement and to guide it into the channels of legitimate class struggle, then scores and hundreds of enterprises will close down. We shall experience the complete paralysis of national life and shall embark upon a long period of irreparable economic disaster when millions will be unemployed, without bread, without a home, and when the crisis will affect one branch of the economy after the other, bringing with it everywhere death, devastation, and misery, partly ending credit and producing financial crises and everyone's ruin. Only then will the masses see the abyss into which they have permitted themselves to be dragged, but by then it will be too late. The state cannot accept the responsibility of granting the working class an exclusively privileged position at the expense of the whole population. The Provisional Government is seeking ways of defusing the explosive situation which now exists between the representatives of labour and capital. At the same time the Government is searching for general measures to regulate national economic life. The Government expects assistance, asks for energetic support from all those to whom the success of the revolutionary cause is dear. If the Government has the necessary power, if everyone feels personally responsible for the fate of Russia, then I have no doubt that Russia will overcome completely the dangers that are threatening her at the present moment.

(b) VIOLENCE IN A PIPE FACTORY*

The campaign launched by the Bolsheviks for the re-election of representatives to the regional soviet has inflamed passions. The re-election was set for Wednesday 17 May. However, since the representatives of the Executive Committee of the Soviet of Workers' and Soldiers' Deputies had decided to hold a meeting with socialist ministers present that day in the pipe factory, the factory committee postponed the election until the 18th. This annoyed the Bolsheviks. Under their influence the forge workers decided not to comply with the decision of the factory committee and arranged the election for the 17th. Hence the work was not started in the forge on the morning of the 17th. The factory committee sent a representative to negotiate when they discovered this. The representative explained that rumours that other shops had supported the decision of the forge workers were false. And apparently he succeeded in explaining the incorrectness of the position taken by the forge workers. However, after he had left, the factory committee were informed again of the unsettled mood in the forge. Comrade Kapanitsky (S.R.), member of the Petrograd Soviet of Workers' and Soldiers' Deputies and the representative on duty of the factory committee, was met in a very hostile manner. The forge workers decided to punish him as a result of his appeal to comply with the decision of the factory committee. Someone suggested throwing him into the furnace. But they later abandoned the plan ('furnaces for other, more important members of the

* From *Rabochaya Gazeta*, 20 May 1917.

Soviet of Workers' and Soldiers' Deputies'). They decided to take Comrade Kapanitsky in a wheelbarrow to the river and drown him. The official representative of the factory committee was then thrown into a wheelbarrow to be taken to the Neva to be drowned. Other shops found out about this and came to rescue their representative. A free fight ensued. The forge workers threw the factory committee representative out of the wheelbarrow. There were many other victims. Finally the workers rescued their representative from the hands of the forge workers.

3/4 THE FUEL SHORTAGE*

Russia needs 80 million puds of coal every fortnight. During the first half of August, 52 million puds were due to be shipped from the Donets region. Only 35 million puds were moved; i.e. the shortfall was 17 million puds, or 32 per cent of the coal intended for shipment.

It appears that during the first half of August the disruption of rail transport played no role in the reduction of shipments. Of course a shortage of railway wagons was felt in some stations. However, at the same time the railways even transported part of the reserves from some mines. And during these two weeks the quantity of coal mined was 17 million puds less than the volume scheduled for shipment.

During the first half of August 1917, 43 million puds of coal were mined. During the same period in 1916 54 million puds of coal were mined. During the same two weeks 7 million puds of coke were produced; the same period in 1916 yielded 11 million puds.

Normally a drop in labour productivity is the reason for such a shortfall. As a matter of fact the productivity of a miner dropped to 207 puds during the first half of August, 10 puds less than during the first half of July 1917 and 40 per cent lower than that attained during the first half of August 1916.

But it would be wrong to regard the drop in labour productivity as the sole reason for the coal crisis, for we are confronted here with the operation of a whole chain of complex causes besides the simple unwillingness of the workers to do their job well. We

* From *Russkiya Vedomosti*, 8 September 1917.

are aware that one cannot reduce everything to the enmity of the workers. Labour productivity began dropping long before the revolution. *Den* has made use of very striking figures from Mr Vukublin's report to the All-Russian Congress on Donets Fuel. During the first half of 1915 the average output per worker in the Donets region was 4,616 puds; during the second half of 1915, 4,400 puds; during the first half of 1916, 3,888 puds; during the second half of 1916, 3,537 puds; during the first half of 1917, 2,858 puds. Labour productivity in pre-revolutionary Russia dropped on average from half year to half year by 9.66 per cent. Over the period January–March 1917 output per worker was 1,553 puds; and over the period April–June 1,355 puds; i.e. the post-revolutionary period reveals a reduction of 12 per cent instead of the previous 9.66 per cent.

Therefore the fall in coal output was brought about, besides workers' disorders, by conditions prevailing in the mining industry; the disruption of transport, the disorganisation of trade and the undermining of the foundations of industry. The special commission which studied the Donets region in August, while stressing the significance of the unorganised, spontaneous movement of the workers, also highlighted some other reasons for the continual drop in the efficiency of the coal mines: the shortage of metal and coal carts, the lack of timber for pit props, the inadequate investment resources, etc. According to the *Torgovo-Promyshlennaya Gazeta* 4.5 to 5 million rubles are needed to produce 10 million puds of coal. Before the war only 2.5 to 3 million rubles were needed.

If we add to this the acute food situation in which the Donets region finds itself, we get a complete picture of the vicious circle confronting industry in the Donets region. An all round lowering of industrial techniques, together with a complete inability to improve the situation in the short run, the confused food situation, all this fosters unrest among the unenlightened working masses. War and revolution have removed the best elements from among them, replacing them with prisoners of war, women and children. Their productivity does not exceed 50 per cent of those they replace. And the spontaneous movement among the workers, which takes the form of unbearable excesses and violence, is an added blow to the technical and financial burdens of the coal mining industry.

Given these circumstances, it is a waste of time to look for culprits. What is needed apparently is a long period of recuperation for industry and an all round raising of the cultural level of the masses.

3/5 AGRARIAN DISORDERS IN EUROPEAN RUSSIA, MARCH–SEPTEMBER 1917*

The table of the Main Land Committee gives a clear picture of the agrarian movement in the various *guberniyas* of European Russia. *Guberniyas* are divided into six groups according to the incidence of agrarian disorders. In the first, the lowest, group, with ten uprisings or less, are the *guberniyas* of Olonets, Vologda, Yaroslavl, Vyatka and Ural *oblast*, Estland, Kovno, Grodno and the Caucasus. In the second group, from eleven to twenty-five uprisings, are the *guberniyas* of Moscow, Vladimir, Kostroma, Perm, Astrakhan, the Don Army *oblast* and the Tauride. In the third group, from twenty-six to fifty uprisings, are Lifland, Petrograd, Novgorod, Tver, Kaluga, Nizhny–Novgorod, Ufa, Kharkov, Ekaterinoslav, Bessarabia, Podoliya, Volhynia and Vilno. In the fourth group, from fifty-one to seventy-five uprisings, are the *guberniyas* of Vitebsk, Smolensk, Orlov, Poltava, Kiev, Kherson, Saratov and Orenburg. In the fifth group, from seventy-six to one hundred uprisings, are Minsk, Tula, Kursk, Voronezh, Tambov, Penza and Simbirsk. Finally, in the sixth, the highest group, 101 and more uprisings, are Pskov, Mogilev, Ryazan, Kazan and Samara *guberniyas*.

Centres of the peasant movement in the central agricultural regions are Ryazan, Kursk, Tambov, Tula and Voronezh *guberniyas*; in the middle Volga; Kazan, Samara, Simbirsk and Penza *guberniyas* and in the western lakes; Pskov, Mogilev and Minsk *guberniyas*. From these centres the peasant movement drops and its intensity decreases as it spreads towards the north, east and south. Leading the movement are regions where semi-serf methods of exploitation of peasants were still strong. We are unable to establish, on the basis of the evidence of the Main Land Committee, the distribution of peasant movements by types in the various regions of Russia.

* From *Krasnii Arkhiv* (Moscow–Leningrad 1926), Vol. 14, pp. 184–5.

3/6 INFLATION*

At the beginning of the war Russia had a monetary system in which the notes issued were more in the nature of gold certificates, the exchange fund being much larger than the statutory requirements. Like all other belligerent countries Russia suspended the gold standard at the outbreak of war. Appeals to the public to deposit gold with the State Bank failed. Banks continued to work normally and no moratorium on outstanding debts had to be granted.

Russian war expenditure was heavy. Over 17,000 million rubles were needed for the period up to August 1916. The ever-increasing war needs had to be met more and more by resorting to the printing press. On the whole the use of the printing press made itself felt only gradually.

Prices, in general, remained relatively stable until the end of 1916. The most important factors in undermining public confidence were the shock of military defeat and the revelations about the mismanagement of the country in 1916. A factor in raising the price of consumer goods was the transfer of labour to industries producing war materials. The loss to the enemy of industrial areas which had been characterised by high productivity (e.g. Poland) and the maldistribution of food products also contributed to the increase of prices. Labour productivity in such industries as textiles dropped as a result (Poland was an important textile area).

Table 3/6. 1 illustrates the movement of prices. (1913=100)

TABLE 3/6. 1†

	1913	100
	1915	130
Jan	1916	155
Jan	1917	300
Oct	1917	755

* From unpublished paper by M. McCauley.

† A. A. Vainshtein, *Tseny i Tsenoobrazovanie v SSSR* (Moscow 1972), p. 30.

Table 3/6. 2 shows the number of notes in circulation
TABLE 3/6. 2* (1914 = 100)

16 Jul	1914	100
1 Jan	1915	181
1 Jan	1916	344
1 Jan	1917	557
1 Mar	1917	609
23 Oct	1917	1158

The rate of inflation can be illustrated by the fact that before the advent to power of the Provisional Government the average monthtly issue of notes (1914–17) was about 300 million rubles. Under the Provisional Government it rose to 1,083 million rubles per month. The so-called Liberty Loan, launched by Kerensky, only met with limited success. Public confidence had collapsed.

3/7 GENERAL BALUEV ON THE FOOD SUPPLY SITUATION*

13 October 1917

The Commander in Chief of the Western Front reports to you that, following threats by the starving population of the city and *uezd* to loot and burn down the army storehouses, the commander of the Vyazma garrison ordered seven wagons of flour to be removed from the storehouses and made available to the population. Requests, supported by remarks about possible excesses and pogroms, are coming in from the food supply committees in the cities near the front line to provide food for the population. Hence the front, already in a very serious condition, is confronted with a great new danger from the starving population. A total breakdown in supply is possible. It is now thirteen days since the ration was fixed at one pound of bread and seven-eighths of a pound of hardtack. During that time there has been a 68 per cent shortfall in deliveries of flour. The hardtack is almost all gone. We shall

* Index based on A. M. Michelson, *Russian Public Finance during the War* (New Haven 1928) p. 379.

* From *Ekonomicheskoe Polozhenie Rossii nakanune Velikoi Oktyabrskoi Sotsialisticheskoi Revolyutsii* (Moscow 1957), Part 2, p. 290.

have to use the field rations, i.e. deny the front its last supplies for use in case of movement. This may result in serious consequences. However, the Ministry of Food, evidently does not realise the seriousness of the situation at the front. It does not provide any tangible help, but merely confirms that the Western Front is in a sorrowful state. Alarming news is arriving from the front about discontent as a result of the reduction of the bread ration. General Baluev adds to this that he considers it his duty to report to you the situation at the front and the mood of the people. He urgently requests that extra measures be taken to provide both the front and the population with foodstuffs, otherwise the most terrible consequences are unavoidable.

3/8   ANTI-SEMITISM IN BESSARABIA*

SOROKY, Guberniya of Bessarabia

Widespread agrarian agitation is being conducted in Soroky *uezd* as well as in other parts of Bessarabia. One of the local agitators put forward the motion that every peasant deputy must, on return-ing from the Congress 'personally choke one landlord'. This same Arman stated that if he is given two land surveyors he will solve the whole agrarian problem in the *uezd* once and for all in a week. The agitation has resulted in a strong agrarian movement. Land is being seized not only from the *pomeshchiks*, but from peasants as well. Resolutions are being passed by Moldavians expelling Malorussians, who bought land from the local *pomeshchiks*, from the *uezd*. Besides Podolians are being recom-mended to return to Podoliya to 'their landlord' and the long cultivated land for which the Podolians have paid instalments to the bank for over a year be abandoned for seizure by Moldavians. The consequence of all this was that by the middle of September the area of land sown to winter wheat was 40 per cent down on 1916. Arable land was even more neglected.

Looting and murder are common occurrences in the *uezd*. The administration is impotent. The militia cannot cope with the situation. The pogrom movement is growing. There is talk of putting all the blame on the Jews. The Soroky Municipal Duma

* From *Russkiya Vedomosti*, 7 October 1917.

cannot meet since the population will not tolerate the situation, that of the thirty-three members of the Municipal Duma, twenty-two are Jews. Once, when a Jew was elected chairman they broke up the meeting and attacked the Duma members. The way rumours from the capital are understood by unenlightened minds may be illustrated by the remark of one woman who said that things would now improve since 'Kerensky had married the republic and a tsar would soon be born to them!'

MAP 1   Russia in Turmoil 1914–17

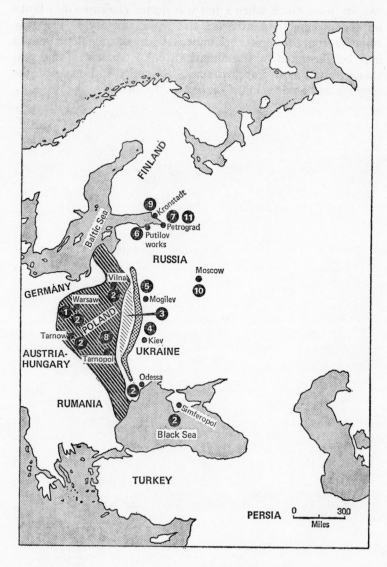

LEGEND

(**1**) 1914. Russian promises of autonomy were too vague to win full Polish loyalty. The Finns and Ukrainians were also disappointed by Russia's reluctance to satisfy their national aspirations

(**2**) 1914–15. Many of Russia's four million Jews welcomed German liberation from Tsarist tyranny and persecution

(**3**) 1915–17. Front line troops grew steadily more defeatist as a result of lack of ammunition, insufficient clothing, poor rations and Bolshevik anti-war propaganda

(**4**) 1916–17. Bands of deserters and marauders lived behind the lines, looting the peasantry and spreading demoralisation among the troops

(**5**) 1916–17. The Tsar lived in increasing isolation at his military head-quarters

(**6**) 1916. Strikes in munition factory suppressed by military force

(**7**) 1917. February revolution. The Tsar abdicated. A Provisional Government continued with the war. The Bolsheviks demanded immediate peace

(**8**) 1917. July mutinies. Hundreds of fleeing Russians were shot down by the Government's orders

(**9**) 1917 July. Sailors and factory workers called for an end to the war

(**10**) 1917 August. Factory workers' strike, demanding an end to the war

(**11**) 1917 October revolution. Bolsheviks seize power and promised immediate peace. All fighting stopped at once, from the Baltic to the Black Sea. A formal armistice came into effect on 22 November 1917

 The Eastern Front 1914–17

MAP 2   The Fall of the Monarchy 1917

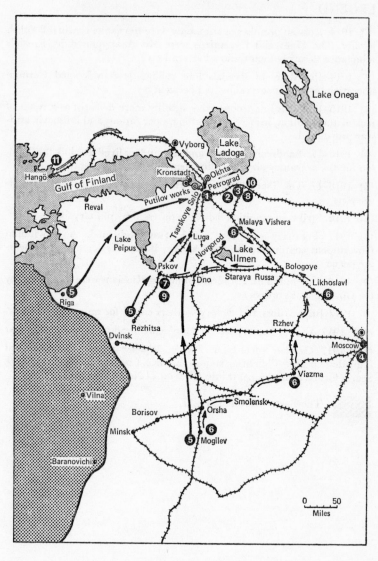

In February 1917 Petrograd was the centre of strikes and demonstrations against the enormous hardships caused by the war. A Provisional Government was set up, and demanded liberal reforms. The Tsar made no serious attempt to restore his authority either by force or by persuasion. Unable even to reach his capital, and having lost the support of his generals, he abdicated. None of the revolutionary parties was prepared for this sudden end to Tsardom. During March and April they gathered in Petrograd from their scattered exiles, and, as delegates to the Council of Workers' and Soldiers' Deputies, acted as a pressure group on the Provisional Government.

LEGEND

(1) Nicholas leaves for Mogilev, his headquarters, 22 February

(2) Strikes in Petrograd, 23–6 February

(3) Troop mutinies in Petrograd, 27 February

(4) Secret police headquarters in Moscow burnt, 27 February

(5) Some troops move on Petrograd, 1 March

(6) Nicholas unable to reach Petrograd, 1 March

(7) Nicholas abdicates, 2 March

(8) A Provisional Government 'rules' side by side with a Council (*Soviet*) of Workers' and Soldiers' Deputies. In the latter the Bolsheviks are in a minority, 3 March

(9) Nicholas put under arrest, 8 March

(10) All-Russian Conference of Soviets rejects Bolshevik motion to end the war by 325 votes to 57, 29 March

(11) Lenin returns to Petrograd from exile, 3 April. 'The robbers' imperialist war is the beginning of civil war in all Europe', he tells the crowd. 'Long live the worldwide socialist revolution'

▓▓▓	Russian territory under German military control in February 1917
◉	Principal strikes (including Petrograd)
➡	Troops sent against the strikers, but disarmed at Tsarskoye Selo and Luga
┼┼┼┼┼	Railways which were largely controlled by railway workers hostile to Tsardom
➡–➡	Route of the Tsar's train, which a railway worker refused to allow to continue to Petrograd. The engine driver obeyed the red signal
⇒	Lenin's route by rail to Petrograd. He had travelled from Switzerland across Germany by train, with the approval of the Kaiser, and thence via Sweden to Finland

PETROGRAD DEATHS IN THE FEBRUARY REVOLUTION
655 Soldiers   587 Citizens   73 Policemen

MAP 3   Lenin's Return to Russia 1917

On 25 July 1914 (old style) Lenin was arrested in Cracow by the Austrians as an enemy alien and spy. He was released on 10 August, the Austrian Government having been persuaded that he was even more an enemy of Tsardom, and could 'render great services' to Austria by fomenting anti-Tsarist troubles.

When revolution broke out in Petrograd in February 1917, Lenin, the Bolshevik leader, was in Switzerland. Wartime was not conducive to travel, nor did his plan to go through Britain prove possible. Instead, the German Government, eager to see dissension and chaos in Russia, agreed with alacrity to his request to travel across 'enemy' territory, and provided him with facilities. Thus Imperial Germany served as a handmaiden to the Russian revolution of October 1917.

'Our tactics: absolute distrust; no support of new Government; Kerensky particularly suspect; to arm proletariat only guarantee; no *rapprochement* with other parties. This last is *conditio sine qua non*.'
(Lenin to Bolsheviks in Sweden, telegram from Berne, 13 Mar 1917)

LEGEND

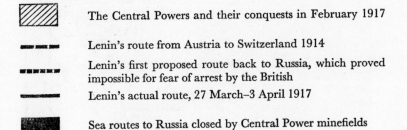

The Central Powers and their conquests in February 1917

Lenin's route from Austria to Switzerland 1914

Lenin's first proposed route back to Russia, which proved impossible for fear of arrest by the British

Lenin's actual route, 27 March–3 April 1917

Sea routes to Russia closed by Central Power minefields

MAP 4 The Location of the Bolshevik Leaders during the
February Revolution 1917

Most of the Social Democratic leaders of both the Bolshevik and Menshevik factions were abroad or in exile when revolution broke out in Russia in 1917. Those who were in Siberia reached Petrograd early in March, following the spontaneous amnesty of all political prisoners. Also returning in March were those living in Sweden. Next to return, in April, were the 'specials' from Switzerland, led by Lenin. Finally, in May, came the 'regulars' who had been in Switzerland, or elsewhere abroad.

The only Bolshevik leaders, none of them very senior, who happened to be in Petrograd at the time of the February Revolution: Molotov, Steklov, Shlyapnikov, Latsis and Zalutski.

(M) =   Mensheviks and others who became Bolsheviks on their return to Petrograd

New York:	*Stockholm:*	*London:*	*Paris:*	*Switzerland*
Bukharin	Kollontai	Litvinov	Antonov-	Lenin
Trotsky (M)	Uritsky (M)	Chicherin (M)	Ovseenko	Lunacharsky (M)
Volodarsky				Radek
				Zinoviev

LEGEND

Territory controlled by Germany and her allies in February 1917

Centre of the February Revolution and scene of all subsequent struggles for power during 1917

The location of the Bolshevik leaders at the time of the February Revolution. The majority were in exile or out of Russia. They all made haste to return to Petrograd.

MAP 5 The War and Revolution, July and August 1917

FINNS
Helsingfors
Gulf of Finland
Reval
Narva
Petrograd
POLISH SOLDIERS
& REFUGEES
Dorpat
Valka
Pskov
ESTONIANS
LATVIANS
Baltic Sea
Mitava
Riga
Yaungulbene
Memel
Vilkomir
Dvinsk
Tilsit
Kovno
Vilna
Smorgon
Moscow
Minsk
GERMAN-OCCUPIED
RUSSIA
Baranovichi
Krevo
Pinsk
Kovel
Rovno
Lemberg
Brody
Kiev
GALICIA
Tarnopol
Berdichev
Kharkov
Stanislau
UKRAINIANS
Poltava
Czernowitz
Ekaterinoslav
AUSTRIA-HUNGARY
Jassy
Kishinev
Nikolaev
Odessa
Kherson
Don
GERMAN-OCCUPIED
RUMANIA
Ismail
0   150
Miles
BULGARIA
Black Sea

In March 1917 the Provisional Government assured Britain and France that it would continue the war against the Central Powers. But the offensive launched on 18 June ended two weeks later in mutiny and failure. Mass demonstrations in Petrograd on 3 and 4 July, though leaderless, showed how hated the war had become, and the Bolsheviks soon dominated the Soviets by their cry of 'Bread and Peace'. The Provisional Government then published evidence of financial dealings between the Bolsheviks and German agents, forced Lenin to go into hiding in Finland, and arrested Trotsky. In August General Kornilov led an army against Petrograd, intending to crush the Soviets and stiffen the Provisional Government against concessions. The Bolsheviks took a leading part in the defence of the city, and greatly increased their military power, having been armed by the Provisional Government. They also gained support among the masses, who feared the return of autocracy.

WAR DEBTS OWED BY RUSSIA TO THE ALLIES BY JULY 1917

To Britain	$ 2,760 million
To France	$ 760 million
To USA	$ 280 million
To Italy	$ 100 million
To Japan	$ 100 million
Total	$ 4,000 million

LEGEND

The eastern front on 18 June 1917

Austrian territory conquered by Russia, 18 June–3 July 1917

Russian proposals for further offensive action during the first half of July

Subject peoples insisting on independence from Russian rule, and gravely hampering the war effort when their demands were rejected or disregarded

Principal areas of mutiny, 4–17 July

Kornilov's unsuccessful attack on the capital, August 1917

Factory groups between Petrograd and the front with increasingly strong Bolshevik influence, July–September 1917

Military units between Petrograd and the front with increasingly strong Bolshevik sections, July–September 1917

85

Map 6 The October Revolution in Petrograd

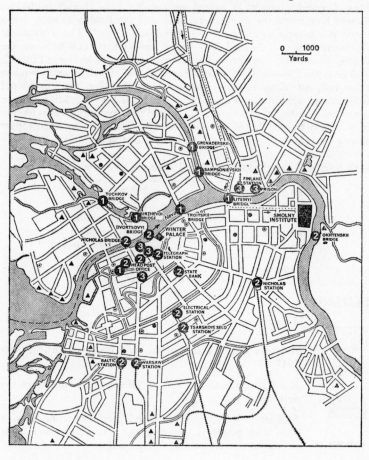

From August to October 1917 the Bolsheviks greatly increased their organisation in factory groups throughout Petrograd, and in many barracks in the city. They concentrated on devising a plan for overturning the Provisional Government, with a *coup d'état*. Lenin was in hiding in a suburb. On the evening of 6 November (24 October old style) he entered the city and put into operation a three-phased plan, worked out by Trotsky, for the capture of key points. This was accomplished by the early hours of 8 November (26 October old style). Lenin's new government, a Council of People's Commissars, declared an immediate end to the war, and declared all land to be handed over to the peasants, thus effectively demobilising the Army. Lenin co-operated with the Socialist Revolutionaries, whose support he needed, and agreed to set up a Constituent Assembly in January 1918. The Bolsheviks suppressed the Assembly when they found themselves in a minority.

The Constituent Assembly, elected on 25–7 November 1917 by secret ballot and universal suffrage, met only once, on 18 January 1918, and was immediately suppressed by the Bolsheviks. The SRs had 370 delegates. The Bolsheviks had 175, plus the support of 40 Left SR supporters.

Socialist Revolutionaries	17	million votes
Bolsheviks	9.8	million votes
Non-Russian parties (i.e. Ukrainians)	7.6	million votes
Mensheviks	1.4	million votes
Other parties	4	million votes

LEGEND

⬤	Garrisons loyal to the Provisional Government
◉	Garrisons supporting the Bolsheviks
▲	Factories in which Bolshevik support was strong, and anti-war feeling high
• • • • • •	Lenin's route into Petrograd on the evening of 6 November. He set up his headquarters at the Smolny Institute
(1)	First objectives, main bridges plus the telegraph station, seized during the night of 6 November
(2)	Second objectives, including the main railway stations, seized during the day of 7 November
(3)	Third objectives, including the headquarters of the Provisional Government in the Winter Palace, seized in the evening of 7 November
– – ➤	The cruiser *Aurora*, which fired blank shells at the Winter Palace on 7 November

MAP 7   The Russian Revolution, November 1917–March 1918

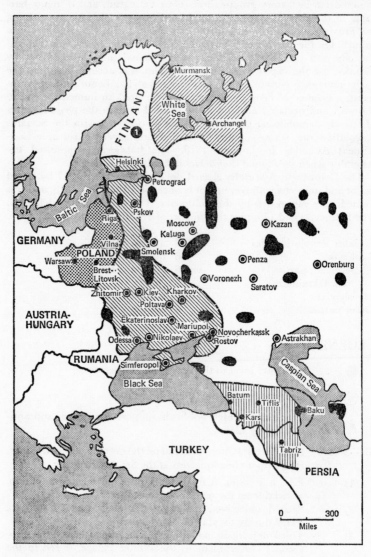

LEGEND

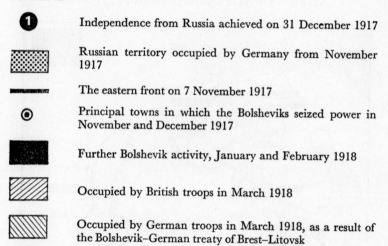

①   Independence from Russia achieved on 31 December 1917

        Russian territory occupied by Germany from November 1917

        The eastern front on 7 November 1917

        Principal towns in which the Bolsheviks seized power in November and December 1917

        Further Bolshevik activity, January and February 1918

        Occupied by British troops in March 1918

        Occupied by German troops in March 1918, as a result of the Bolshevik–German treaty of Brest–Litovsk

        Occupied by Turkish troops in March 1918

MAP 8   The War against Bolshevism 1918–19

The anti-Bolshevik armies, even at the height of their success in 1919, were too disunited in aims and methods to prevail over the Bolshevik 'Red Army' with its combination of Communist ideology and the national defence of mother Russia against the foreign foe.

LEGEND

▬▬▬	Under Bolshevik rule, November 1918
■■■	Principal armies attempting to destroy Bolshevism
▲▲▲	Maximum advance of the anti-Bolshevik forces 1918–19
▨▨▨	Remnant of anti-Bolshevik forces, defeated 1920–1
▬ ▬ ▬	Established Russian frontiers, March 1921–October 1939

MAP 9   The Anti-Bolshevik Attack on Petrograd 1919

An unexpected threat to the Bolshevik régime was the attack on Petrograd in September 1919, led by a former Tsarist General, Yudenich. With 18,500 troops, and a few British tanks, he drove back the 25,000 Red Army troops to within sight of Petrograd. But he failed to cut the Moscow–Tosno–Petrograd railway; as a result, Trotsky was able to enter the city, organise its defence, and launch a counter-attack which drove Yudenich back to Estonia. The Bolsheviks then signed their first independence treaty with Estonia, largely to prevent any further such attacks.

LEGEND

Main attacks by anti-Bolshevik forces, September–October 1919

Naval support given to the anti-Bolsheviks by Britain and France

Line held by the Red Army, 21 October 1919

MAP 10   Foreign Intervention in Northern Russia 1918–19

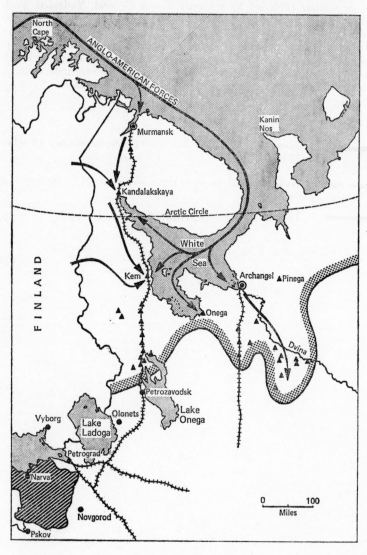

British, American, Canadian, Italian and Serb troops all landed in Northern Russia in 1918. They were joined by the Finnish troops under Mannerheim. But none were able to reach Petrograd, or to link up with the other interventionist forces along the Urals.

LEGEND

⊚ Bases held by foreign troops 1918–19

▲ Towns and villages occupied during the various advances 1918–19. When the foreign troops withdrew, the local anti-Bolshevik Russians were unable to resist any longer

▨ Farthest advance of foreign troops during 1918–19

▨ Farthest advance of anti-Bolshevik attack on Petrograd, October 1919

MAP 11 Makhno and the Anarchists 1917–20

Nestor Makhno, the Ukrainian anarchist, was imprisoned for terrorism in 1907, at the age of eighteen. Released in February 1917, he organised a peasant army and established control over a large area of southern Russia. He defeated the Austrians at Dibrivki (September 1918) and the Ukrainian nationalists at Ekaterinoslav (November 1918). In 1919 he allied with the Bolsheviks, defeating two anti-Bolshevik armies, Denikin's at Peregonovka (September 1919) and Wrangel's in the Crimea (June 1920). Makhno himself was then attacked continuously by the Bolsheviks and fled (November 1920) via Rumania to France, where he died in 1935.

LEGEND

◉   Centres of the Confederation of Anarchist Organisations (*Nabat*) 1918

●   Anarchist conferences, with dates

○   Makhno's Headquarters 1918–20

➡   Makhno's principal military activities

MAP 12   The Russo-Polish War 1920

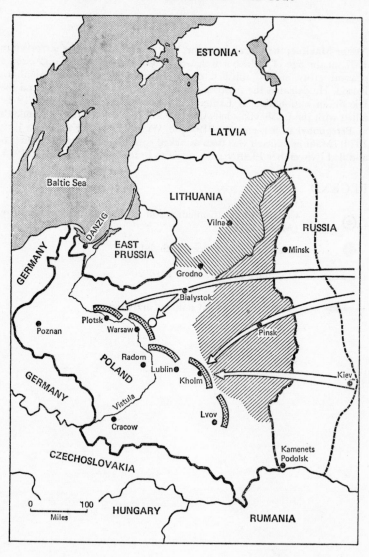

LEGEND

Poland's established frontiers, June 1920

The eastern extent of Polish conquests, April, May and June 1920

Russian attacks following the Polish occupation of Kiev in June 1920

Polish lines of defence, August 1920

The 'Miracle of the Vistula'. Russian armies were defeated; they retreated to Russia

Seized by Poland from Lithuania, October 1920

Annexed by Poland from Russia, Treaty of Riga, March 1921

Poland's eastern frontier from 1921 to 1939

MAP 13   The Ukraine 1917–21

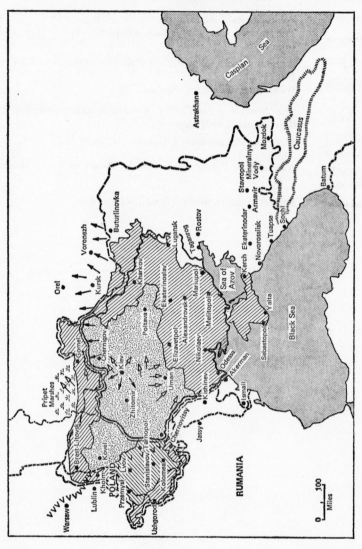

LEGEND

 The Ukrainian State, which declared its independence from Russia in November 1917. After the Brest–Litovsk Treaty (March 1918) it was under German military occupation until December 1918. Then it reasserted its independence against strong Bolshevik, White Russian, Anarchist and Polish opposition

 The West Ukrainian Republic, established in November 1918 from former Austro–Hungarian territory

 Territories annexed to the independent Ukraine during 1918

 Territory claimed by the Ukrainian nationalists as part of the 'ethnographic' Ukraine

 Boundary of the Ukrainian Soviet Socialist Republic 1921

 Western boundary of the Soviet Union 1921–39

 Western boundary of the Soviet Union since 1945

 Farthest northern advance of Denikin's anti-Bolshevik armies, November 1919. Denikin's Great Russian policies failed to gain him much Ukrainian support

Farthest eastern advance of the Polish Army in June 1920

Farthest western advance of the Red Army by August 1920

MAP 14   The Border States 1919–20

In 1919, Pilsudski, Head of State of the new Polish Republic, tried to unite the Border States and nationalities against Bolshevik Russia. His proposed Union of Border States failed, partly because of Poland's dispute with Lithuania over Vilna, but largely because of the reconquest of the Ukraine, the Crimea, the Don, the Kuban and Transcaucasia by the Red Army.

LEGEND

▬▬▬▬▬▬ Russia's western border in 1914

 States and areas intended as part of the 'Union of Border States' in 1919, under Polish leadership

(1) Independent from Russia 1918. Formerly part of the ancient Polish–Lithuanian Union, which Pilsudski hoped to revive

(2) Poland, which had re-won its independence in 1918, obtained French, but not British support for its stand against the Bolsheviks

(3) Former Austrian territory occupied by the Poles 1919, in defiance of the Paris Peace Conference

(4) Base for the Russian anti-Bolshevik army of Baron Wrange 1919–20

(5) The three independent Transcaucasian Republics, formerly part of Tsarist Russia and opposed to Russian Bolshevik rule. They received envoys from Poland in February 1920. Absorbed by the Bolsheviks 1920–1

(6) Base for the Russian anti-Bolshevik army of Denikin. The British urged Denikin to co-operate with the Poles, but in vain

(7) Prominent in the fight against the Bolsheviks, forming the first volunteer White Army. Supported by the Poles

(8) In May 1920 the Poles captured Kiev and hoped to ally with the Ukrainian nationalists against the Bolsheviks. The Poles were driven out of the Ukraine by the Bolsheviks in June 1920

(9) Former Russian territory occupied by the Poles 1919. Not regained by the Russians until 1939

(10) Claimed by both Poland and Lithuania. Occupied by Poles, April 1919, by the Bolsheviks July 1920, and again by the Poles, October 1920. The Poles refused to give it to Lithuania

(11) Independent from Russia 1918. Beholden to the Poles for capturing Dvinsk for them, Latvia supported Pilsudski's scheme

(12) Independent from Russia 1918. The base for the unsuccessful attack on Petrograd in 1919 by the Russian anti-Bolsheviks under Yudenich

(13) In November 1917 Finnish Bolsheviks seized Helsingfors and South Finland. The Tsarist General Mannerheim and German-trained Finnish troops smashed the Communist régime and occupied all Finland by mid-1918

MAP 15   Famine and Relief 1921

As a result of three years of war, a year of German occupation, a further two years of civil war, and the severe drought of 1920, large areas of Russia were starving by 1921. Railways, livestock, food stores and farm machinery had all been depleted enormously. The high death rate during the total of six years fighting had left many peasant homes without a breadwinner. The result was the famine of 1921, in which perhaps as many as ten million people died.

104

LEGEND

▬▬▬ The Soviet frontier in 1921

▦ Principal famine area

▨ Area where famine conditions were widespread

+++++ Railways used to transport foreign relief

◉ Ports used by American Relief Administration, which provided the highest proportion of all foreign food supplies

○ Town in which a woman shopkeeper was sentenced to twenty-five years' imprisonment for selling human flesh to the hungry

Numbers being fed by foreign relief organisations

American Relief Administration	3,758,446
Society of Friends	212,000
Swedish Red Cross	84,750
Nansen's Organisation	100,000
Save the Children Fund	236,000
International Federation of Trade Unions Relief Commission	28,174
Workers' International Relief Commission	40,000
American Mennonites	5,000
	4,454,570

Relief contributions from soldiers of the Red Army, as reported

In gold	3,539 rubles, 2 pounds sterling, 58 rings, 6 watches, 2 pairs of earrings
In silver	2,685 rubles, 1 watch, 11 Crosses of St George
In valuables	72 gold and silver articles, 1 diamond
In paper money	1,158 million Soviet rubles, 2,657 Tsarist rubles, 5,260 Kerensky rubles
Necessaries	21,885 articles, foodstuffs, 2,510 tons. Cloth 7,400 yards. Bark shoes, 15,000 pairs. Horned cattle, 272 head

Relief sent by the British Society of Friends

3,670 bags of flour
32 bales of clothing
150 sacks of white sugar
58 barrels of cod liver oil
200 bags rock cocoa

455 cases of chocolate
3,482 cases condensed milk
93 bags rice
670 bags beans
310 bags peas

MAP 16   The Spread of Soviet Rule in Central Asia 1917–36

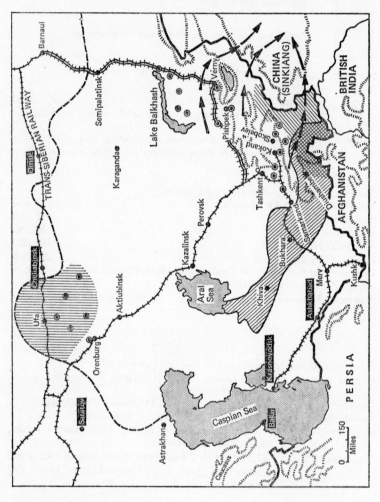

Tsarist rule in Central Asia was established between 1850 and 1914. In 1917 the predominately Muslim peoples of this vast region sought independence. But by 1924 the Soviet government had re-established Russian rule, and by 1936 the whole area was divided into Soviet republics, bound to Moscow by direct military, political and economic ties.

LEGEND

Railways completed by 1914, important instruments of Russian imperial control

The Turkestan–Siberian (*Turksib*) railway, opened 1930, an important instrument of Russian colonisation and Soviet control

The Russian imperial frontier in 1914

Approximate northern limit of Turkic-speaking peoples

Under firm Bolshevik control from November 1917 (Tashkent)

Centres of anti-Bolshevik revolt and of independent governments which denounced Russian colonial rule and hoped to build a separate Turkic Muslim state

Towns occupied by British and other foreign troops 1917–19

Bashkiria, area of a nationalist uprising 1917; of an alliance with the anti-Bolsheviks 1918; of the acceptance of Bolshevik assurances of autonomy 1919; and of the suppression by the Bolsheviks of all national resistance 1920

The Soviet Peoples' Republics of Bukhara and Khiva, established in 1917, preserving their independence from Bolshevik rule, and linked to Petrograd by Treaties of Alliance

The flight of Kazakh nomads, first from Tsarist military conscription (1916), then from Soviet forced collectivisation (1932). Over one million Kazakhs fled from their homelands 1916–32

Area of anti-Soviet revolt 1923–31, suppressed by armed force

MAP 17 Independent Transcaucasia 1917–21

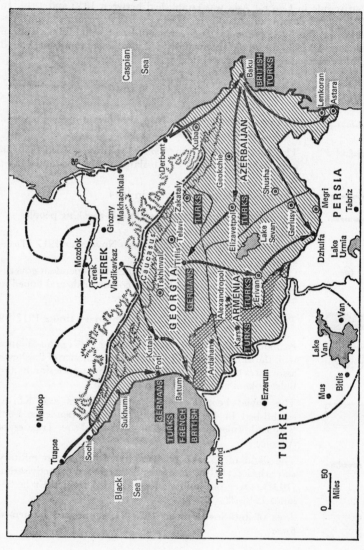

In March 1917, when Tsarist rule had been broken, a Transcaucasian Federative Republic was declared. After a mere two months of independence it was occupied by the Turks, who ruled Transcaucasia until May 1918, when Georgia, Armenia and Azerbaijan declared themselves independent states and sought first German, and then British and French protection. In the north Caucasus region a Terek People's Soviet Socialist Republic, set up under firm Bolshevik control in January 1918, was conquered by anti-Bolshevik Russians under Denikin in May 1919. In December 1919 the British evacuated Transcaucasia and the Bolsheviks reconquered the northern Caucasus. After signing an alliance with Turkey early in 1920, the Bolsheviks invaded Transcaucasia and conquered Azerbaijan by May 1920, Armenia by December 1920, and Georgia by April 1921. Soviet Republics were then established under strict control from Moscow.

LEGEND

The Transcaucasian Federative Republic, March 1917–May 1918

The Terek People's Soviet Socialist Republic January 1918–May 1919

The three independent Transcaucasian Republics 1918–20

Armenian territorial claims which helped to bring Lenin and Ataturk together

Principal foreign occupying or protecting powers 1918–20

The Bolshevik conquest of Transcaucasia 1920–1

Centres of anti-Bolshevik revolt suppressed by armed force

Ceded by Russia to Turkey (Treaty of Kars, March 1921)

109

MAP 18   The Independent Far Eastern Republic 1920–2

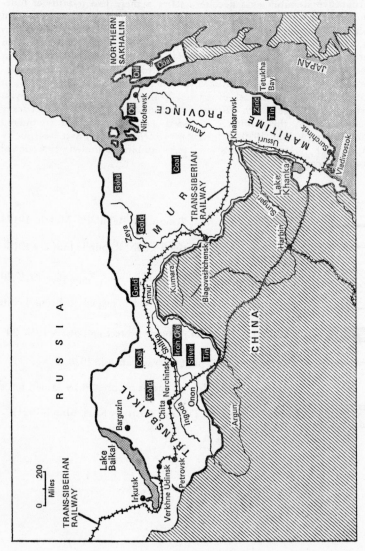

The area from Lake Baikal to Vladivostok was occupied after the October Revolution by a variety of anti-Bolshevik forces, including 72,000 Japanese, 7,000 Americans, 6,400 British, 4,400 Canadians and token forces of French and Italians. A Russian anti-Bolshevik régime was set up by Admiral Kolchak in 1918. In 1920 a Far Eastern Republic was declared in Chita, under firm Bolshevik control, but in an independent guise. During 1922, as the foreign troops departed, the Republic extended its control to Vladivostok. In 1922 the Republic was formally annexed to the Soviet Union. The region is rich in mineral resources, as well as being an exporter of furs and fish.

Population in 1922

Russians	1,620,000
Chinese	
Japanese	300,000
Koreans	
Mongols	250,000
Tungus	50,000
Jews	25,000

LEGEND

▬▬ Boundary of the Far Eastern Republic in 1922

▮ Principal mineral deposits being worked by 1922

111

4 The October Revolution

*The Kornilov revolt quickened the pace of events in Petrograd.
The Bolsheviks won increasing support and in September they
were the majority party in both the Petrograd and Moscow soviets.
It was one thing however to dominate the soviets and quite
another to stage a successful uprising. Trotsky (4/3) regards the
formation of a military revolutionary committee as a major break-
through. It was an organ of the Petrograd soviet and thus would
help to legitimise the takeover.*

*The decision to stage an insurrection met with opposition in the
Central Committee. Kamenev and Zinoviev went so far as to make
public their opposition (4/2). They regarded the Bolshevik initiative as much too risky. They thought the decision had been
reached too hastily. The Bolsheviks were overrating their own
strength and support throughout the country and seriously under-
estimating the power of Kerensky and his supporters to hit back.
Kamenev and Zinoviev wanted a revolution but at a later date.*

*Lenin had advocated a revolution ever since April when he
had published his policy in Pravda. Kamenev had been a consistent doubter, Zinoviev also. The majority, however, followed
Lenin. Lenin, in Finland, was impatient for action. (4/1.)
Trotsky, in Petrograd, had some awkward questions to answer
(4/4). The day of revolution was set for October 25 to coincide
with the opening of the Second Congress of Soviets. All power
was at last to come to the soviets. The new state was to be a
Soviet state.*

4/1 LENIN CALLS FOR AN UPRISING, 12–14 SEPTEMBER 1917*

A letter to the Central Committee and the Petrograd and Moscow
Committees of the RSDLP(B)

The Bolsheviks, having obtained a majority in the Soviets of
Workers' and Soldiers' Deputies of both capitals, can and *must*
take state power into their own hands.

They can do so because the active majority of revolutionary
elements in the two chief cities is large enough to carry the people
with it, to overcome our opponents' resistance to smash them, and
to gain and retain power. For the Bolsheviks, by immediately
proposing a democratic peace, by immediately giving the land to
the peasants and by re-establishing the democratic institutions
and liberties which have been distorted and shattered by Kerensky,
will form a government which *nobody* will be able to overthrow.

The majority of the people are *on our side*. This was proved
by the long and painful course of events from May 6 to August 31
and to September 12. We gained a majority in the Soviets of the
metropolitan cities because the people came over *to our side*. The
vacillation of the Socialist Revolutionaries and Mensheviks and
the increase in the number of internationalists within their ranks
prove the same thing.

The Democratic Conference represents *not* a majority of the
revolutionary people, but *only the compromising upper strata of
the petty bourgeoisie*. Let us not be deceived by the election
figures; elections prove nothing. Compare the elections to the city
councils of Petrograd and Moscow with the Moscow strike of
August 12. Those are objective facts regarding that majority of
revolutionary elements that are leading the people.

The Democratic Conference is deceiving the peasants; it is giving
them neither peace nor land.

A Bolshevik government *alone* will satisfy the peasants'
demands.

Why must the Bolsheviks assume power *at this very moment*?

Because the imminent surrender of Petrograd will reduce our
chances a hundred times.

* From Lenin, *Polnoe Sobranie Sochinenii* (Moscow 1962) Vol. 34, pp.
239–41.

And it is *not in our power* to prevent the surrender of Petrograd while the army is headed by Kerensky and Co.

Nor can we 'wait' for the Constituent Assembly, for by surrendering Petrograd Kerensky and Co. *can* always obstruct its convocation. Our Party alone, by seizing power, can secure the Constitutent Assembly's convocation; it will then accuse the other parties of procrastination and will be able to substantiate its accusations.

A separate peace between the British and German imperialists must and can be prevented, but only if we act immediately.

The people are tired of the vacillations of the Mensheviks and Socialist Revolutionaries. It is only our victory in the metropolitan cities that will carry the peasants with us.

We are concerned now not with the 'day', or 'moment' of insurrection in the narrow sense of the word. That will be only decided by the common voice of those who are *in contact* with the workers and soldiers, with *the masses*.

The point is that now, at the Democratic Conference, our Party has virtually *its own congress*, and this congress (whether it wishes to or not) *will* decide the *fate of the revolution*.

The point is to make the *task* clear to the Party. The present task is an *armed uprising* in Petrograd and Moscow (with its region), the seizing of power and the overthrow of the government. We must consider *how* to bring this about without expressly spelling it out in the press.

We must remember and weigh Marx's words about insurrection, '*Insurrection is an art*,' etc.

It would be naïve to wait until the Bolsheviks achieve a 'formal' majority. No revolution ever waits for *that*. Kerensky and Co. are not waiting either, and are preparing to surrender Petrograd. It is the wretched vacillations of the Democratic Conference that are bound to exhaust the patience of the workers of Petrograd and Moscow! History will not forgive us if we do not assume power now.

There is no apparatus? There is an apparatus – the Soviets and the democratic organisations. The international situation *right* now, on *the eve* of the conclusion of a separate peace between the British and the Germans, is *in our favour*. To propose peace to the nations right now means *to win*.

By seizing power both in Moscow and in Petrograd *at once* (it doesn't matter which comes first, possibly Moscow), we shall win *absolutely and unquestionably.*

N. Lenin

4/2 KAMENEV AND ZINOVIEV OPPOSE UPRISING, 11 OCTOBER 1917*

About the present situation

As regards the whole political situation, the Bolshevik walk-out from the pre-parliament presented our party with the question: *what will happen next?*

A current is forming and growing in workers' groups which sees the only way out in an immediate declaration of an armed uprising. Now all the timescales have coincided so that if one is to speak of such an uprising, one has plainly to fix a date and moreover for the immediate future. This question is already being debated in one form or another in all the periodical press, in workers' meetings and is occupying the minds of a wide circle of party workers. We, in our turn, regard it as our duty and our right to speak out on this question with full frankness.

We are most profoundly convinced that to declare at once an armed uprising would mean to stake not only the fate of our party, but also the fate of the Russian and the international revolution. There is no doubt that there are such historical situations that an oppressed class has to acknowledge that it is better to join battle and lose than to surrender without a fight. Is the Russian working class in such a position now? *No, and a thousand times no.*

As a result of the huge growth of the influence of our party in the cities and especially in the army, such a situation has arisen at the present moment that the wrecking of the Constituent Assembly is becoming more and more impossible for the bourgeoisie. Thanks to the army, and to the workers, we are holding a revolver to the temple of the bourgeoisie. The bourgeoisie has been put in such a situation that if they thought of making an attempt to wreck the Constituent Assembly now, it would again push the

* From *Protokoly Tsentralnogo Komiteta R.S.D.R.P. (B) Avgust 1917– Fevral 1918* (Moscow 1958), pp. 87–92.

petty bourgeois parties in our direction and the revolver would have fired . . .

It is said that: (1) the majority of the people in Russia are already for us and (2) the majority of the international proletariat are for us. Alas ! neither one nor the other is untrue, and this is the crux of the matter.

A majority of workers and a significant part of the army in Russia are for us. But all the rest are in question. We are all convinced, for example, that if it now comes to elections to the Constituent Assembly, then the majority of peasants will vote for the SRs. What is this, chance? The mass of soldiers supports us not because of our war slogan but because of our peace slogan. This is an extremely important circumstance which if we do not take account of it we risk basing all our calculations on false premises. If we take power now alone and are forced (as a consequence of the whole world situation) to wage a revolutionary war, the mass of soldiers will flee from us. Of course, the best elements among young soldiers will stay with us, but the mass of soldiers will defect . . .

Those same delegates from the front who are now conducting such an agitation against the war are asking our speakers openly not to speak of a revolutionary war because this will put the soldiers off. This is an extremely important symptom . . .

And now we come to the second assertion, that supposedly, the majority of the international proletariat are already on our side. This, unfortunately, is not true. The uprising in the German fleet has enormous symptomatic significance. The portents exist for a serious movement in Italy. But from there to some degree of active support for the proletarian revolution in Russia, a Russia which is declaring war on the whole bourgeois world, is still very far. It is extremely harmful to overrate one's forces. We have doubtless been given much and much will be required from us. But if we now lose the battle, having staked everything, we shall inflict a cruel blow also to the international proletarian revolution, growing extremely slowly but none the less without any doubt growing. But meanwhile only the growth of revolution in Europe would make it necessary for us, without any vacillations, to take power immediately into our own hands. This is also the only guarantee of the triumph of an uprising of the proletariat in Russia. This will come but it isn't here yet . . .

But everyone who does not wish only to speak of an uprising is obliged to assess also its chances soberly. And here we regard it as our duty to say that at present to underestimate the strength of our adversary and overestimate our own strength would be the most harmful thing of all. The strength of our adversary is greater than it appears ...

The strength of the proletarian party, of course, is very considerable, but the decisive question is, is the mood among the workers and soldiers of the capital really such, that they themselves see salvation already only in street fighting and are bursting to go on to the streets. No. This mood does not exist ...

Under these conditions such a posing of the question about the transfer of power to the proletarian party would be a great historical falsehood: it must be either now or never!

No! The party of the proletariat will grow, its programme will become clearer to even wider masses. It will have the opportunity of continuing its merciless unmasking of the policy, on a yet greater scale, of the Mensheviks and SRs, who have ceased to advance on the path leading to a real transfer of power to the majority of the people. And there is only one way that it can nullify its successes in present circumstances, and that is by taking the initiative for an uprising itself and in so doing subjecting the proletariat to the blows of the whole united counter-revolution, supported by petty-bourgeois democracy.

We raise a warning voice against this ruinous policy.

4/3 TROTSKY'S SPEECH AT A SESSION OF THE
PETROGRAD SOVIET ON THE QUESTION OF
THE MILITARY REVOLUTIONARY
COMMITTEE, 16 OCTOBER 1917*

Comrades! We have never been farther from Broido and his party and never have the tactics of the Mensheviks been so disastrous, as at present.

Comrade Trotsky cites the statement of Rodzyanko to a member of the staff of *Utro Rossii* that the surrender of Petrograd, according to him, could have its positive side. In Petrograd, as

* From L. Trotsky, *Sochineniya*, Vol. 3, Part 2, 1917 (Moscow–Leningrad 1925), pp. 14–16.

in Riga, the Germans would 're-establish order', dissolve the soviets, annihilate the Baltic Fleet and strangle at birth the Russian revolution.

Here in the pre-parliament people will not say such things, of course.

Comrades, we foresaw the Kornilov revolt in good time and therefore protested against the withdrawal of troops from Petrograd. Broido and his comrades hurriedly agreed then to carry out Kerensky's order, but the day after, in order to defend the Winter Palace, they had to appeal for help to the Kronstadters, whom they had previously branded counter-revolutionaries.

Then they kept quiet about the 18th June which, as we prophesied, turned into a terrible disaster, preparing the ground for the events of the 3rd–5th July.

Comrades! It is said that we are setting up a headquarters so as to seize power. We make no secret of this. A whole stream of speakers from the front have spoken here and they have all declared that if there is no armistice in the near future, the frontline troops will turn tail and stream to the rear.

But what are the Mensheviks' prospects?

The whole Allied press has ridiculed Skobelev, the question of a conference has been dropped, and this last straw, which they had tossed to the army, has broken.

We are sending our delegation to the front, so that the soldiers will understand us. We shall tell them that we are not demagogues but their true friends.

The pogrom movement is a movement of the masses which are desperate and in particular of their least conscious part.

An unskilled labourer, arriving from his village, as he stands for hours in queues, naturally begins to hate those who are better dressed and richer than he is, since a rich man, by paying twice over, obtains all the goods he needs without ration cards. His hatred is thus transferred also to those who are better educated than he is, who is of a different religion, etc. We understand these unskilled labourers and treat them differently from the bourgeois scum who would like to execute them.

If revolutionary power punished all marauders, then the possibility of any pogroms would thereby be reduced significantly.

Here people have been singing the praises of the All-Russian Executive Committee of Peasant Deputies which is opposed to the congress of soviets. We know, however, that this committee, as a result of its policies, has prepared the ground for peasant uprisings and agrarian disturbances.

If this committee is opposed to us, then it is also opposed to those peasants whose legs they have been pulling for seven months. When we have the choice of either Avksentev or the poorest peasants, then we must state that we are for the peasants and against their committee.

Now we are being presented with a categorical demand to withdraw troops from Petrograd and we have to reply *yes* or *no*.

We must inform the soldiers if they should leave or treat the order to leave with distrust. Broido has not answered this question. We say, however, that we must know where we are going. If they are to die, then they must die as conscious citizens, who know whither and for what purpose they are going to their death.

In the second speech Comrade Trotsky mentioned, replying to the representatives of the front, that the whole army had been seized by a single mood, it spoke with one voice, demanding immediate peace.

This is at one entirely with our feeling and with our actions. It is not true, when people tell us that we are isolating the pro-letariat. We see clearly, on the basis of evidence, that millions of our brothers in the trenches are entirely in accord with our demands.

We shall live together, fight and die together, if this is the only way to attain our demands.

4/4 TROTSKY'S STATEMENT TO THE PETROGRAD SOVIET*

A statement about an 'initiative' at a session of the Petrograd soviet.
18 October 1917

Lately all the press has been full of reports, rumours and articles about a coming initiative which is an event sometimes attributed to the Bolsheviks and sometimes attributed to the Petrograd soviet.

The decisions of the Petrograd soviet are published for general information. The soviet is an elective institution, every member of which is responsible to the workers or soldiers who elected him.

* From ibid., pp. 31–3.

The revolutionary parliament of the proletariat and revolutionary garrison cannot keep its decision secret from the workers and soldiers.

We are not concealing anything. I declare in the name of the soviet: we have not been planning any kind of armed initiative. However, if the course of events forced the soviet to take an initiative, workers and soldiers would respond as one man to its initiative.

Bourgeois newspapers are naming the 22nd October as the day of the initiative. All newspapers are spreading this 'intuitive' piece of prophecy. However the 22nd October was unanimously agreed by the Executive Committee as a day of agitation, propaganda and rallying the masses under the banners of the soviet and as a day for making collections for the soviet.

It has been stated, further, that I have signed an order for 5,000 rifles from the Sestroretsky factory. Yes, I signed the order because of a decision already adopted in the days of the Kornilov revolt so as to arm the workers' militia. And the Petrograd soviet will continue to organise and to arm the proletarian guard.

But all this information, all these facts have been surpassed by the *Den* newspaper.

Comrade Trotsky announces the 'plan' of the Bolshevik initiative which was to take place last night, printed in yesterday's copy of *Den*. The 'plan' gives details of routes, along which the army of Bolsheviks was to march and states the targets which have to be seized. Nor does it forget to mention that the insurgents from the districts of Novaya Derevnya should arrest and bring with them 'dark elements'. (During the reading there is laughter in the hall.)

I wish to hear, so as to know exactly, the precise route which each army has to take ... (Laughter.)

Comrades, this statement does not need any commentary, just as the newspaper which printed this does not need anyone to describe its aims.

The aim of the campaign is clear.

We are in conflict with the government and it may take on a very acute form. This is a question of the withdrawal of troops. You can see how the bourgeois press is trying to create around the Petrograd soldiers and workers an atmosphere of enmity and suspicion and to evoke hatred at the front for Petrograd soldiers.

The congress of soviets is another thorny question. Governmental circles know our point of view as regards the role of the congress of soviets. The bourgeoisie knows that the Petrograd soviet will propose to the congress that it should take power into its own hands, propose a democratic peace to the belligerent peoples and give land to the peasants. They are trying to disarm Petrograd, by withdrawing its revolutionary garrison. They are hastening, before the congress opens, to arm and to station, at different points, all those who are loyal to them, in order that they may put in motion all their forces, to bring to nothing the representations of the workers, soldiers and peasants. Just as an artillery bombardment prepares an attack against the army, so the present campaign of lies and calumny is preparing an armed assault on the congress of soviets.

We must be on our guard. We have entered upon a period of most acute struggle. One must constantly expect an attack by counter-revolutionaries.

However at the first attempt by them to disrupt the congress of soviets, at the first attempt to attack, we shall answer with a counter-attack which will be merciless and which we shall carry through to its conclusion.

4/5 THE MILITARY REVOLUTIONARY COMMITTEE OF THE PETROGRAD SOVIET APPEALS TO THE PEOPLE OF PETROGRAD*

To the people of Petrograd –

For the information of workers, soldiers and all citizens of Petrograd we declare:

In the interests of the defence of the revolution and its conquests against attacks by counter-revolution, commissars have been appointed by us in military units and at strategic points in the capital and its environs. Orders and instructions, which are being distributed to these points are to be carried out only with the sanction of our authorised commissars. Commissars, as representatives of the soviet are inviolable. Opposition to commissars is opposition to the Soviet of Workers' and Soldiers' Deputies. The

* From L. Trotsky, *Sochineniya*, Vol. 3, Part 2, 1917, p. 45.

soviet has taken all measures to protect revolutionary order against attacks by counter-revolutionaries and thugs. All citizens are invited to give every form of support to our commissars. In the event of disturbances arising one should turn to the commissars of the Military Revolutionary Committee in the nearest military unit.

                                        Military Revolutionary Committee

24 October 1917

4/6   STANKEVICH ON THE EVENTS OF 24 OCTOBER 1917*

I arrived in Petrograd on 24 October loaded with all sorts of reports and materials. Kerensky met me in great good humour. He had just returned from a meeting of the Council of the Republic, where he had delivered a powerful speech against the Bolsheviks and had received the usual general ovation.

'Well, how do you like Petrograd?' he asked me on arrival.

I expressed my bewilderment.

'What, don't you know that an armed uprising is under way here?'

I laughed since the streets were absolutely quiet and there was no sign of any kind of uprising. Although preoccupied, he also had a somewhat ironical attitude towards the uprising. I told him that an end had to be made to the endless shocks within the country and that resolute measures should be taken against the Bolsheviks. He said that he was of the same opinion and that now no kind of Chernovs could help either the Kamenevs or the Zinovievs, if one could only cope with the uprising. But on the latter there was so little doubt that Kerensky immediately agreed that I should summon Dukhonin to Petrograd. I sent the necessary telegram straight away.

Kerensky asked me to go to the Council of the Republic to see what was going on and to discuss with the leaders the final form and the firmness of the resolution.

The Mariinsky Palace was full to overflowing. As well as the members of the Council there were many representatives of the

* From V. B. Stankevich, *Vospominaniya 1914–1919 g.* (Berlin 1920), pp. 258–61.

'world of officialdom' and of the military in the lobbies and in the boxes. Excitement could be felt. The parties conferred in their factions, trying to reach agreement among themselves but without success since the SRs rejected in their own group a fifth resolution and evidently were losing hope of agreeing on anything. Among other things, I began to speak of the necessity of organising a civil defence force from among the students but the Mensheviks recoiled from me as if I had been infected with the plague.

'The government has already made a lot of stupid mistakes and you want even to organise a White Guard.'

Then the voting on the resolutions began, haphazardly, without prior agreement. A resolution drawn up by Dan, stating that the Council held both the government and the Bolsheviks responsible for the Bolshevik uprising and suggesting the transfer of the defence of the country and the revolution to some kind of committee of safety made up of representatives of the Municipal Duma and of the parties, was adopted. I came immediately to the conclusion that such a resolution was nothing but a refusal to support the government and I expressed the view that the government would resign. After I had informed Kerensky of the resolution by telephone, I went straight away to the Winter Palace. Kerensky was amazed and excited and stated that under such conditions he would not remain a single moment more as head of the government. I supported his decision warmly and phoned Avksentev and other party leaders. They came to the Winter Palace. Kerensky's decision utterly amazed them since they regarded the resolution as purely theoretical and fortuitous and did not believe that it would have practical results. Avksentev was especially amazed when Kerensky stated that he was transferring power to him, as chairman of the Council. Discussions started and they went on all night . . .

However, next morning it became clear that events had taken such a turn that the government crisis could not be resolved in the usual manner; almost the whole city was in the hands of the insurrectionists. I found Kerensky at Military Headquarters. He had not been to bed and now proposed to leave. We accompanied him. He went with his ADCs in his own car in full military dress. The government and an ever-decreasing number of officers remained in the Winter Palace and at Military Headquarters. I sat down to draft an appeal to the army. The government, under the chairmanship of Konovalov, in session in the Winter Palace, approved my text. I went immediately to the telegraph office and sent the appeal to Stavka. I contacted Dukhonin, who during the night had received news from Headquarters about the uprising, as well. Dukhonin assured me that all necessary measures had been taken to send troops to Petrograd and that some units were due to arrive at any moment. I returned to the government and reported on my negotiations. The government discussed the problem of whom to appoint as Governor General of Petrograd. After a few arguments and some hesitation, Kishkin was selected. The latter immediately began to confer with General Bagratuni and Palchinsky.

All this time, sad and alarming news was coming in by telephone. The railway stations had been occupied. The telegraph and telephone exchange had been taken over. The Mariinsky Palace had been occupied and the members of the Council, who had gathered there for a meeting to review yesterday's resolution, thrown out.

4/7   THE PETROGRAD SOVIET WELCOMES THE REVOLUTION*

Resolution of an extraordinary session of the Petrograd soviet on the report of the overthrow of the Provisional Government.
25 October 1917

The Petrograd Soviet of Workers' and Soldiers' Deputies welcomes the victorious revolution of the proletariat and the garrison of Petrograd, and especially underlines the solidarity, organisation, discipline and the complete unanimity which the masses showed in this uprising as remarkable for its bloodlessness and for its success.

The Soviet, expressing its unshakeable conviction that the proletarian and peasant government, which, as the Soviet government, will be created by the revolution and which will provide support for the urban proletariat from the whole mass of the poorest peasantry, that this government will resolutely march towards socialism, the one and only means of saving the country from the unprecedented disasters and horrors of the war.

* From L. Trotsky, *Sochineniya*, Vol. 3, Part 2, 1917, pp. 58–9.

The new proletarian and peasant government will propose immediately a just democratic peace to all the belligerent peoples.

It will abolish immediately the landlords' ownership of land and will hand it over to the peasants. It will create workers' control over the production and distribution of goods, it will establish social control over banks, as well as simultaneously merging them into one state enterprise.

The Petrograd Soviet of Workers' and Soldiers' Deputies calls on all the workers and peasants of Russia to support selflessly, with all their strength, the proletarian and peasant revolution. The Soviet expresses its conviction, that the urban workers, in alliance with the poorest peasants, will display inflexible discipline, necessary for the victory of socialism. The Soviet is certain that the proletariat in western European countries will aid us to carry the cause of socialism through to a complete and lasting victory.

4/8 THE REVOLUTION IN THE BALTIC FLEET*

EXTRACTS FROM THE DIARY OF CAPTAIN I. I. RENGARTEN

26 October

13–00. The thing has happened. The Provisional Government has fallen. Last night we received a wireless message to that effect.

We had a little conference here this morning: Rasvozov, Baron Korf, Cherkassky, Shchastny, Onipko, Demchinsky and I. Korf put forward his plans: he said that, since with the disappearance of the Provisional Government he was no longer representing anybody here and had no means at his disposal to defend Russian interests, he was divesting himself of his authority and ceasing to take part in any activities; but he qualified this statement by placing himself personally at the disposal of the Chief.

We all agreed with him (it must be noted that Baron Korf is for Governor-General Nekrasov, who is at present at Petrograd).

The Chief declared that he was still maintaining his former attitude of devoting himself entirely to military and naval interests.

14–00. I have just read some new telegrams signed 'The Assembly of Soviets.' The death penalty is abolished; all those arrested

* From C. E. Vulliamy, ed., *The Red Archives* (London 1929), pp. 155–6.

for political crimes have been set free. All the Ministers, with the exception of Kerensky, have been arrested. Kerensky has fled. An order has been issued calling upon everyone to assist in his capture.

Proclamations addressed to railway workers enjoin them to maintain order, and prevent interruptions of communications.

The front has been granted the right of free propaganda.

16–00. There is a rumour of a new government having been formed with Lenin as President and Trotsky as Minister of Foreign Affairs.

17–45. At 15-29 we took down a radio message from Petrograd, in which the Petrograd Soviet of Workers' and Soldiers' Deputies invites all committees of army corps to send representatives to the Assembly of Soviets at the ratio of 1 to 25,000.

27 October.

I have spent the morning with Rasvozov, as has been my habit of late. Cherkassky, Demchinsky, and Shchastny were with us.

The official news is as follows: On the initiative of the 'Baltic Fleet' a committee for the administration of the naval department has been set up. Captain of the First Class, Modest Ivanov, has been proposed as candidate for membership in the Supreme Naval Court, and has wired his assent without delay.

Admiral Leskov [?] appears to be the other candidate.

Some 'Extraordinary Committee of Inquiry' has been set up, which has arrested Colonel Nordman [the Chief of the Intelligence Department of the Commander-in-Chief's Staff] and incarcerated him in the Niulandsky prison, on grounds of 'political unreliability.'

17–40. *Tiens!* That is new! I hear loud steps approaching my cabin, and presently there emerges a boy dressed in a soldier's coat, offering me papers – *The News, The Tide, The Social-Revolutionary* – the orthodox press of our time. A newsboy on board ship – a trifling example of change in our transient life!

The C.C.B.F. has heard that Petrograd is being besieged by troops sent from the front. . . .

28 October.

A whole series of events has happened during the night. We have received two wireless messages under the signature of the Presiding Minister, Kerensky, with the notification that he is proceeding to Petrograd at the head of the troops which are still loyal to the country, and that the troops of the Petrograd Soviet and the sailors have capitulated. In another telegram he denounces the activities of the Soviet troops as the rebellious violence of a band of criminals.

4/9 TROTSKY AFTER THE EVENT*

Reminiscences of the October revolution
7 November 1920

Trotsky: I shall begin my reminiscences with the session of the soldiers' section. (I don't remember exactly whether it was the presidium of the soldiers' section or the executive committee of the Petersburg soviet.) It was communicated at this session that the HQ of the military district was demanding the dispatch of about a third of the regiments of the St Petersburg garrison to the front. This was apparently a session of the executive committee. The left SR Verba was there and of our people there were Mekhonoshin and Sadovsky. As soon as this demand was made known, we started to whisper among ourselves that this would involve removing the most revolutionary and bolshevist regiments. The task now was to exploit this decision in every way possible, as the question of the armed uprising had already been decided by that time. We stated that we were willing to submit to this decision if it was required by military needs but beforehand it was necessary to check if the Kornilov movement was involved in it or not. And we decided to put forward the demand to create an organ which would check, from the military point of view, whether this was really dictated by military consideration or whether it was a politically motivated decision. The soldiers' section was a political organ of the garrison and was not suited to such a function. Hence in order to carry out this check we set up a kind of counter HQ, a purely military institution. Afterwards the Mensheviks enquired whether, in setting up this organisation, we were breaking off relations with the HQ of the St Petersburg district. We replied that we were not, our representative remained there. At this session there was the left SR Lazimir (who died later on the southern Russian front), a young comrade

* From L. Trotsky, *Sochineniya*, Vol. 3, Part 2, 1917, pp. 90–100.

who had worked in the commissariat of the old army. He was one of those left SRs who at once followed us. He supported us at this session and we seized on him. The demand to set up a military revolutionary committee came, as it were, not from us but from a left SR. Old Mensheviks, more experienced in political affairs began to say that this was nothing else than the organisation of an armed uprising.

One of the prominent old Mensheviks was also there, a former member of their Central Committee (CC) of the RSDRP. He denounced us with exceptional venom. In general terms, we proposed to Lazimir to draft a plan for the organisation of the military revolutionary committee and he embarked upon this. Whether he realised that this involved a conspiracy or whether he only reflected the inchoate revolutionary mood of the left wing of the SRs, I do not know. More likely the latter. In any case he took on this work at a time when the other left SRs had adopted a suspicious and temporising attitude towards the matter. Apparently they didn't obstruct it. When he had produced his draft, we put it right, marking, in every way possible, the revolutionary-insurgent nature of the institution. The following evening the document was laid before the St Petersburg soviet and was accepted.

The question of the creation of a military revolutionary committee was raised by the Bolshevik military organisation. In September 1917, when the military organisation was discussing the question of an armed uprising, it came to the conclusion that it was necessary to create a non-party 'soviet' organ to lead the uprising. Comrade Lenin was informed about this decision by me. The time was extremely propitious for us. . . . We discussed the question in the CC and basing ourselves on the facts, we were coming to the conclusion, that if such an important question as the withdrawal of the garrison could bring the conflict to an open revolution, then, precisely, this circumstance would help us enormously to set in motion the familiar method of revolution, since we had a plan to bring it about by purely conspiratorial means. This idea naturally recommended itself the more so since the majority of the garrison was on our side and we had to make use of this mood. Now we were in the process of obtaining a purely military beginning to the great conflict, on the basis of which we could launch the uprising . . .

Kozmin: I remember that the soviet was continually in session after the 18th October and I remember you were giving constant orders about where everything was to be distributed. Perhaps you could tell us about that time and how this was done.

Trotsky: The arms situation was as follows. The prime source of weapons was the Sestroretsky factory. When a delegation of workers came and stated that they needed weapons I said: 'You know that the arsenal is not in our hands.' They replied: 'We have been to the Sestroretsky factory.' 'Well, what happened?' 'They said that if the soviet issued an order, they would hand over weapons.' This was the first test. I issued an order for 5,000 rifles and they received them the same day. This was published in all the bourgeois newspapers. I remember very well that in *Novoe Vremya* there was almost a leading article or mention was made of it in one of the articles. This very act legalised our orders on military weapons. Subsequently, this matter went ahead, at what amounts to full speed. It was after the revolution when we, the military revolutionary committee, began to appoint commissars in all military institutions, in all military units and in all commissariats where there were weapons. There our commissars provided the party with a military organisation and the control of weapons then naturally passed into our hands . . .

The second congress of soviets opened on the 25th. Then Dan and Skobelev entered Smolny and passed precisely through the room where Vladimir Ilich and I were sitting. He had a kerchief tied round him, as if he had toothache. He had huge glasses and was wearing a dirty cap and looked quite odd. But Dan whose eye was experienced and trained, when he had caught sight of us, looked now from one side and now from the other side, nudged Skobelev with his elbow, winked and carried on. Vladimir Ilich also nudged me and said: 'They have recognised us, the scoundrels.'

But it was not dangerous because at that time we were masters of the situation.

We continued the military revolutionary committee's game with the HQ of the district. We had negotiations with them on how to establish mutual relations with the commissars to avoid friction between the soldiers' section and the garrison. They put forward a plan that their commissar should be the district commissar. The fact that we appointed the regimental commissars was unimportant but what was vital was that they should be subordinate to their commissar.

We continued these discussions and they made the newspapers. *Novoe Vremya* or *Rech* reported: 'Apparently an agreement will be reached.' Vladimir Ilich, when he had read these newspapers was in an extremely angry mood with us. The first question he put on his arrival was: 'Is this really true?' 'No, this is to camouflage the game', we reassured him. At that time the Post Office, bank and Inzhenerny castle had already been taken and the Winter Palace was being surrounded. Hence our position was more or less assured. But then early in the morning when machine guns were growling everywhere, suddenly men and women workers from the printing works arrived to inform me that *Pravda* had been closed down. They began to invite us to every kind of wilful action. This was either the 24th or 25th. They asked: 'What's all this? Podvoisky, tear off the seals'. 'Yes, we shall start type setting, only give us protection.' This request 'give us protection' spurred us on also. We had as many regiments as you like. We drew up an order immediately. 'The valiant Volynsky regiment is responsible for guaranteeing the freedom of the proletarian press. The government has closed down the newspapers *Pravda* and *Rabochy i Soldat*. The executive committee of the soviet annuls this order and lays on the valiant Volynsky regiment the responsibility of restoring our rights . . .'

Podvoisky: The decisive session when Zinoviev and Kamenev opposed the rising was on the 13th.

Trotsky: This session took place at the flat of Sukhanov, the Menshevik. It was the night of the 14th/15th. But if it was on that date, then, comrades, there was little time between the congress of soviets and the session at which Martov made his enquiries. No, it was earlier. The first time that SRs came from the district HQ and told us that there was an order to withdraw three regiments; that was in the executive committee. And perhaps it was in the executive committee of the soviet of the soldiers' section?

Sadovsky: It appears this took place in the presidium. There was a session, chaired by Zavade.

Trotsky: I wasn't at the session of the important workers. I was at the preliminary conference with comrade Lenin, and Zinoviev and Kalinin were going there. When the question was put to Kalinin if the workers were going to rise, he answered affirmatively that the chance must not be lost. At that time discussions with Vladimir Ilich dealt rather with the problem of when the uprising could be started. A definite period was decided upon for the beginning of the uprising by military conspiratorial means . . . There was no record of the proceedings, apart from a counting of votes The debates were on matters of principle and the comrades who spoke, more than might be supposed, argued against an armed uprising, going so far as to deny the power of the soviets. Objections amounted to the point that an armed uprising could be victorious and then what? . . . but we would not be able to retain our positions for social-economic reasons, etc. In this way the question was treated in great depth. Comparisons were made with the July days, it was said that the masses might not come on to the streets and we would beat a retreat. Then there were arguments that we would not be able to cope with the food problems, that we would perish in the first two weeks, that St Petersburg would remain our island, that Vikzhel, the engineers, the specialists and the intelligentsia would throttle us. The debates were very passionate but now, after the event, it is very difficult to recall all the arguments. What was most striking, comrades, was that when people began to deny the possibility of an uprising at the present time then our opponents in their arguments went even so far as to deny soviet power. We asked them: 'But what is your position?' They answered, 'agitation, propaganda, the rallying of the masses, etc.' 'Well, but what after that?' I cannot remember how the voting went, but I know that there were 5 or 6 votes *against*. There were considerably more votes *for*, about 9. However, I do not vouch for these figures. The session lasted all night. We began to disperse at dawn. Some comrades and I stayed to sleep.

Two varying attitudes to the uprising. On the one hand, the Petersburgers (those who worked in the St Petersburg soviet) linked the fate of this uprising with the course of the conflict over the withdrawal of the garrison. Vladimir Ilich was not afraid of an uprising and even insisted on linking the fate of the uprising not only with the course of the conflict in St Petersburg alone. This was not another attitude but rather a different approach to the problem. Our point of view was the St Petersburg one, that St Petersburg would start the thing in this way, but Lenin was thinking of an uprising not only in St Petersburg, but in the whole country. And he didn't ascribe such a great place and significance exclusively to the uprising of the St Petersburg garrison.

The 15th October was designated the day of the uprising.

4/10   THE RED GUARDS*

The Red Guard contributed little to the Bolshevik seizure of power in Petrograd in October 1917. It was poorly organized and weak in numbers, and lacked training; the outcome of events owed less to it than to the mood of the Petrograd garrison, the Provisional Government's lack of a dependable armed force, the establishment of a Bolshevik majority in the Petrograd Soviet, and in general to the weakness of the opposition faced by the Bolsheviks. William Brown's comments on the Red Guard are not untypical for observers of this period:

> There was nothing very impressive about the appearance of the Red Guard. They were just such men as one would expect to see taking part in an insurrectionary uprising against established government, sure to be put down in a few hours, or at most in a few days, like the draft riots in our own [i.e. the American] Civil War. Many of them were mere boys. The idea that these men were to wield power in Russia for a long time to come had not even occurred to us. That was an idea which needed only to present itself to be immediately rejected as absurd and impossible.

In view of the above it might appear rather pointless to indulge in the sterile intellectual exercise of determining how numerous the Red Guard was in Russia in October 1917. However, there are important reasons for studying the Red Guard in such detail.

Firstly, even if the Red Guard was not a crucial factor in the establishment of Bolshevik power in the capital city, in the provinces it was of much greater importance, especially in areas where no troops were stationed. Secondly, the Red Guard consisted of those sections of the industrial working class, and sometimes of peasants and intellectuals, who were willing to establish

* From D. N. Collins, *Soviet Studies*, Vol. 24, No. 2 (October 1972), pp. 270, 271, 280.

Soviet power by force of arms. Without a study of the Red Guard it is impossible to obtain a clear idea of the social and political forces which helped the Bolsheviks to power.

Thirdly, the Red Guard formed the basis of the Red Army. No account of the history of the Civil War or of the Red Army itself is complete without an investigation of the forces of which it was originally composed.

Finally, an investigation of the role played by the Red Guard in the provinces and in Petrograd may compel historians to revise currently held opinions about the role of the industrial working class in the revolution before October; for example, the Red Guard was closely connected with the movement for workers' control of industry.

It is worthless discussing the significance of an organisation if its dimensions are not known. Consequently, one of the first priorities in an investigation of the Red Guard—and the subject of this note—is the determination of its size . . .

In the above discussion of the relative merits of estimates of the numbers of Red Guards in various localities in Russia an attempt has been made to discover whether it is possible to determine Red Guard numbers with any degree of accuracy. It would appear that approximate numbers are available, and that it is possible to establish the validity of some estimates. However, in the present state of knowledge it is impossible to be more precise than to give a figure of between 70,000 and 100,000 (the figure eventually arrived at by Verkhos) for the total number of Red Guards. It is evident that there is no basis for the assertion that there were 200,000 Red Guards prior to the Bolshevik seizure of power.

5 War, Civil War and Intervention

The October revolution did not bring peace to the embattled Russian armies. Peace as the Bolsheviks discovered, can only be secured if both warring camps desire it. Some in Soviet Russia did not want peace, if it meant leaving the Kaiser intact. One of the arguments used by Lenin to justify the seizure of power in October had been that the spark of a Russian revolution would kindle the flame of revolution in the capitalist countries and this would set the world alight. Some radical spirits in the Bolshevik Central Committee and in the Left Socialist Revolutionary Party were for a war of liberation against Germany. Lenin was wary of such revolutionary fervour. He knew that the Russian soldiers who had been promised peace and land would not take kindly to being asked not only to continue the war but to take it into Germany herself. He was not for peace at any price but he regarded short-term concessions as acceptable since sooner or later the German proletariat would rise and sweep away their imperial masters. Lenin believed that the victorious German revolution was on the immediate horizon. He was defeated in the Central Committee and threatened resignation before he had his way and the peace of Brest–Litovsk was signed.

The treaty meant the temporary loss of the Ukraine, and on top of this Czechoslovak prisoners of war seized many towns on the Trans-Siberian railway from Samara to Irkutsk in May 1918. A non-Bolshevik government was established in Samara in June and the Whites were building up their forces. The civil war had begun.

The Allied powers decided in July 1918 to intervene in Soviet Russia. They wished to stop German penetration of the country and they wanted to aid the Czechoslovaks. When an armistice was signed with the Central Powers in November 1918, the Allies had to decide whether to withdraw their forces or to side with the Whites. They chose the latter course.

The civil war can be divided into three phases: (1) February to November 1918, (2) November 1918 to December 1919, (3) January to November 1920.

During the first phase, the eastern front was the most significant. The fronts in the north and southeast did not register much activity. Admiral Kolchak overthrew the Directorate which had been established in Ufa and proclaimed himself supreme ruler of Russia in November 1918.

The second phase saw action on the northwestern, eastern, south-eastern, southwestern and southern fronts. Bitter fighting was the keynote everywhere. The high point of White progress was achieved in October 1919 when Denikin's cavalry reached Orel, 200 miles southwest of Moscow. Yudenich reached the suburbs of Petrograd in late October 1919. The Reds scored notable victories to force Denikin back to the Don in October 1919 and Kolchak was forced to retreat to Irkutsk in December.

Phase three is dominated by the Polish invasion in May 1920 and Wrangel's drive north from the Crimea in June. The Reds met defeat near Warsaw and conceded territory to the Poles at the treaty of Riga in March 1921. By the end of the year Soviet Russia has been cleared of all large anti-Bolshevik forces.

One of the most colourful army commanders thrown up by the civil war was Nestor Makhno. He was an ally of the Reds in 1919 but was never a Bolshevik. He is usually described as a green or an anarchist. Trotsky's vivid analysis of his movement (5/25c) reveals the thorn in the flesh he was to the Reds. Makhno's reply (5/25d) demonstrates that his gifts were better expressed on the battlefield than on paper.

CHRONOLOGY OF THE CIVIL WAR

Phase I

1918

February	S.E.	Volunteer Army retreats from Don to Kuban
March	S.E.	Collapse of Cossack government of General Kaledin

May	S.E.	Germans reach Rostov-on-Don; Skoropadsky régime in Ukraine
28 May	East	Czechoslovaks seize many towns on Trans-Siberian Railway from Samara to Irkutsk
8 June	East	Formation of democratic government at Samara on the Volga
July	East	Formation of moderate conservative government at Omsk, Siberia
2 August	North	Allied occupation of Archangel; formation of democratic government under Chaikovsky
6 August	East	Czechoslovaks and Whites take Kazan; highpoint of first White advance westward
August	S.E.	Volunteer Army resumes offensive, takes Novorossiisk in Kuban
September	East	Ufa conference; formation of five-man Directorate
8 October	East	Red Army takes Samara on its advance eastwards
18 November	East	Kolchak's *coup d'état*, becomes 'Supreme Ruler' of Russia

Phase II

11 November		Armistice between Allies and Central Powers; discussions in Paris on extending or curtailing commitments in Russia begin
13 November	West	Ukrainian nationalists under Petlyura revolt, overthrow Skoropadsky régime
27 November	South	Bolsheviks proclaim provisional Ukrainian Soviet Government
1919		
January	N.W.	Soviet troops advance into Baltic provinces
March	East	Kolchak captures Ufa on drive westwards to Volga; halted 26 April
6 April	S.W.	Red Army takes Odessa after evacuation

		of French forces (28 March, Allied Council decides against extended inter vention)
19 May	S.E.	Denikin takes offensive; mutiny of Soviet commander Grigorev and of Makhno, partisan leader (4 June); Red troops fall back to north
9 June	East	Red counter-offensive against Kolchak; Ufa recaptured
16 June	N.W.	First offensive by Yudenich against Petrograd fails
25 July	East	Advancing Reds take Chelyabinsk in Urals
August	South	Advancing Whites reach Tambov, S.E. of Moscow, also take Kiev and Odessa
14 October	South	Highpoint of Denikin's advance; cavalry reaches Orel, 200 miles southwest of Moscow
22 October	N.W.	Highpoint of Yudenich's second advance, reaches suburbs of Petrograd
20 October	South	Red counter-offensive begins; Denikin pushed back to Don.
December	East	Kolchak retreats to Irkutsk; democratic government formed; partisan uprisings help advancing Reds

Phase III

1920

4 January	East	Kolchak resigns as 'Supreme Ruler'; handed over to pro-Bolsheviks 15 January; shot 7 February
February	North	Fall of White government at Archangel
March	South	Denikin's army evacuated from Kuban to Crimea; Wrangel takes over command
May	West	Polish invasion; Kiev falls 6 May
June	South	Wrangel drives north from Crimea
July	West	Red counter-offensive; Minsk, Vilno taken; push towards Warsaw

| August | West | Poles rally and drive Reds across the frontier; Armistice signed 12 October |
| October | South | Red final offensive against Wrangel in Crimea; evacuation 14 November |

1921

| 18 March | | Treaty of Riga signed by Poland and Soviet Russia |

5/1 GERMAN SUBVENTIONS FOR THE BOLSHEVIKS*

The State Secretary to the Foreign Ministry Liaison Officer
at General Headquarters
Telegram No. 1925

AS 4486   Berlin, 3 December 1917

The disruption of the Entente and the subsequent creation of political combinations agreeable to us constitute the most important war aim of our diplomacy. Russia appeared to be the weakest link in the enemy chain. The task therefore was gradually to loosen it, and, when possible, to remove it. This was the purpose of the subversive activity we caused to be carried out in Russia behind the front – in the first place promotion of separatist tendencies and support of the Bolsheviks. It was not until the Bolsheviks had received from us a steady flow of funds through various channels and under different labels that they were in a position to be able to build up their main organ, *Pravda,* to conduct energetic propaganda and appreciably to extend the originally narrow basis of their party. The Bolsheviks have now come to power; how long they will retain power cannot be yet foreseen. They need peace in order to strengthen their own position; on the other hand it is entirely in our interest that we should exploit the period while they are in power, which may be a short one, in order to attain firstly an armistice and then, if possible, peace. The conclusion of a separate peace would mean the achievement of the desired war aim, namely a breach between Russia and her Allies. The amount of tension necessarily caused by such a breach

* From Z. A. B. Zeman, *Germany and the Revolution in Russia 1915–1918* (London 1958), pp. 94–5.

would determine the degree of Russia's dependence on Germany and her future relations with us. Once cast out and cast off by her former Allies, abandoned financially, Russia will be forced to seek our support. We shall be able to provide help for Russia in various ways; firstly in the rehabilitation of the railways; (I have in mind a German Russian Commission, under our control, which would undertake the rational and co-ordinated exploitation of the railway lines so as to ensure speedy resumption of freight movement), then the provision of a substantial loan, which Russia requires to maintain her state machine. This could take the form of an advance on the security of grain, raw materials, &c., &c., to be provided by Russia and shipped under the control of the abovementioned commission. Aid on such a basis – the scope to be increased as and when necessary – would in my opinion bring about a growing *rapprochement* between the two countries.

Austria–Hungary will regard the *rapprochement* with distrust and not without apprehension. I would interpret the excessive eagerness of Count Czernin to come to terms with the Russians as a desire to forestall us and to prevent Germany and Russia arriving at an intimate relationship inconvient to the Danube Monarchy. There is no need for us to compete for Russia's good will. We are strong enough to wait with equanimity; we are in a far better position than Austria–Hungary to offer Russia what she needs for the reconstruction of her state. I view future developments in the East with confidence but I think it expedient for the time being to maintain a certain reserve in our attitude to the Austro–Hungarian government in all matters including the Polish question which concern both monarchies so as to preserve a free hand for all eventualities.

The above-mentioned considerations lie, I venture to believe, within the framework of the directives given me by His Majesty. I request you to report to His Majesty accordingly and to transmit to me by telegram the All-highest instructions.

KÜHLMANN

5/2　FORMATION OF THE RED ARMY*

28 January 1918

The old army was an instrument of class oppression of the working people by the bourgeoisie. With the transition of power to the working and exploited classes there has arisen the need for a new army as the mainstay of Soviet power at present and the basis for replacing the regular army by the arming of the whole people in the near future, and as a support for the coming socialist revolution in Europe.

I

In view of the aforesaid, the Council of People's Commissars resolves to organize a new army, to be called the Workers' and Peasants' Red Army, on the following principles:

(1) The Workers' and Peasants' Red Army is built up from the most conscious and organized elements of the working people.

(2) Access to its ranks is open to all citizens of the Russian Republic who have attained the age of 18. Every one who is prepared to devote his forces, his life to the defence of the gains of the October Revolution, the power of the Soviets, and socialism can join the Red Army. Joining the ranks of the Red Army requires characteristics from army committees or democratic public organizations standing on the platform of Soviet power, Party or trade union organizations, or at least two members of these organizations. Joining by whole units calls for mutual guarantee and a signed vote.

II

(1) The Workers' and Peasants' Red Army soldiers are fully maintained by the State and receive, on top of that, 50 rubles monthly.

(2) Invalid members of the families of Red Army soldiers who formerly were their dependants are provided with everything

* From Y. Akhapkin, ed., *First Decrees of Soviet Power* (London 1970), pp. 86–7.

necessary according to the local consumer quotas, in keeping with the decisions of the local bodies of Soviet power.

III

The supreme authority for the Workers' and Peasants' Red Army is the Council of People's Commissars. Direct guidance and administration of the army is concentrated in the Commissariat of Military Affairs and the special All-Russia Board attached to it.

Chairman of the Council of People's Commissars
V. ULYANOV (LENIN)

5/3   SOVIET TROOPS TAKE KIEV*

4 February 1918

To all, all, all

Soviet troops entered Kiev on 29 January. The troops were under the direction of Yury Kotsyubinsky, Deputy to the People's Secretary for Military Affairs, Shakhrai. The Kiev garrison with all its artillery has sided with Kotsyubinsky's troops and has declared the Kiev Rada of Vinnichenko and Porsh deposed. The General Secretariat of the Kiev Rada headed by Vinnichenko, abandoned by everyone, has gone into hiding. Odoevsky, who attempted to get together a compromise General Secretariat, has been arrested. The Central Executive Committee of the Soviets of the Ukraine together with its People's Secretariat in Kharkov has been proclaimed the supreme authority in the Ukraine. The following have been adopted:

Federal union with Russia and complete unity with the Council of People's Commissars in matters of internal and external policy. The Central Executive Committee of the Soviets of the Ukraine and the People's Secretariat moved to Kiev on 3 February. The Army Radas of the South-Western and Roumanian Fronts have disbanded themselves voluntarily.

* From J. M. Meijer, *The Trotsky Papers 1917–1922* (Mouton, The Hague 1964) (hereafter Meijer), Vol. 1, pp. 24, 26.

The representatives of both fronts have acknowledged the All-Ukrainian Central Executive Committee and the People's Secretariat as the sole authority in the Ukraine.

An All-Ukrainian Congress of Soviets of Workers', Soldiers' and Peasants' Deputies will meet shortly in Kiev.

All the cities and guberniyas of the Ukraine without exception have stated that they agree to take part in it: Kharkov, Ekaterinoslav, Kiev and Podoliya, Kherson guberniya and Poltava, Chernigov guberniya and the Donets Basin, Odessa and Nikolaev, all coastal towns and the whole Black Sea Fleet, and the entire front and rear of the Ukraine.

The Congress is to be summoned and opened by the All-Ukrainian Central Executive Committee.

Orenburg has been occupied by Soviet troops finally.

Dutov, together with a handful of adherents, has gone into hiding. All government establishments in Orenburg have been occupied by Soviet troops. The Orenburg Soviet of Workers', Solders' Peasants' and Cossacks' Deputies has been declared the local authority.

Simferopol has been occupied by Soviet troops. All authority on the peninsula is in the hands of the All-Crimean Soviet of Workers', Soldiers' and Peasants' Deputies.

> Chairman of the Council of People's Commissars,
> Vladimir Ulyanov (Lenin).

5/4   THE SEARCH FOR PEACE

THE DECREE ON PEACE*

8 November 1917

The Workers' and Peasants' government, created by the revolution of October 24–25 and basing itself on the Soviets of Workers' Soldiers' and Peasants' Deputies, calls upon all the belligerent peoples and their governments to start immediate negotiations for a just, democratic peace.

By a just or democratic peace, for which the overwhelming

* From Akhapkin, pp. 20–1.

majority of the working class and other working people of all the belligerent countries, exhausted, tormented and racked by the war, are craving – a peace that has been most definitely and insistently demanded by the Russian workers and peasants ever since the overthrow of the Tsarist monarchy – by such a peace the government means an immediate peace without annexations (i.e. without the seizure of foreign lands, without the forcible incorporation of foreign nations) and without indemnities.

The Government of Russia proposes that this kind of peace be immediately concluded by all the belligerent nations, and expresses its readiness to take all resolute measures now, without the least delay, pending the final ratification of all the terms of such a peace by authoritative assemblies of the people's representatives of all countries and all nations.

In accordance with the sense of justice of democrats in general, and of the working classes in particular, the Government conceives the annexation or seizure of foreign lands to mean every incorporation of a small or weak nation into a large or powerful state without the precisely, clearly and voluntarily expressed consent and wish of that nation, irrespective of the time which such forcible incorporation took place, irrespective also of the degree of development or backwardness of the nation forcibly annexed to the given state, or forcibly retained within its borders, and irrespective, finally, of whether this nation is in Europe or in distant, overseas countries.

If any nation whatsoever is forcibly retained within the borders of a given state, if, in spite of its expressed desire – no matter whether expressed in the press, at public meetings, in the decisions of parties, or in protests and uprising against national oppression – it is not accorded the right to decide the forms of its state existence by a free vote, taken after the complete evacuation of the troops of the incorporating or, generally, of the stronger nation and without the least pressure being brought to bear, such incorporation is annexation, i.e. seizure and violence.

The Government considers it the greatest of crimes against humanity to continue this war over the issue of how to divide among the strong and rich nations the weak nationalities they have conquered, and solemnly announces its determination immediately to sign terms of peace to stop this war on the terms indicated, which are equally just for all nationalities without exception.

At the same time the Government declares that it does not regard the above-mentioned peace terms as an ultimatum; in other words, it is prepared to consider any other peace terms, and insists only that they be advanced by any of the belligerent countries as speedily as possible, and that in the peace proposals there should be absolute clarity and the complete absence of all ambiguity and secrecy.

The Government abolishes secret diplomacy, and, for its part, announces its firm intention to conduct all negotiations quite openly in full view of the whole people. It will proceed immediately with the full publication of the secret treaties endorsed or concluded by the government of landowners and capitalists from February to October 25, 1917. The Government proclaims the unconditional and immediate annulment of everything contained in these secret treaties in so far as it is aimed, as is mostly the case, at securing advantages and privileges for the Russian landowners and capitalists and at the retention, or extension, of the annexations made by the Great Russians.

Proposing to the governments and peoples of all countries immediately to begin open negotiations for peace, the Government, for its part, expresses its readiness to conduct these negotiations in writing, by telegraph, and by negotiations between representatives of the various countries, or at a conference of such representatives. In order to facilitate such negotiations, the Government is appointing its plenipotentiary representative to neutral countries.

The Second All-Russian Congress of Soviets

5/5 COMPULSORY MILITARY TRAINING*

22 April 1918

One of the main objects of Socialism is to deliver mankind from the burden of militarism and from the barbarity of bloody clashes between nations. The goal of Socialism is universal disarmament, eternal peace and fraternal cooperation of all the peoples inhabiting the earth.

* From Akhapkin, pp. 121–3.

This goal will be achieved when power in all the strongest capitalist countries passes into the hands of the working class, which will wrest the means of production from the exploiters, turn them over to all working people for common use, and establish a Communist system as the unshakeable foundation of the solidarity of all mankind.

At the present time it is in Russia alone that state power belongs to the working class. In all the other countries the imperialist bourgeoisie is at the helm. Its policy is aimed at suppressing the communist revolution and enslaving all weak nations. The Russian Soviet Republic, surrounded on all sides by enemies, has to create its own powerful army to defend the country, while engaged in remaking its social system along communist lines.

The Workers' and Peasants' Government of the Republic deems it its immediate task to enlist all citizens in universal labour conscription and military service. This work is meeting with stubborn resistance on the part of the bourgeoisie, which refuses to part with its economic privileges and is trying, through conspiracies, uprisings and traitorous deals with foreign imperialists, to regain state power.

To arm the bourgeoisie would mean to generate constant strife within the army, thereby paralysing its strength in the fight against the external enemies. The parasitic and exploiter elements who do not want to assume the same duties and rights as others cannot be given access to arms. The Workers' and Peasants' Government will find ways of making the bourgeoisie share, in some form or other, the burden of defending the Republic, upon which the crimes of the propertied classes have brought unheard-of trials and calamities. But in the immediate transitional period military training and arms will be given only to workers and to peasants who do not exploit the labour of others.

Citizens of 18 to 40 years of age who have undergone compulsory military training will be registered as subject to military service. At the first call of the Workers' and Peasants' Government they will have to take up arms and join the ranks of the Red Army, which consists of the most devoted and selfless fighters for the freedom and independence of the Russian Soviet Republic and for the international socialist revolution.

1. Military training is compulsory for the citizens of the Russian Soviet Federative Republic of the following ages: (1) school age, whose youngest limit is determined by the People's Commissariat of Public Education; (2) preparatory age, from 16 to 18 years, and (3) call-up age, from 18 to 40 years.

Female citizens are trained, with their consent, on an equal footing with males.

NOTE. Persons whose religious convictions do not allow the use of arms are trained only in those duties which do not involve the use of arms.

2. Training of persons of the preparatory and call-up ages is entrusted to the People's Commissariat for Military Affairs, and that of the school-age category to the People's Commissariat for Public Education, with the closest cooperation of the Commissariat for Military Affairs.

3. Military training is compulsory for workers employed in factories, workshops, at agricultural estates and in villages, and peasants who do not exploit the labour of others.

4. In the provinces compulsory military training is organised by area, *guberniya, uezd* and *volost* military commissariats.

5. The trainees are in no way recompensed for the time spent in compulsory training; instruction shall be organised, as far as possible, in such a way so as not to divert the trainees from their normal permanent occupation.

6. Instruction shall be conducted continuously for eight weeks, at least 12 hours per week. The terms of training for special arms, and the procedure for refresher call-ups, will be determined in special regulations.

7. Persons who have been given training in the regular army can be excused from compulsory training after passing an appropriate test, with the issue of certificates that they have undergone a course of compulsory training.

8. Instruction shall be given by trained instructors in accordance with a programme approved by the People's Commissariat for Military Affairs.

9. Persons who avoid compulsory training or neglect their duties stemming therefrom shall be called to account.

Chairman of the Central Executive
Committee, YA. SVERDLOV

5/6   FIGHTING IN SVIYAZHSK*

13 August 1918

From: Sviyazhsk – Eastern Front Staff HQ

To: Moscow – Chairman of the Council of People's Commissars, Lenin

Stubborn fighting is in progress here. To date the numbers of those killed are to be counted in tens, those wounded in hundreds. On our side we have a certain numerical preponderance in artillery. On his side the enemy is superior in organisation and in the accuracy of his fire. The allegation that our men do not want to fight is a lie. Wherever there is a good or tolerably good commander and good commissars, the soldiers fight. The presence of workers who are Communists is most beneficial. There are many supremely devoted and courageous men among them. When the Commander wants to say that such and such a post is occupied by a reliable person, he says: I have got a Communist there. I am not going to attempt to predict what tomorrow may bring. But I have no doubt of victory.

Trotsky

5/7   FIGHTING AT KAZAN

(a) MOBILIZATION OF PEASANTS AND WORKERS IN KAZAN GUBERNIYA†

To the Peasants and Workers of Kazan *Guberniya*

The enemies of the working people, the landlords, capitalists, officers and their hirelings, the Czechoslovaks, are attempting to mobilise the working population of Kazan *guberniya* to fight against workers and peasants.

By this document I declare the following so that in the future no one may plead ignorance of the revolutionary laws and degrees of Soviet power:

---

* From Meijer, Vol. 1, p. 79.

† From L. Trotsky, *Kak Vooruzhalas Revolyutsiya* (Moscow 1923), Vol. 1, p. 241.

1. Anyone who is mobilised by the Czechoslovak White Guards and joins the army of the enemies of the people, commits a most serious state crime.

2. All workers and peasants who have joined, under duress, the ranks of the hostile army must immediately go over to the side of the Soviet troops. By doing this they will be guaranteed a full pardon.

3. Those peasants and workers who have sold themselves to the White Guards and who do not voluntarily lay down their arms will be shot together with their officers, and the sons of the bourgeoisie and landlords. All their property will be handed over to the wounded and maimed Red Army men and the families of fallen soldiers of the Workers' and Peasants' Army.

Workers and peasants of Kazan guberniya! The word of the Soviet power is firm. Its punishment is severe. Do not give a single soldier to the corrupt Guards. Give everything to the defence of Soviet power!

27 August 1918

(b) THE STRUGGLE FOR KAZAN*

From: Moscow

To: Sviyazhsk – Trotsky

c. 21 August 1918

I am amazed and alarmed at the slowing down in the operations against Kazan; what is particularly bad is the report of your having the fullest possible opportunity of destroying the enemy with your artillery. One should not take pity on the city and put off matters any longer, as merciless annihilation is what is vital once it is established that Kazan is enclosed in an iron ring.

Lenin

The enemy's artillery is not weaker than ours.

* From Meijer, Vol. 1, p. 90.

5/8   TROTSKY INSISTS ON STALIN'S RECALL*

4 October 1918

From: Tambov

To: Moscow – Chairman of the Central Executive Committee.

I categorically insist on Stalin's recall. Things are going badly on the Tsaritsyn Front, despite a superabundance of military forces. Voroshilov is able to command a regiment, but not an army of fifty thousand men. None the less I will retain him as Commander of the Tenth Tsaritsyn Army on condition that he places himself under the orders of the Commander of the Southern Front, Sytin. Right up to this day the Tsaritsyn people have failed to send even operational reports to Kozlov. I had required them to submit operational and intelligence reports twice daily. If this is not carried out tomorrow I shall commit Voroshilov and Minin for trial and announce this in an army order. So long as Stalin and Minin remain in Tsaritsyn, according to the constitution of the Military Revolutionary Council they merely enjoy the rights of members of the Military Revolutionary Council of the Tenth Army. For the purpose of launching an attack there remains only a short while before the autumn weather makes the roads impassable, when there will be no through road here either on foot or on horseback. Operations in strength are impossible without coordination of operations with Tsaritsyn. There is no time for diplomatic negotiations. Tsaritsyn must either obey or get out of the way. We have a colossal superiority in forces but total anarchy at the top. This can be put to rights within 24 hours given firm and resolute support your end. In any event this is the only course of action that I can envisage.

Trotsky

* From Meijer, Vol. 1, pp. 135, 137.

5/9   EX-TSARIST OFFICERS MAY SERVE IN RED ARMY*

13 October 1918

From: Kozlov

In view of changed circumstances, a certain section of the officer class is displaying its readiness to work in the service of the Soviets. On this I propose the following: in those cases where there are no direct, serious charges against the arrested officers, that the question be put to them: do they agree to serve the Red Army and the Red Fleet. That, in the event of an affirmative answer, they be put at my disposal. That, at the same time, their family position be ascertained and they be warned that, in the event of treachery or desertion to the enemy's camp on their part their families will be arrested, and that a signature to this effect be obtained from them. By this means we shall lighten the load on the prisons and obtain military specialists, of whom there is great need. Please communicate instructions accordingly to all the commissions under your orders.

Chairman of the Military
Revolutionary Council, Trotsky

5/10   STALIN REPORTS VICTORIES AT TSARITSYN†

23 October 1918

To: Trotsky

Stalin arrived today and brought news of three major victories of our troops in the vicinity of Tsaritsyn: one of them ten versts from Tsaritsyn, another the annihilation of four enemy regiments by the Steppe Army at Svetly Yar, which, as it turns out, had been summoned up by the Tsaritsyn people, and the third near Muzga, where four enemy regiments were also annihilated.

* From ibid., Vol. 1, p. 149.
† From ibid., Vol. 1, pp. 159, 161.

Stalin has persuaded Voroshilov and Minin, whom he considers very valuable and irreplaceable workers, to stay on and accord full compliance to the orders from the centre; the sole cause of their dissatisfaction, according to his words, is the extreme delay in the delivery of shells and small-arms ammunition, or their non-delivery, which is also having a fatal effect on the Caucasian army, two hundred thousand strong and in excellent fighting spirit.

Stalin would very much like to work on the Southern Front; he expresses great apprehension that people whose knowledge of this Front is poor may commit errors, of which he cites numerous examples. Stalin hopes that in the course of his work he will manage to convince people of the correctness of his approach, and he is not putting up any ultimatum about the removal of Sytin and Mekhonoshin but agrees to work jointly with them on the Revolutionary Council of the Southern Front and also expresses the wish to be a member of the Higher Military Council of the Republic.

In informing you, Lev Davydych, of all these statements of Stalin, I ask you to think them over and let me have a reply, firstly, as to whether you agree to talk matters over personally with Stalin, for which purposes he is ready to visit you, and, secondly, whether you consider it possible under given, specific conditions to put aside former differences and arrange to work together as Stalin so much desires.

As far as I am concerned, my belief is that it is essential to make every effort towards arranging to work together with Stalin.

Sverdlov

5/11   ORDER TO RED TROOPS ON SOUTHERN FRONT*

ORDER

Of the Chairman of the Revolutionary War Council of the
Republic to the troops and Soviet institutions
on the Southern Front.
24 November 1918. No. 65

* From Trotsky, *Kak Vooruzhalas Revolyutsiya*, Vol. 1, p. 358.

Krasnov and the foreign capitalists which stand behind his back, have thrown on to the Voronezh front hundreds of hired agents who have penetrated, under various guises, Red army units and are carrying on there base work, corrupting and inciting men to desert. In a few shaky units on the Voronezh front one can actually observe the marks of demoralisation, cowardice and self-interest. While, on all other fronts, in all other armies, Red troops are chasing the enemy and advancing, on the Voronezh front often senseless, criminal retreats and the break-up of whole regiments are taking place constantly.

I declare that from now on an end must be put to this by using merciless means.

1. Every scoundrel who incites anyone to retreat, to desert, or not to fulfil a military order, will be shot.

2. Every soldier of the Red Army who voluntarily deserts his military post, will be shot.

3. Every soldier, who throws away his rifle or sells part of his equipment, will be shot.

4. Military police detachments to arrest deserters will be stationed in the whole front line strip. Every soldier who offers resistance to these detachments, must be shot on the spot.

5. All local soldiers and committees of the poor are obligated on their part to take all measures to capture deserters. Deserter patrols are to be carried out twice every 24 hours, at 8 o'clock in the morning and 8 o'clock in the evening. Captured deserters are to be handed over to the HQ of the nearest unit or to the nearest military commissariat.

6. Those guilty of harbouring deserters are liable to be shot.

7. Houses in which deserters are found will be burnt down.

Death to self-seekers and to traitors!

Death to deserters and to the agents of Krasnov!

Long live the honest soldiers of the Workers' Red Army!

5/12   LACK OF DISCIPLINE IN PERM*

31 December 1918

From: Moscow

To: Kozlov and to the Chairman of the Military Revolutionary
Council, Trotsky, wherever he is.

A number of party reports have come in from the Perm area
about the catastrophic state of the army and about drunkenness. I
am sending them on to you. Would you please go there. I had
thought of sending Stalin; I am afraid that Smilga will be lenient
with Lashevich, who, it is said, is also drinking and is in no fit
state to restore order. Telegraph your opinion.

Lenin

5/13   THE SHOOTING OF COMMISSAR
PANTELEEV†

11 January 1919

To: Kremlin, Moscow – Chairman of the Central Executive
Committee, Sverdlov. On the subject of the shooting of
Commissar Panteleev

In reply to the question as to where and in what circumstances
the Commissar of the Second Petrograd Nomernoi Regiment,
Panteleev, was executed by shooting, Comrade Slaven, formerly
Army Commander and now Front Commander, states:

> Commissar Panteleev, together with the regimental com-
> mander, abandoned the position at the head of a considerable
> part of the strength of his regiment and later turned up on
> board a steamship that had been seized by the deserters in
> order to effect their unauthorised departure from Kazan
> towards Nizhny. He was shot not for his regiment having
> abandoned their position but for having himself abandoned the
> position, in company with the regiment. The documents on

* From Meijer, Vol. 1, p. 228.
† From ibid., Vol. 1, p. 253.

this affair are with the Political Commissar of the Fifth Army, Mikhailov. (Signed) Slaven.

> Chairman of the Military
> Revolutionary Council, Trotsky

5/14   REPORT ON MEDICAL SERVICES*

> 7 April 1919
> (Samara)

To: Alexander School, Moscow
Call up Velmer and obtain, if possible, an immediate answer.

For: The People's Commissariat of Health, The Chief Administration of Sanitary Services, and the Chairman of the Council of Defence, Lenin.

The state of the medical services in the Fifth Army defies description. There are no doctors, no drugs, no hospital trains. The wounded are transported in cattle trucks. All the evidence suggests that the work of the Chief Administration of Sanitary Services does not measure up as regards drive and intensity to the work of the other Services of the Red Army. Owing to the shortage of doctors, the mobilisation of fifth-year students was held up. Only latterly, after prolonged representations, has the order been issued. To leave wounded men without care or attention is the surest way of causing the army to disintegrate. I request the Council of Defence to prompt the Chief Administration of Sanitary Services to take such measures as will, at least to some degree, meet the immediate requirements of the Front. Doctors, hospital trains and drugs are needed.

> Chairman of the Military
> Revolutionary Council, Trotsky

* From ibid., Vol. 1, p. 343.

5/15   SUPPLY DIFFICULTIES

(a) ZINOVIEV DEMANDS BOOTS*

15 April 1919

To: Simbirsk, from Smolny, Petrograd
Top priority for Trotsky, at present whereabouts, only.

Two months ago at a special conference in Petrograd, in which
Trotsky and Krasin took part, it was decided to issue 30 thousand
pairs of boots immediately to the Seventh Army. For six weeks
various government offices have been impeding their issue with
formalities. The most energetic protests are being received from
the Seventh Army; the men go about unshod while the boots
are lying around in Petrograd. One consignment has been sent
off. The latest delay has been brought about by a member of the
People's Commissariat of Supply, Frumkin. In his special telephonic message, No. 1715, he, totally illegally and without any
necessity whatsoever, imposed a categoric ban on the issue of the
boots in question. This is sabotage of the worst sort. Frumkin's
telephonic message has today been countermanded. However, a
delay did result and the same can recur at any given moment. This
procrastination exasperates the soldiers. I have been making endless applications that Frumkin be called to account. I ask that
the Military Revolutionary Council hold an investigation as to
who caused this two months' hold-up.

Zinoviev

(b) LENIN ON HORSES†

31 May 1919

From: Chairman of the Council of People's Commissars of the
R.S.F.S.R. Kremlin, Moscow

To: Podvoisky

You have not yet supplied the 2,500 horses which were already
promised some weeks ago. You forwarded 500 of them in such a

* From ibid., Vol. 1, pp. 357, 359.
† From ibid., Vol. 1, p. 494.

way that it is still not known where they are. The 1,500 horses for Petrograd have not yet arrived. Put pressure on the apparatus to see that all 4,000 horses are delivered within seven days and specially routed by direct consignment. Send tanks. They are very badly needed. Send them to Moscow. Where are the workers' replacement drafts for the Southern Front? They have not arrived yet. Send transport straight away. Telegraph how much transport you will be supplying within the next seven days and within the next two weeks. Fewer promises, more deeds. The main thing is to check that orders are actually carried out; and inform us of what actually has arrived at its destination.

Lenin

5/16   THE SITUATION IN PETROGRAD

(a) THE ORDER TO REMOVE THE OFFICE FOR THE PREPARATION OF STATE PAPERS FROM PETROGRAD*

27 May 1919

To: Petrograd – Defence Committee

Recognising the necessity, arising from the military situation, of carrying out in the shortest possible time, the total evacuation of the Petrograd Office for the Preparation of State Papers, apart from the paper mill and such other of its branches as are difficult to evacuate and not of vital importance for production purposes, the Council of Defence recommends the Commission of Five for the Evacuation of Petrograd to carry through this evacuation, irrespective of any partial improvements in the position on the Petrograd Front. In this matter the Council of Defence recommends the Commission of Five to lay down a maximum period during which the evacuation is to be carried out, to supply all the necessary means and to see that all is completed within that period. The task of laying down the order in which the machinery is to be dismantled and speeding up the evacuation in the maximum period provided for is assigned to the Subcommission for

* From ibid., Vol. 1, p. 256.

the evacuation of the Office, acting in accordance with the instructions of the People's Commissariat of Finance.

Chairman of the Council of Defence,
V. Ulyanov (Lenin)

(b) THE ORDER TO DEFEND PETROGRAD*

ORDER

Of the Chairman of the Revolutionary Military Council
of the Republic, to Red Army men, commanders and
commissars defending Petrograd.
20 October 1919   Petrograd

Red Army men, commanders, commissars. The fate of Petrograd will be decided tomorrow. While the Red Army has gone over to a decisive and victorious offensive in the south and has retaken Orel and has routed Mamontov's ten regiments, a string of failures in Petrograd has forced our troops to roll back as far as the Pulkovsky positions. They must not retreat any further. Petrograd must not be surrendered. Even a temporary surrender of Petrograd would mean the loss of thousands of workers' lives and innumerable cultural treasures. Petrograd must be defended, no matter the cost.

All measures have been taken. Fresh units have been brought up. They guarantee us an enormous numerical superiority. The cadre of commanders has been revitalised and renewed. The best battle-hardened workers have been enrolled to fight. All that is necessary for victory is available. All that is necessary is that you should wish and promise this victory. That will guarantee it.

Remember: the great honour of defending this city, in which the revolution of workers and peasants was born, has fallen to your lot.

Forward!

Take the offensive!

Death to the hirelings of foreign capital!

Long live red Petrograd!

* From Trotsky, *Kak Vooruzhalas Revolyutsiya*, Vol. 2 (Part 1), p. 405.

5/17   MOBILISE THE WORKERS!*

9 May 1919

From: Moscow

To: Kiev – Kamenev, Ioffe, Rakovsky

The C.C. considers the most important task of the next fortnight to be the mobilisation of not less than 20,000 workers for the purpose, not of forming new units, but of incorporating them into the best cadres on the Southern Front. All the workers in Kharkov and Ekaterinoslav must be drafted. Comrades Kamenev and Ioffe must apply all their efforts to this work. It is essential that Comrade Kamenev makes sure that this is done in Kharkov and Ekaterinoslav, and Comrade Ioffe likewise from Kiev. What now matters as a whole is to gain time. The mobilisation must be fully completed within fourteen days. Party workers must be forcibly inspired with the thought that the fate of the revolution depends on the success of this mobilisation. Extensive agitation and energetic and rapid organisational measures are what is needed. The men mobilised must be sent off in company drafts as soon as possible and the necessary number of Communists included in each such draft. A stock of uniforms, even if not of the proper issue, must be laid in beforehand. The dispatch of the company drafts must not meet with delay for want of uniforms. Party Committees and Trade Unions must be brought in on the mobilisation and assigned specific tasks. The C.C. regards the figure of 20,000 as the minimum and the fortnight allowed for this as the maximum for rescuing our position on the Southern Front. This task must be performed with exceptional energy. Report without delay all measures taken by you. Telegraph the results achieved to the C.C. every three days.

Lenin

* From Meijer, Vol. 1, pp. 408, 410.

5/18 TROTSKY'S RESIGNATION REFUSED*

5 July 1919

From: The Central Committee of the Russian Communist Party (Bolsheviks) Kremlin, Moscow.

Having examined Comrade Trotsky's statement and having given it thorough consideration, the Orgburo and Politburo of the CC have come to the unanimous decision that they are totally unable to accept Comrade Trotsky's resignation or grant his request.

The Orgburo and Politburo of the CC will do everything they can to provide for the work on the Southern Front – the most difficult, dangerous and important of the fronts at the present time – which Comrade Trotsky chose for himself, to be arranged as to best suit Comrade Trotsky and to yield the greatest benefit to the Republic. As People's Commissar for Military Affairs and Chairman of the Military Revolutionary Council Comrade Trotsky has full power to take action and equally so as a member of the Military Revolutionary Council of the Southern Front in conjunction with the Front Commander (Egorev) whom he himself put forward and the CC confirmed.

The Orgburo and Politburo of the CC grant Comrade Trotsky every opportunity of striving for, by every possible means, what he considers as an adjustment of the line on the military question and, if he so wishes, of endeavouring to speed up the summoning of a party congress.

Being firmly convinced that Comrade Trotsky's resignation is absolutely impossible at the present moment and would cause the Republic the greatest harm, the Orgburo and Politburo of the CC emphatically recommend Comrade Trotsky to refrain from raising this question again and to carry on performing his function, cutting them down to the maximum extent, should he so desire, with a view to concentrating his work on the Southern Front.

In view of this, the Orgburo and Politburo of the CC decline to agree either to Comrade Trotsky leaving the Politburo or to his giving up the post of Chairman of the Military Revolutionary

* From ibid., Vol. 1, pp. 590, 592.

Council of the Republic (People's Commissar for Military Affairs).

> Signed:
> Lenin, Kamenev, Krestinsky, Kalinin,
> Serebryakov, Stalin, Stasova

5/19 RED VICTORIES IN THE URALS*

17 July 1919

From: Council of People's Commissars of the R.S.F.S.R., Kremlin, Moscow

To: Simbirsk – Military Revolutionary Council of the Eastern Front, Lashevich, Yurenev

I congratulate you on your victories. Special measures should be taken: firstly, against stealing of arms by Ural workers so as to prevent the development of a disastrous partisan mentality; secondly, so that the Siberian partisan movement does not demoralise our troops. Telegraph your opinion and report whether collaboration with the new front commander is amicable and send more details on Bashkir affairs.

Lenin

5/20 TROTSKY ON MILITARY DISCIPLINE†

COMMANDERS MUST KNOW HOW TO OBEY

In one of the Ukrainian sectors on the Southern Front a commander of a rifle brigade gave an order to a commander of a cavalry regiment who was subordinate to him to dispatch some horsemen to a flank. The commander of the cavalry regiment answered: 'I have no cavalry for you and you have a whole brigade of infantry.' This case characterises a system of

* From Lenin, *Polnoe Sobranie Sochinenii*, Vol. 51 (Moscow 1965), pp. 15, 16.

† From Trotsky, *Kak Vooruzhalas Revolyutsiya*, Vol. 2 (Part 1), p. 89.

relations under which important and decisive victories cannot be won.

The order to dispatch the cavalrymen was given in the name of the commander of a brigade, the brigade's chief of staff, a former lieutenant-colonel, a modest but conscientious fellow. The commander of the cavalry regiment doubtless regarded himself as a 'communist', otherwise he would hardly have decided to give such an insolent answer. In a few remote places communist commanders (i.e. false communists) regard everything as permissible, especially when they are dealing with non-communist commanders. This outrage should be extirpated, the sooner and more mercilessly, the better.

A communist commander must be a model of discipline. Discipline signifies a certain conscious link and subordination among people, who are striving towards a common goal. The commander of a regiment, who instead of carrying out a battle order, replies insolently to his superior commander, besides all else, will never establish the necessary subordination in his own regiment. Petty tyrants may frighten people, but they are incapable of establishing firm control.

Under the answer of the commander of the cavalry regiment which has been cited, there was only his signature. But where was the signature of the commissar? If there had been a well-disciplined commissar in the regiment, then he would not only have refused to sign an order so incompatible with proper organisation, he would have demanded that the commander of the regiment immediately carry out the battle order. Had the commander refused he would have arrested him on the spot. Evidently in the present case the commissar was not available, but the commander of the cavalry regiment, regarding himself as a communist, did not conform to any regulations and infringed a battle order and even did not inform the commissar about this.

Perhaps, incidentally, there was no commissar at all in this regiment, since someone somewhere thought that commissars were only necessary where there were 'military specialists'. A gross delusion! There ought to be a commissar in every regiment. But supervision of certain commanders, who in their own words are 'extremely revolutionary', is just as necessary as supervision of doubtful 'military specialists'.

A communist commander is always a most precious acquisition for our Red Army. He must only be a genuine communist, i.e. a man of duty and discipline from head to foot. However, we have, amongst officers still a considerable number of commanders who demand unquestioning subordination to themselves but are completely unsubordinated to their own immediate superior. Moreover, they justify themselves, either by their party-mindedness, or by reference to some kind of special mandate from authoritative soviet officials. Such false communists are more damaging to the army than the worst traitors from the officer corps of the White Guards. A traitor causes an army material loss, goes over to the side of the enemy, but that's not all, whereas a false communist poisons the consciousness of his unit by criminal demagogy. Although refusing to carry out an order, he will brag about his 'party-mindedness', yell about the interests of the revolution and at the same time treacherously undermine the co-ordination of military operations.

Not all Makhnovites are anarchists. Some falsely consider themselves communists. Makhnovites under the communist flag are much more dangerous than under an anarchist or left-SR flag.

Only when we have cleansed the Red Army of disorganising elements shall we be able to guarantee its complete steadfastness in battle.

18 July 1919
Village Vorozhba

5/21   STALIN COMPLAINS ABOUT OVERWORK AND LENIN REBUKES HIM

(a)*

20 February 1920

To: Kremlin, Moscow – to Lenin

It is not clear to me why concern for the Caucasus Front should be primarily my responsibility. Procedurally, the reinforcement of the Caucasus Front is entirely the concern of the Military

* From Meijer, Vol. 2, p. 67.

Revolutionary Council of the Republic, the members of which, according to my information, are in good health, and not that of Stalin who is already overloaded with work as it is.

Stalin

(b)*

20 February 1920

To: Stalin

It is your job to speed up the arrival of reinforcements from the South-Western Front for the Caucasus Front. You should help in every way you can and not pick a quarrel about departmental fields of competence.

Lenin

5/22   THE SITUATION IN THE UKRAINE†

Moscow, 26 April 1920

To: Lenin

The situation in the Ukraine demands the most serious attention. Banditry is rampant. Two Galician brigades have mutined and have turned their arms against us. As well as military measures, extensive ideological measures are necessary. A very considerable number of local political workers must be transferred to the Ukraine at once. It is equally essential that staunch political workers from departments at the centre should be seconded there for duty. We cannot permit a new 'misunderstanding' in the Ukraine: this time it would be too costly. I recommend taking drastic measures.

Trotsky

* From Lenin, *Polnoe Sobranie Sochinenii*, Vol. 51 (Moscow 1965), pp. 139–40.

† From Meijer, Vol. 2, p. 149.

5/23   THE WAR AGAINST POLAND

(a)*

ORDER

Of the Chairman of the Revolutionary Military Council
of the Republic to Red troops, fighting against the
Polish White Guards.

14 August 1920   No. 233   Moscow

Heroes! You have inflicted a shattering blow on White Poland, which was attacking us. Nevertheless the criminal and frivolous Polish government does not want peace. Pilsudski and his agents know that nothing is threatening the independence of Poland. We, the Russia of workers and peasants, are willing to give her wider frontiers than envisaged by the Entente. But Pilsudski fears the approach of the day when he will have to justify the war to the Polish people and is hoping for the intervention of France and England. For this reason, the Polish government is evading peace negotiations. Not daring to admit this openly, it is playing hide and seek. Its delegates do not turn up on time, but, if they do, then they are without plenary powers. The radio station in Warsaw does not accept our answers or the Polish government pretends that it has never seen them even when there are the receipts from the radio station in Warsaw.

We desire peace now, just as on the first day of the war. But because of this, we must wean the government of Polish bankrupts away from playing hide and seek with us.

Red troops, forward! Heroes, advance against Warsaw!

Long live victory!

Long live independent and fraternal Poland!

Long live the workers' and peasants' Red Army!

* From Trotsky, *Kak Vooruzhalas Revolyutsiya*, Vol. 2 (Part 2), p. 166.

(b) LENIN ON BOUNTY FOR HANGED POLES*

August 1920

Note from Comrade Lenin to Comrade Sklyansky at a meeting.

A superb plan. Complete it *together* with Dzerzhinsky. Under the guise of 'Greens' (and we will pin it on them later) we shall move forward 10–20 versts and hang the *kulaks,* priests and landowners. Bounty : 100,000 rubles for each man hanged.

Lenin

5/24   LENIN ON THE NAVY†

21 March 1921

To: Comrade Trotsky

Should we not close down the navy *completely* for a year? What is its purpose? And give the *coal* to the railways or textile factories, to provide the peasants with cloth? I think that here we should be prepared to take decisive measures. Let the navy suffer. The Soviet régime will benefit.

Lenin

5/25   MAKHNO

(a)‡

22 May 1919

From Kharkov

To: Moscow – Sklyansky for Comrade Lenin
It is essential to organise a large detachment, consisting of, roughly, one reliable Cheka battalion, several hundred Baltic Fleet sailors who have the getting of coal and bread at heart, a supply detachment of Moscow or Ivanovo–Voznesensk workers

---

* From Meijer, Vol. 2, p. 278.
† From ibid., Vol. 2, p. 414.
‡ From ibid., Vol. 1, p. 459.

and some thirty senior Party workers, for the purpose of obtaining supplies of bread and coal from the Mariupol area and disciplining Makhno's anarchist bands. Only on this condition will an advance in the Mariupol–Taganrog direction become possible.

Chairman of the Military
Revolutionary Council, Trotsky

(b)*

Kharkov, 17 December 1920

To: The C.C.

The Politburo

The Chairman of the Council of People's Commissars – Comrade Lenin

The Chairman of the Military Revolutionary Council – Trotsky

The results of the hard fighting with Makhno's detachments have been finally established today. On 14 December Makhno broke through the triple ring with which he was invested and moved northwards with up to 7,000 fighting men and eight field guns. In the Fedorovka sector he came up against the troops of the fourth defensive line and, after a violent battle, which began on the evening of 16 December and lasted until late at night on the 18th (sic), was utterly defeated. We captured eight field guns and a lot of equipment, prisoners, and arms of all sorts. All the infantry was for the most part annihilated; part of it was dispersed and is now being rounded up. Makhno himself, with a detachment of 300–400 horsemen, has managed to escape for the time being. Our cavalry is following hard on his track, with orders to pursue him relentlessly in whatever direction he moves, until his detachment is entirely wiped out and he himself is captured. We have despatched a special shock group of political workers, of up to 450 members, under the leadership of Comrade Antonov, the People's Commissar for Internal Affairs of the Ukraine, to the area where Makhno's movement operated, for the final liquidation of banditry and the strengthening of the Soviet apparatus.

* From ibid., Vol. 2, p. 367.

Judging by the mood of extreme fatigue and demoralisation among Makhno's men that we have captured, there is every reason for supposing that a mortal blow has been inflicted on Makhno's movement and all that remains for Comrade Antonov's group to do is to secure the position.

Commander of the Southern Front, Frunze
Member of the Military Revolutionary Council,
S. Gusev

(c) 'THE MAKHNO MOVEMENT'*

There is Soviet Russia, there is Soviet Ukraine. And besides these there exists a little-known state: Gulyai–Pole. The headquarters staff of a certain Makhno rule there. First of all, he had under his command a partisan detachment, then a brigade, then it appears a division, but now all this has all but been redyed into a special insurgent 'army'. But against whom are the Makhno insurgents rebelling? That is the question to which one must give a clear answer, an answer in word and in deed.

Makhno and his supporters regard themselves as anarchists and because of this they 'reject' state power. Does this therefore make them enemies of Soviet power? Apparently, for *Soviet power is the state power of workers and working peasants.*

But the Makhnovites cannot bring themselves to say openly that they are opposed to Soviet power. They are cunning and evasive: *local* Soviet power they say they accept but they reject *central* power. But all the local Ukrainian soviets recognise the central power which they themselves have elected. Therefore the Makhnovites in fact reject not only the central Ukrainian power but also the power of all the local Ukrainian soviets. What then do they recognise? They recognise the power of the Gulyai–Pole Makhnovite soviets, i.e. the authority of a circle of anarchists in a place, where it has succeeded in temporarily establishing itself. That is actually the entire explanation of the political wisdom of the Makhnovite movement.

However the Makhnovite 'army' needs cartridges, rifles, machine guns, artillery, wagons, railway engines and . . . money. All these things are concentrated in the hands of Soviet power

* From Trotsky, *Kak Vooruzhalas Revolyutsiya*, Vol. 2 (Part 1), pp. 189–91.

which produces them and distributes them under its own direction. Therefore the Makhnovites have to turn to that very power which they reject and request money and cartridges.

But since the Makhnovites quite justifiably fear that Soviet power might deprive them of everything they need to live, they have decided to secure their independence, by seizing the great riches of the country, subsequently to enter into a relationship with the rest of the Ukraine as though on the basis of a pact.

Mariupol county is rich in coal and grain. But since the Makhnovites control the Mariupol railway network, they are refusing to allow coal and grain to leave except in exchange for other supplies. It has come about that while rejecting 'state power', created by the workers and peasants of the whole country, the Makhnovite leadership has organised its own little semi-piratical power, which dares to bar the way of Soviet power in the Ukraine and in the whole of Russia. Instead of the economy of the country being expediently organised according to a general plan and intention and instead of a co-operative, socialist and equal distribution of all necessary products, the Makhnovites are attempting to establish the rule of gangs and bands. According to them a man can keep what he has seized. But then subsequently he can exchange it for something he hasn't got. This is not product exchange, it is commercial robbery.

The Makhnovites shout: 'Down with party-mindedness, down with the communists, long live non-party soviets!' But this you know is a miserable lie. Makhno and his companions-in-arms are not non-party people at all. They are of an anarchical persuasion and dispatch circulars and letters herding all anarchists into Gulyai–Pole so as to organise their own anarchic power there. If they hoist the non-party flag it is only in order to pull the wool over the eyes of the most benighted and backward peasants who understand nothing about parties. But in fact the non-party banner serves as the best possible cover for *kulak* elements. The *kulaks* do not dare to admit openly that they belong to the party of the Black Hundreds because they fear they will be violently dealt with. Therefore, they flaunt more readily the fact that they do not belong to a party. But now the SRs, the worst elements of the Mensheviks, Kadets and all counter-revolutionaries in general, who find it too dangerous to appear in the street in their natural guise take cover behind their refusal to join a party.

Communists do not hide their faces or furl their banners. Openly they present themselves as a party to working people. Workers and peasants have come to recognise the communists in action, by experience and in grievous struggle. It is precisely for this reason the party of Bolshevik communists has acquired a decisive influence among the working masses and thereby also in the soviets.

Counter-revolutionaries of all hues hate the communist party. Makhnovites also share precisely the same feeling towards communists. Hence the tremendous support which all thugs and Black Hundred rascals feel for the 'non-party' banner of the Makhnovites. The Gulyai–Pole *kulaks* and the Mariupol speculators echo with enthusiasm the words of the Makhnovites: 'We do not recognise the state power which demands our coal and grain. Whatever we have seized we keep . . .' In this respect, as in all others, the Makhnovites are no different from the Grigorevites. Grigorev also rebelled against central power in the name of local non-party soviets, i.e. against the organised will of the whole working class, in the name of individual *kulak* groups and bands. But it was not for nothing that Grigorev, when he raised the banner of a savage pogrom-like rebellion and setting out to exterminate communists, called upon 'daddy' Makhno to conclude with him a pogrom alliance. It is true that Makhno declined. But not at all for reasons of principle. Makhno openly called for an uprising against Soviet power at the Gulyai–Pole congress of anarchists. If he did not rebel with Grigorev it was only because he was afraid, realising evidently, the complete hopelessness of an open revolt.

Makhno's 'army' is the worst form of partisan activity, although there are within its ranks quite a few good ordinary soldiers. One cannot find a hint of order or discipline in this 'army'. There is no organisation for supplying the 'army'. Provisions, uniforms and ammunition are seized wherever they are to be found and are expended anyhow. This 'army' also fights according to inspiration. It does not carry out any orders. Individual groups advance when they can, i.e. when there is no serious opposition. But at the first firm push from the enemy they run off in all directions, surrendering to an enemy, small in numbers, stations, cities and military equipment. The blame for this falls completely on muddle-headed and dissolute anarchical commanders.

Commanders are elected in this 'army'. The Makhnovites shout wheasingly: 'Down with appointed officers!' This only deludes the more benighted elements among their own soldiers. One can only speak of appointed persons in a bourgeois society, when Tsarist officials or bourgeois ministers nominate commanders at their discretion who kept the mass of soldiers subject to the bourgeois classes. There is no other power in Russia apart from the power of those elected by the whole working class and working peasantry. It follows that, commanders, nominated by the central Soviet power, are nominated according to the will of the working millions. But the Makhnovite commanders reflect the interests of a minute anarchical group, which relies on the *kulaks* and obscurantism.

The anti-popular character of the Makhnovite movement is most clearly revealed by the fact that the Gulyai–Pole 'army' is actually called the 'Makhnovite army'. *There armed men gather not around a programme nor under an ideological banner but around a man.*

Exactly the same thing happened also with Grigorev. In the Soviet Ukraine and in Soviet Russia regiments and divisions are a weapon in the hands of the whole working class. In the Gulyai–Pole state the armed detachments are a weapon in the hands of citizen Makhno. We have seen what this leads to. The personal 'army' of ataman Grigorev, first of all marched with Petlyura's 'army', then came over to the Soviet side, and then led by Grigorev it rebelled in the name of Grigorev himself. Armed masses, uncomprehending and deceived by the absence of a party are becoming a blind tool in the hands of adventurers.

Such is the Gulyai–Pole state and the Gulyai–Pole 'army'. Scratch a Makhnovite and one will discover a Grigorevite. But most often of all even to scratch him is not necessary: a shameless *kulak* who barks at communists or a petty speculator plainly and simply gives himself away.

Soviet power is the dictatorship of the proletariat which has transformed state power into a weapon of socialist reconstruction. At the same time Soviet power has to protect our socialist country from the frenzied onslaughts of the bourgeoisie. Should one think in such a situation, of permitting the existence of armed bands which form themselves around atamans and little fathers on the territory of a Soviet republic, bands which do not recognise the will of the proletariat, which seize what they want and fight with who ever they wish? No, it is time to finish with this anarchical *kulak* profligacy, to act resolutely, once and for all, so that nobody should want to have anything more to do with it.

2 June 1919   Kupyansk–Kharkov

(d)*

To: Voroshilov, HQ of 14th army

To: Trotsky, Chairman of the Revolutionary Military Council, Kharkov

To : Lenin and Kamenev, Moscow

In connection with order No. 1824 of the Military Revolutionary Council of the Republic, I sent a telegram to the HQ of the 2nd army and to Trotsky in which I asked to be released from the post which I fill. In now reiterating this request I consider myself obliged to give the following explanation for it. Regardless of the fact that I and the insurgents fought exclusively against the White Guard gangs of Denikin, preaching to the people only love for freedom and independent help, the whole official Soviet press and also the party press of the Bolshevik communists as well, have been spreading false information about me, information not worthy of a revolutionary. I have been portrayed both as a bandit and as a collaborator with Grigorev and as a conspirator against the soviet republic in the sense of seeking to re-establish the capitalist order. Thus in number 51 of the newspaper *V Puti* Trotsky, in an article entitled 'The Makhno movement', poses the question: 'Whom are the Makhnovite insurgents rebelling against?' and throughout the whole article tries to prove that the Makhnovite movement is, in essence, a front against soviet power and does not say a single word about the real White Guard front which reached a length of more than 100 versts and on which, in the course of over six months, the insurgents sustained and still sustain innumerable sacrifices. In the aforementioned order No. 1824 I am proclaimed a conspirator against the soviet republic and an organiser of revolt *à la* Grigorev.

* From P. Arshinov, *Istoriya Makhnovskogo Dvizheniya (1918–1921gg.)* (Berlin 1923), pp. 126–7.

I consider it an inalienable right of the workers and peasants, won by the revolution for themselves, to convene congresses to discuss and decide private as well as public affairs. Therefore the banning of such congresses by the central power, to proclaim them to be illegal (Order No. 1824) is a direct and barefaced violation of the rights of the workers.

I fully appreciate the attitude of the central state authority towards me. I am absolutely convinced that this authority considers all insurgent activity incompatible with its state activity. At the same time the central authority regards insurgent activity as being connected with me and transfers to me all enmity which is felt towards insurgency. As an example of this one may cite the aforementioned article by Trotsky in which he, besides a deliberate lie, expresses too much that is personal and hostile towards me.

The hostile and recently the aggressive conduct of the central authority towards insurgency, which I have noted, is leading, with fatal inevitability, to the creation of a special internal front, on both sides of which will be the toiling masses, which believe in the revolution. I consider this the greatest, eternally inexcusable crime against working people and I consider it my duty to do all that is possible to avert this crime. The most reliable way to avert the crime which is about to be perpetrated by the central power, in my opinion, is for me to leave my post. I think that when I have done this the central power will cease suspecting me, and all revolutionary insurgents as well, of an anti-soviet conspiracy and will treat seriously and in a revolutionary manner insurgents in the Ukraine as a living, active offspring of a mass, social revolution and not as a hostile camp with which, hitherto, they have had ambiguous, mistrustful relations, bargaining over every cartridge, or otherwise simply sabotaging it by withholding indispensable equipment and ammunition, thanks to which the insurgents often suffered incredible losses in men and in revolutionary territory, which, however, would have been readily avoidable if the central power's relationship with it had been different. I propose that you take from me my account books and relieve me of my duties.

village Gyaichur

9 June 1919
Makhno

5/26   DENIKIN'S PROCLAMATION*

In connection with my order No. 175 of this year, I order the Special Conference to adopt as the basis of its activity the following positions:

1. United, Great, Indivisible Russia. Defence of the faith. Establishment of order. Reconstruction of the productive forces of the country and the national economy. Raising labour productivity.

2. Struggle with bolshevism to the end.

3. Military dictatorship. Reject all pressure from political parties. Punish all opposition to authority, both from the right and from the left. The question of the form of rule is a matter for the future. The Russian people will establish supreme authority without pressure and without it being imposed. Unity with the people.

Immediate union with the Cossacks by establishing a South Russian authority. In so doing by no means dissipate the rights of an All-State authority. Draw Transcaucasia into a Russian state.

4. Foreign policy: only a national Russian policy. Without paying attention to the vacillations which sometimes arise on the Russian question among our Allies, side with them. Because another combination is morally inadmissable and unrealisable in practice.

Slavonic unity.

In return for aid, not a single inch of Russian land.

5. All forces and all resources for the army, for the struggle and for victory.

Every kind of support for the families of soldiers.

Organs of supply are to pass over finally to independent activity, ultilising all the resources of the country which are still rich and not counting exclusively on help from outside.

Increase our own production.

Procure uniforms and supplies from the well-to-do.

Provide the army with an adequate quantity of money, preferably in the presence of everyone. Simultaneously punish mercilessly

* From A. I. Denikin, *Ocherki Russkoi Smuty* (Berlin 1926) Vol. 5, pp. 280–1.

'requisition without payment' and the misappropriation of 'military booty'.

6. Internal policy:

Manifestation of solicitude for the population without distinction. Continue work on the agrarian and labour law in the spirit of my declaration; also the law of the zemstvo. Assist social organisations whose purpose is the development of the national economy and the amelioration of economic conditions (co-operatives, trade unions, etc.).

Suppress the anti-state activity of certain of these, not hesitating to adopt extreme measures.

Aid the press which is with us, tolerate the dissenting press, annihilate the destructive press.

No class privileges, no preferential support, administrative, financial or moral.

Do not only frighten people with threats of severe measures for mutiny, the leadership of anarchical movements, speculation, robbery, bribe-taking, desertion, and other mortal sins, but carry out these measures with the active involvement of the Department of Justice, the Chief Military Procurator, the Department of Internal Affairs and Control. The death penalty is the most fitting punishment.

Accelerate and simplify the process of rehabilitation of those who are not completely at ease with bolshevism, the Petlyurist movement, etc. If it has just been a mistake and they are suitable for the cause, then they should be pardoned.

Appointment to service is exclusively to be based on the man's suitability for the job, rejecting wild fanatics both on the right and on the left. Local bureaucracy; for deviation from the policy of the central power, for acts of violence, for abitrariness, for settling scores with the population, and equally for inactivity; do not merely suspend but punish. Enlist the local population for self-defence.

7. Restore the morale of the front and the military rear by the work of specially appointed generals with wide powers, by field courts martial and by the use of extreme repressive measures. Violently purge counter-intelligence and the criminal investigation department, put into them legally trained (refugee) personnel.

8. Strengthen the ruble, improve transport and production chiefly for state defence.

The burden of taxation should fall mainly on the well-to-do and also on those not liable for military service. Barter is to be employed solely to obtain military equipment and for goods which are necessary for the country.

9. The temporary militarisation of water transport to use it fully for the war; not destroying, however, the commercial industrial machine.

10. Alleviate the position of the bureaucracy and the families of officials at the front by partial transfer to allowances in kind (through the efforts of the Board of Provisions and the Department of Military Supplies). Maintenance is not to be less than the subsistence minimum.

11. Propaganda is to serve exclusively the direct purpose of popularising the ideas being advanced by authority, the unmasking of the essence of bolshevism, the raising of popular self-consciousness and will for the struggle with anarchy.

Taganrog   14 December 1919

6 Politics in a Socialist State

When the Bolsheviks attained power in October 1917, Russia was at war. After managing to conclude a disadvantageous peace, she was forced into a civil war in the spring of 1918 and by the end of 1918 had to contend with intervention from the Allied powers. The Ukraine was a German sphere of influence until November 1918, then Greens, Reds and Whites fought over its fate. The Ukraine was vital from the point of view of industry and food production. So was the Volga region and the North Caucasus. The Bolsheviks found themselves pinned into an area the centre of which was Moscow. Northern Russia, including Moscow, is normally a food deficit zone.

Given these conditions it is hardly likely that conditions were conducive to the creation of a new style democracy. The Bolsheviks based their support on the industrial proletariat and the poor peasants. Since there was little food in the cities many of the workers went back to their villages to stay alive. Peasants were unwilling to sell their surplus stocks for rapidly devaluing paper money. If these factors did not make the situation difficult enough the Reds found themselves in the midst of a savage civil war. They were fighting for their very existence. Defeat of the Soviet government could spell death for them.

Lenin's blueprint for a socialist administration which he had drawn in State and Revolution, *written in August 1917, was hardly applicable to the Russia of 1917. The left-wing Bolsheviks expected a socialist state straight away. Lenin looked forward to state capitalism until the economy had been developed sufficiently to introduce socialism.*

Terror breeds terror. The Left Socialist Revolutionaries were violently opposed to the peace with imperial Germany. They assassinated the German ambassador and many Bolsheviks. The attempt on Lenin's life was bound to have violent repercussions. The advent of the Red Terror, Bolshevik counter-terror, actually predates the attempt on Lenin's life. However, it is synonymous with the Cheka, the Extraordinary Commission, originally set up in December 1917 (6/3) and led by Dzerzhinsky. It became one of the most feared organisations in Soviet Russia and was the strong arm of the communist party. Eventually it was to be used against the party itself.

The October revolution placed power in the hands of the soviets. However, the first Soviet government only contained members of the Bolshevik faction of the Russian Social Democratic Labour Party. Left Socialist Revolutionaries did join the government shortly afterwards but left after the signing of the Brest–Litovsk peace. This almost complete monopoly of the government was not to the liking of other socialists. Trade unions such as the railwaymen's union actively opposed the Bolsheviks. Factory committees were often deaf to Bolshevik pleas.

Soviets were expected to play a key role in the new society (6/5). Tension between the communist party and the soviets grew as the economic and military situation worsened. The Bolsheviks had to forge another instrument to guide the country, the party committee. The Red Army and the party saved Soviet Russia from complete destruction. The tense situation made party discipline of primary importance. Firm, resolute leadership at the centre, and this was usually evident, had to be mirrored at the local level. The exigencies of war led to a great centralisation of power. The centre was fearful that its decisions were not being carried out correctly. The local official was impatient to be rid of the tight supervision which surrounded him. Everyone had embarked on a task which was new to him. The rules of the game had to be developed by experiment. A certain amount of opposition was tolerable during the critical civil war days but when the war was over, Lenin and the Central Committee moved quickly to stifle it. Much of the strife was over the role of the trade unions in a Soviet society. Lenin put 'the lid' on opposition at the tenth party congress in March 1921 (6/14c and d). After the Kronstadt uprising he was in a ruthless mood.

The Bolsheviks hoped that the socialist revolution would be victorious in Europe during the desperate years after the October revolution. They had expected the Germans and others to come to their aid in constructing a socialist society. The Bolsheviks

*established the Communist International and attempted to create
parties elsewhere in their own image. (6/15a)*

6/1 A PEOPLE'S COURT*

The revolutionary court of the Viborg district was sitting for the
first time. The courtroom was full to overflowing. Questions such
as: 'What kind of a court is it going to be?' could be heard. 'It will
be alright, better than before. Wait, brothers, have patience.' It
was clear to everyone that the genuinely guilty would be punished
... because everyone was equal before the law.

The judges, who were workers and soldiers, took their places.
One could see that they were excited since they appreciated their
responsibilities.

The defendants were brought in. A member of the Red Guard
showed them politely to their seats and offered them cigarettes.
They smoked and chatted. How different from the old court!

One of the judges addressed the assembly in a friendly manner
and explained the basic concepts of the court and invited the
audience to aid the judges in their deliberations. The chairman
of the court Chakin stated that the procedure would be as
follows: Both sides would put their case, then the audience would
be permitted to contribute, two for and two against conviction.
The court accepted the procedure straight away.

The first defendant was Belyaev, a soldier-militiaman, accused
of firing his rifle while drunk. When asked for an explanation, he
replied: 'Comrades, I was very drunk and I may have fired the
rifle, but I don't know. I give my word that it won't happen
again.'

The chairman of the court invited a member of the audience to
speak for the prosecution. After a moment two men came forward
and spoke about the damage a man could do with a rifle in these
exciting days and recommended that the accused be punished.

When the judge asked for someone to speak for the defence, no
one volunteered for a long time. Eventually a worker requested
permission to speak. He argued that the 'ill luck of the poor
soldier could have befallen anyone' and proposed that he be
found not guilty but be dismissed from the militia. The audience

* From *Izvestiya*, 21 November 1917.

concurred amid shouts of 'That's right, that's fair!'. After a short
period of consultation the chairman of the court acquitted
Belyaev but dismissed him from the militia. But he warned him
that if he committed the same offence again he would be severely
punished. After hearing the decision of the court, Belyaev turned
to the audience and said: 'Thank you kindly, comrades,' and
solemnly left the court.

6/2   DECREE ON THE JUDICATURE*

5 December 1917

The Council of People's Commissars resolves:

(1) To abolish the existing general judicial institutions, such
as district courts, court chambers and the Senate Directing with
all its departments, the military and naval courts of all designa-
tions, and commercial courts, replacing these by courts established
through democratic elections.

A special decree will be issued on the order of continuation of
pending cases.

All terms shall be suspended from October 25 of this year,
until the issue of a special decree.

(2) To suspend the operation of the existing institution of
justices of the peace, replacing justices of the peace, hitherto
elected indirectly, by local courts as represented by a permanent
local judge and two alternate assessors invited to every session in
accordance with special lists. Local judges shall henceforth be
elected on the basis of direct democratic suffrage; pending such
elections they shall be elected by district and *volost* Soviets of
Workers', Soldiers' and Peasants' Deputies or, in the absence of
such, by *uezd*, city and *guberniya* Soviets.

The same Soviets draw up lists of alternate assessors and
determine the order of their attendance at sessions.

The former justices of the peace are not deprived of the right
to be elected—should they so desire—local judges, both provision-
ally by the Soviets and definitively in democratic elections.

The local courts try all civil cases involving sums of not more
than 3,000 rubles, and criminal cases punishable with not more

* From Akhapkin pp. 44–6.

than two years of prison and involving a civil suit not exceeding 3,000 rubles. Judgements passed by the local courts are final and without appeal. In cases where a recovery of more than 100 rubles or a prison term of more than seven days has been adjudged, a cassation request is allowed, with the *uezd* court or, in the capitals, the metropolitan congress of local judges, serving as the cassation instance.

In the army in the field criminal cases are tried by local courts elected in the same manner by regimental councils or, in the absence of such, by regimental committees.

A special decree will be found on court procedure to be followed in other cases.

(3) To abolish the existing institutions of court investigators, the procurator's surveillance, and official and private counsellors at law.

Pending the reorganization of the entire court procedure, preliminary criminal investigation shall be conducted personally by local judges, whose warrants for apprehension and bringing to trial shall be subject to approval by a full local court.

The functions of prosecution and defence, also in the preliminary investigation stage, and those of attorneys in civil cases, can be performed by all citizens, without distinction of sex, who are of good character and enjoy civil rights.

(4) Current cases and proceedings of judicial institutions, and those before officers of preliminary investigation, the procurator's surveillance and councils of the bar, as well as the archives and property of these institutions, are taken over by special commissars elected by the local Soviets of Workers', Soldiers' and Peasants' Deputies.

The junior and clerical personnel of the abolished institutions shall be obliged to continue in office, performing under the general direction of the commissars, all the necessary work on the referral of pendent cases and informing on fixed days, persons concerned about the progress of their cases.

(5) The local courts adjudicate in the name of the Russian Republic and abide by the laws of the overthrown governments in so far as such laws have not been abrogated by the revolution and do not contradict revolutionary conscience and revolutionary legal awareness.

NOTE. All laws contravening the decrees of the Central Executive Committee of the Soviets' of Workers, Soldiers' and Peasants' Deputies and also the minimum programmes of the Russian Social-Democratic Labour Party and the Socialist-Revolutionary Party shall be considered invalid.

(6) The sides involved in disputes over civil and private criminal matters may apply to the arbitration court. The order of arbitration will be determined by a special decree.

(7) The right of pardon and reinstatement in rights of convicted criminal offenders will rest henceforth with the judicial authority.

(8) In order to fight the country-revolutionary forces and to protect the revolution and its gains against them, and also for the purpose of trying cases of marauding and pillage and the sabotage and other misdeeds of merchants, industrialists, officials and other persons, worker-and-peasant revolutionary tribunals shall be instituted consisting of a chairman and six alternate assessors elected by the *guberniya* or city Soviets of Workers', Soldiers' and Peasants' Deputies.

Special investigation commissions shall be instituted by the same Soviets to conduct preliminary inquiry into such cases.

All the hitherto existing investigation commissions are abolished and their cases and proceedings are turned over to the new investigation commissions to be set up by the Soviets.

Chairman of the Council of Peoples
Commissars, V. Ulyanov (Lenin)

6/3   ESTABLISHMENT OF THE CHEKA*

20 December 1917

The Commission is to be called the All-Russian Extraordinary Commission for the Struggle with Counter-Revolution and Sabotage and is to be attached to the Council of People's Commissars.

The duties of the Commission are to be as follows:

1. To investigate and nullify all acts of counter-revolution and sabotage throughout Russia, irrespective of origin.

* From *Pravda*, 18 December 1927.

2. To bring before the Revolutionary Tribunal all counter-revolutionaries and saboteurs and to work out measures to combat them.

3. The Commission is to conduct the preliminary investigation only, sufficient to suppress (the counter-revolutionary act). The Commission is to be divided into sections: (1) the information (section) (2) The organisation section (in charge of organising the struggle with counter-revolution throughout Russia) with branches, and (3) the fighting section.

The Commission shall be set up finally tomorrow. Then the fighting section of the All-Russian Commission shall start its activities. The Commission shall keep an eye on the press, saboteurs, right Socialist Revolutionaries and strikers. Measures to be taken are confiscation, imprisonment, confiscation of cards, publication of the names of the enemies of the people, etc.

> Chairman of the Council of People's Commissars,
> V. Ulyanov (Lenin)

6/4   REVOLUTIONARY TRIBUNALS*

1 January 1918

1. The Revolutionary Tribunal shall have jurisdiction over persons (a) who foment uprisings against Workers' and Peasants' power, who actively oppose it or who incite others to oppose or disobey it; (b) who use their position as government or public servants to hinder or disorganise the regular flow of work in their institutions or enterprises in which they are employed or were employed (sabotage, concealment of documents or property, etc); (c) who halt or restrict the production of goods without the requisite authority . . . (e) who do not carry out the decrees, decisions, instructions and other published orders of the organs of Workers' and Peasants' power, if such an act merits a trial before the Revolutionary Tribunal.

2. The Revolutionary Tribunal shall take into consideration the circumstances of the case and the dictates of revolutionary conscience when deciding punishment.

* From *Sobranie Uzakonenii i Rasporyazhenii Rabochego i Krestyanskogo Pravitelstva 1917* (Petrograd 1918), pp. 179–81.

3. (a) The Revolutionary Tribunal is to be elected by the Soviets of Workers', Soldiers' and Peasants' Deputies and is to consist of one permanent chairman, two permanent substitutes, one permanent secretary and two permanent substitutes and forty jurymen. All persons, except the jurymen, shall be elected for three months and may be recalled by the Soviets before they have completed their term. (b) Jurymen shall be elected for one month . . .

4. Sessions of the Revolutionary Tribunal are to be held in public.

5. Verdicts shall be according to the majority vote of the members of the Revolutionary Tribunal . . .

11. Verdicts of the Revolutionary Tribunal are final. If the procedure laid down in these instructions is not followed or evidence of overt injustice in the verdict is discovered, the People's Commissar of Justice shall have the right to request the Central Executive Committee of the Soviet of Workers', Soldiers' and Peasants' Deputies to order a second and final trial.

People's Commissar of Justice
I. Z. Steinberg

6/5   ON THE RIGHTS AND DUTIES OF SOVIETS*

6 January 1918

1. The Soviets of Workers', Soldiers', Peasants' and Farm Labourers' Deputies are the local organs (of power) and are completely independent in local matters but always act in accordance with the decrees and decisions of the central soviet power and of the larger bodies (*uezd, guberniya* and *oblast* soviets) of which they form a part.

2. To soviets as well as to organs of power there fall the tasks of administration and service in every sphere of local life, administrative, economic, financial, cultural and educational.

3. In the field of administration, soviets must carry out all decrees and decisions of the central power, adopt measures to notify the population, to the greatest possible extent, of these

* From *Istoriya Sovetskoi Konstitutsii (v Dokumentakh) 1917–1956* (Moscow 1957), pp. 96 and 97.

decisions, issue obligatory decrees, carry out requisitions and con-
fiscations, impose fines, suppress counter-revolutionary organs of
the press, effect arrests and disband social organisations which
propagate active opposition to or the overthrow of soviet power.
Note: Soviets shall prepare a report for the central soviet power
of all the measures taken by them and provide information on the
most important events of local life.

4. Soviets shall elect from among their members an executive
organ (executive committee, presidium) which shall be charged
with putting into effect all its decisions and all its current administrative work.

Note:

(a) Military Revolutionary Committees as fighting organs,
which came into being during the revolution, are disbanded.

(b) As a temporary measure, the appointment of commissars
is permitted in those *guberniyas* and *uezds* where the power of
the soviet has not been sufficiently established or where soviet
power is not fully recognised.

5. Soviets as organs of administration may grant credit from
state resources for three months, on the presentation of detailed
estimates.

The People's Commissariat of Internal Affairs

6/6   THE DISSOLUTION OF THE CONSTITUENT ASSEMBLY*

19 January 1918

At its very inception, the Russian revolution produced the Soviets
of Workers', Soldiers' and Peasants' Deputies as the only mass
organization of all the working and exploited classes capable of
giving leadership to the struggle of these classes for their complete
political and economic emancipation.

Throughout the initial period of the Russian revolution the
Soviets grew in number, size and strength, their own experience
disabusing them of the illusions regarding compromise with the
bourgeoisie, opening their eyes to the fraudulence of the forms
of bourgeois-democratic parliamentarism, and leading them to
the conclusion that the emancipation of the oppressed classes was

* From Akhapkin, pp. 74–5.

unthinkable unless they broke with these forms and with every kind of compromise. Such a break came with the October Revolution, with the transfer of power to the Soviets.

The Constituent Assembly, elected on the basis of lists drawn up before the October Revolution, was expressive of the old correlation of political forces, when the conciliators and Constitutional-Democrats were in power.

Voting at that time for candidates of the Socialist-Revolutionary Party, the people were not in a position to choose between the Right-Wing Socialist-Revolutionaries, supporters of the bourgeoisie, and the Left-Wing Socialist-Revolutionaries, supporters of Socialism. Thus the Constituent Assembly, which was to have crowned the bourgeois parliamentary republic, was bound to stand in the way of the October Revolution and Soviet power.

The October Revolution, which gave power to the Soviets and through them to the working and exploited classes, aroused frantic resistance on the part of the exploiters, and in putting down this resistance it fully revealed itself as the beginning of the socialist revolution.

The working classes learned through experience that old bourgeois parliamentarism had outlived its day, that it was utterly incompatible with the tasks of Socialism, and that only class institutions (such as the Soviets) and not national ones were capable of overcoming the resistance of the propertied classes and laying the foundations of socialist society.

Any renunciation of the sovereign power of the Soviets, of the Soviet Republic won by the people, in favour of bourgeois parliamentarism and the Constituent Assembly would now be a step backwards and would cause a collapse of the entire October Workers' and Peasants' Revolution.

By virtue of generally known circumstances the Constituent Assembly, opening on January 18, gave the majority to the Party of Right-Wing Socialist-Revolutionaries, the party of Kerensky, Avksentev and Chernov. Naturally, this party refused to discuss the absolutely precise, clear-cut and unambiguous proposal of the supreme body of Soviet power, the Central Executive Committee of the Soviets, to recognize the programme of Soviet power, to recognize the Declaration of Rights of the Working and Exploited People, to recognize the October Revolution and Soviet power. By doing so the Constituent Assembly severed all ties with the Soviet Republic of Russia. The withdrawal from such a Constituent Assembly of the groups of Bolsheviks and Left-Wing Socialist-Revolutionaries, who now are in an indisputably vast majority in the Soviets and enjoy the confidence of the workers and the majority of the peasants, was inevitable.

Outside the Constituent Assembly, the parties which have the majority there, the Right-Wing Socialist-Revolutionaries and the Mensheviks, are waging an open struggle against Soviet power, calling in their press for its overthrow and thereby objectively supporting the exploiters' resistance to the transition of land and factories into the hands of the working people.

Obviously, under such circumstances the remaining part of the Constituent Assembly can only serve as a cover for the struggle of the bourgeois counter-revolution to overthrow the power of the Soviets.

In view of this, the Central Executive Committee resolves:

The Constituent Assembly is hereby dissolved.

6/7 THE RED TERROR

(a) THE RED TERROR LEGALISED*

5 September 1918

The Soviet of People's Commissars, after having heard the report of the chairman of the Extraordinary Commission to Fight Counter-Revolution concerning the activities of the Commission, finds, that in the present situation, the protection of the rear by terror is an urgent necessity. In order to strengthen the activity of the Extraordinary Commission and to introduce into it more balance, the greatest possible number of responsible party comrades must be drafted in; it is necessary to protect the Soviet Republic from class enemies by isolating them in concentration camps. All those involved in White Guard organisations, plots and revolts are to be shot. The names of all those shot and the reason for their execution should be published.

People's Commissar of Justice
Kursky

* From *Sobranie Uzakonenii i Rasporyazhenii Rabochego i Krestyanskogo Pravitelstva* (Moscow 1918), p. 789.

(b) VICTIMS OF THE RED TERROR*

In 1918, persons arrested on the charges of counter-revolution, crime in office, speculation, use of forged and other people's documents, etc., numbered 47,348.

In 1919, the activities of the Cheka developed, and the number of persons arrested reached 80,662. The greatest number of arrests during that year (14,761) took place in November, and the smallest (4,301) in July.

Out of the total number of persons arrested in 1919, 21,032 were classed as counter-revolutionaries, while 19,673 were arrested for crime of office.

Out of the 128,010 arrested in 1918–19, 54,250, or 42 per cent were freed without any subsequent consequences; 8 per cent of the total number of persons under arrest consisted of hostages. Nearly 11 per cent were sentenced to compulsory labour, 28 per cent retained in prison, and nearly 8 per cent sent into concentration camps.

In 1918, 6,185 persons were executed, and 3,456 in 1919, the total number during the two years being 9,641 persons. The greatest number of persons executed in any month in 1919 was 609 in September, and the smallest 187 in August.

During 1918 and 1919 7,068 persons were shot on the charge of counter-revolution, 632 for crime of office, 217 for speculation, 1,204 for crime.

In 1918 no one was shot for assuming a false name, for crossing the frontier without permit, for using forged documents, etc. while in 1919, 248 persons were shot for these offences.

(c) NERVOUS OFFICIALS*

One rule must be observed by the Extraordinary Commissions: it is necessary that its members should be frequently relieved of their duties, transferred to some other post, to some other profession. The conditions of work have a terrible effect on the nervous system, and paralyse the sensitiveness of the officials. As a

* From *Ezhenedelnik Vserossiskoi Chrezvychainoi Kommissii* (February 1920).
* From *Zhizn*, 4 September 1919.

consequence, even a man with a heart of adamant cannot but be affected by the work. The productivity of the work done by the Extraordinary Commissions depends on the possibility of the workers being able to get relief by working at some other occupation. It is only necessary to keep the machinery going, relieving the members not all at once, but gradually.

(d) LOCKHART AND RED TORTURE*

Tell us why you did not subject this Lockhart to the most refined tortures, in order to get the information and addresses which this 'goose' must be full of? In that way you could have easily discovered a whole number of counter-revolutionary organisations . . .

Tell us why, instead of subjecting him to such tortures, the mere description of which would have sent a thrill of cold horror through counter-revolutionaries, you allowed him to leave the Extraordinary Commission . . .

(Letter from Nolim Soviet, Vyatka *Guberniya*)

(e) DZERZHINSKY†

Dzerzhinsky was a silent, gloomy man. Tall, spare, with grey shifty eyes. He spoke in monosyllables or very shortly. When Shcheglovitov inquired of him the reason of his trial, he answered, 'Simply because you were one of the Tsar's ministers,' and to the same question of Diestler, a Right Socialist Revolutionary, 'Why, because you are a Socialist Revolutionary'. A few moments later he signed their death warrant. He signed scores of such warrants every day whilst sipping glasses of tea, always with the same gloomy air and casting anguished glances around.

(f) RED TERROR AND THE COSSACKS‡

The Central Committee of the Communist party sent to the Kamensky Executive Committee the following secret circular which we reproduce in full.

* From *Ezhenedelnik*, No. 3 (1919).
† From Russian Press Bureau, Bulletin No. 41, 2 October 1919, Omsk.
‡ From Sir B. Pares, Private Papers.

The latest events on the various fronts of the Cossack districts, advance into the interior of Cossack settlements and the increasing resistance of the Cossack troops, forces us to issue instructions to the workers of the party regarding the nature of their work in restoring and strengthening the Soviet Government in the districts indicated. Taking into consideration the experience of a year of civil war with the Cossacks, we have to face the fact that the only way is a pitiless fight with all the wealthy Cossacks by destroying them one by one. No compromise or half measures are possible and therefore we must:

(1) Institute a wholesale terror against the wealthy Cossacks and peasants, and having destroyed them altogether, carry out a pitiless mass terror against the Cossacks in general who took any direct or indirect part in the fight against the Soviet government.

(2) Confiscate corn and make them bring all their surpluses to prescribed centres. This refers to corn as well as all other rural products.

(3) Take all measures to help newly-arrived poor settlers, organising settlements wherever possible.

(4) Put all newly arrived settlers on an equal footing with the Cossacks in land and other respects.

(5) Carry out complete disarmament, shooting anyone who has any arms after the date of surrender.

(6) Arm only the reliable elements.

(7) Arm detachments to be posted in Cossack villages until complete order is restored.

6/8 MURDER OF THE TSAR*

In view of the fact that Czechoslovak bands are threatening the red capital of the Urals, Ekaterinburg, and bearing in mind that the crowned executioner, if he goes into hiding, may escape the people's court, the executive committee executing the will of the people, had decided: shoot the ex-Tsar, Nikolai Romanov, guilty of innumerable bloody crimes.

* From P. Gilliard, *Tragicheskaya Sudba Russkoi Imperatorskoi Familii* (Tallinn 1921), pp. 20–1.

The decision of the executive committee was carried out during the night of 16/17 July (1918).

The Romanov family has been transferred from Ekaterinburg to another, safer place.

Presidium of the Ural Soviet of Workers',
Peasants' and Red Army Deputies

6/9   DECREE ON THE PRESS*

9 November 1917

In the trying critical period of the revolution and the days that immediately followed it the Provisional Revolutionary Committee was compelled to take a number of measures against the counter-revolutionary press of different shades.

Immediately outcries were heard from all sides that the new, socialist power had violated a fundamental principle of its programme by encroaching upon the freedom of the press.

The Workers' and Peasants' Government calls the attention of the population to the fact that what this liberal façade actually conceals is freedom for the propertied classes, having taken hold of the lion's share of the entire press, to poison, unhindered, the minds and obscure the consciousness of the masses.

Every one knows that the bourgeois press is one of the most powerful weapons of the bourgeoisie. Especially at the crucial moment when the new power, the power of workers and peasants, is only affirming itself, it was impossible to leave this weapon wholly in the hands of the enemy, for in such moments it is no less dangerous than bombs and machine-guns. That is why temporary extraordinary measures were taken to stem the torrent of filth and slander in which the yellow and green press would be only too glad to drown the recent victory of the people.

As soon as the new order becomes consolidated, all administrative pressure on the press will be terminated and it will be granted complete freedom within the bounds of legal responsibility, in keeping with a law that will be broadest and most progressive in this respect.

However, being aware that a restriction of the press, even

* From Akhapkin, pp. 29–30.

at critical moments, is permissible only within the limits of what is absolutely necessary, the Council of People's Commissars resolves:

GENERAL PROVISIONS ON THE PRESS

1. Only those publications can be suppressed which (1) call for open resistance or insubordination to the Workers' and Peasants' Government; (2) sow sedition through demonstrably slanderous distortion of facts; (3) instigate actions of an obviously criminal, i.e. criminally punishable, nature.

2. Publications can be proscribed, temporarily or permanently, only by decision of the Council of People's Commissars.

3. The present ordinance is of a temporary nature and will be repealed by a special decree as soon as normal conditions of social life set in.

> Chairman of the Council of People's Commissars,
> VLADIMIR ULYANOV (LENIN).

6/10   DECLARATION OF THE RIGHTS OF THE PEOPLES OF RUSSIA*

15 November 1917

The October Revolution of workers and peasants began under the common banner of emancipation.

The peasants are emancipated from landowner rule, for there is no landed proprietorship any longer – it has been abolished. The soldiers and sailors are emancipated from the power of autocratic generals, for generals will henceforth be elected and removable. The workers are emancipated from the whims and tyranny of capitalists, for workers' control over factories and mills will henceforth be established. All that is living and viable is emancipated from the hated bondage.

There remain only the peoples of Russia, who have been and are suffering from oppression and arbitrary rule, whose emancipation should be started immediately, and whose liberation should be conducted resolutely and irrevocably.

In the epoch of tsarism the peoples of Russia were systematically

* From ibid., 31–2.

incited against one another. The results of this policy are known: massacres and pogroms, on the one side, and slavery of the peoples, on the other.

There is no return to this infamous policy of incitement. From now on it is to be replaced by a policy of voluntary and sincere alliance of the peoples of Russia.

In the period of imperialism, after the February Revolution, which had given power to the Constitutional-Democrat bourgeoisie, the undisguised policy of incitement ceded place to the policy of cowardly distrust towards the peoples of Russia, the policy of petty excuses for persecution and provocation covered up with utterances about 'freedom' and 'equality' of the peoples. The results of this policy are known: increased national enmity, undermined mutual confidence.

This reprehensible policy of lie and distrust, petty persecution and provocation must be done away with. From now on it shall be replaced by an open and honest policy leading to the complete mutual confidence of the peoples of Russia.

Only this confidence can lead to a sincere and firm alliance of the peoples of Russia.

Only thanks to this alliance can the workers and peasants of the peoples of Russia be welded into a single revolutionary force capable of holding out against any encroachments on the part of the imperialist-annexationist bourgeoisie.

Proceeding from these premises, the First Congress of Soviets in June of this year proclaimed the right of the peoples of Russia to free self-determination.

In October of this year the Second Congress of Soviets re-affirmed this inalienable right of the peoples of Russia more resolutely and definitely.

Carrying out the will of these Congresses, the Council of People's Commissars has resolved to base its activity in the matter of the nationalities of Russia on the following principles:

1. EQUALITY AND SOVEREIGNTY OF THE PEOPLES OF RUSSIA.

2. THE RIGHT OF THE PEOPLES OF RUSSIA TO FREE SELF-DETERMINATION, UP TO SECESSION AND FORMATION OF AN INDEPENDENT STATE.

3. ABOLITION OF ALL AND ANY NATIONAL AND NATIONAL-RELIGIOUS PRIVILEGES AND RESTRICTIONS.

4. FREE DEVELOPMENT OF NATIONAL MINORITIES AND ETHNIC
GROUPS INHABITING RUSSIA.

Concrete decrees stemming herefrom will be worked out immediately after the establishment of the Commission for the Affairs
of Nationalities.

In the name of the Russian Republic,
> People's Commissar for Nationalities Affairs,
> JOSEPH DZHUGASHVILI-STALIN.
> Chairman of the Council of People's
> Commissars, V. ULYANOV (LENIN).

6/11 PATRIARCH TIKHON ANATHEMATISES THE BOLSHEVIKS*

Tikhon,

By the grace of God Patriarch of Moscow and All Russia, to the
beloved in the Lord, archpriests, priests and all faithful children of
the Russian Orthodox Church

> 'May the Lord deliver us from this evil' Galatians 1.4

The Holy Orthodox Church of Christ in Russia is passing through
grievous times: a persecution of Christian truth has been undertaken by the open and secret enemies of that truth who strive to
destroy Christianity and instead of Christian love everywhere sow
the seeds of hatred, enmity and fratricidal strife.

The precepts of Christ of love for one's neighbour are forgotten
and flouted; daily we receive reports of the terrible and savage
murders of quite innocent people, even people on their sick beds,
guilty only of doing their duty to their country and devoting all
their energy to the good of the people. All this is done not only
under the cover of night but even openly in broad daylight with a
hitherto unheard of insolence and merciless cruelty, without any
trial and flouting every right and legality; it is done in our time
in almost every town and village of our country, in the capitals
and distant provinces (in Petrograd, Moscow, Irkutsk, Sevastopol,
etc.).

All this fills our heart with the deep and painful grief and obliges

* From A. I. Vvedensky, *Tserkov i gosudarstvo* (Moscow 1923), pp.114–16.

us to address ourself to these dregs of humanity with a stern denunciation and warning according to the instruction of the apostle 'rebuke them that sin before all that others also may fear' (1 Timothy 5.20).

Come to your senses, you madmen, cease your bloody massacres. What you are doing is not only cruel, it is truly the doing of Satan for which Hell's fire awaits you in the next life beyond the grave and the awful curse of posterity in this life on earth.

By the authority vested in us by God we forbid you the sacraments, anathematise you if you bear Christian names and are orthodox by birth.

We adjure all true children of the Orthodox Church to have no dealings with these dregs of humanity: 'Therefore put away from among yourselves that wicked person' (1 Cor. 5.13).

A most cruel persecution has also been launched against the Holy Church: the sacraments consecrating the birth of man or blessing christian marriage are openly declared unnecessary and superfluous, holy churches are subjected to destruction by guns (the holy cathedrals of the Moscow Kremlin) or pillaging and desecration (the chapel of the Saviour of Petrograd); monasteries deemed holy by a christian people (like the Alexander-Nevsky and Pochaevsky monasteries) are seized by the godless rulers of darkness of this age and declared public property; schools maintained by the Church for training priests and religious instructors are declared superfluous and are turned into schools of atheism or even hotbeds of immorality.

The property of monasteries and churches has been seized on the pretext that they are the property of the people, but without any right or even the desire to consult the legal will of the people themselves. And finally, the power that promised to bring justice and truth to Russia, to guarantee freedom and good order, everywhere demonstrates nothing but the most unbridled licence and ceaseless violence to all and in particular the Orthodox Church.

What limits are there to this mockery of the Church of Christ? How and by what means can this attack by her bitter foes be halted?

We call upon you all, believers and true children of the Church: rise up in defence of our insulted and oppressed Holy Mother.

The enemies of the church seize power over it and its property by force of arms – oppose them with the force of your faith, a

mighty cry of the whole people which will halt the madmen and
show them that they have no right to call themselves the cham-
pions of the people's good, the builders of a new life at the behest
of the people's reason, for they are working directly against the
conscience of the people.

And if it is necessary to suffer in the cause of Christ, we call
upon you, beloved children of the Church, to accept these suffer-
ings with the words of the Apostle 'Who shall separate us from the
love of Christ? Shall tribulation, or distress, or persecution, or
famine, or nakedness, or peril, or sword?' (Romans 8.35.)

And you brother archpriests and priests, do not delay your
spiritual action for even an hour, with burning faith call upon
your children to defend the trampled rights of the Orthodox
Church, set up without delay spiritual unions, call them to join
voluntarily the ranks of the spiritual warriors who will oppose the
external force with the force of their holy inspiration, and we
firmly trust that the enemies of the Church of Christ will be
shamed and dispersed by the strength of Christ's cross, for the im-
mutable promise of the divine bearer of the cross himself was 'I
shall build my church, and the gates of hell shall not prevail against
it' (Matthew 16.18).

Tikhon Patriarch of Moscow and All Russia, 1 February, 1918.

6/12   NEGOTIATIONS WITH THE GERMANS*

Moscow, 7 April 1921

To: The Chairman of the Military Revolutionary Council of the
Republic – Comrade L. D. Trotsky

Dear Comrade,

The negotiations with the German group of which you know,
on the basis about which we spoke in Moscow, have led so far to
the following results. This group considers it first of all essential
to co-operate with us in restoring our war industry, in the following three particular fields: building an air force, building a sub-
marine fleet, and arms production. The group has approached,
in the strictest secrecy, the firms of 'Blohm und Voss' (submarines),

* From Meijer, Vol. 2, pp. 441, 443.

'Albatroswerke' (air force) and 'Krupp' (arms), who are prepared to provide both their technical resources and the necessary equipment. Immediate plans are being worked out, and it is proposed that, on the 20th Neumann, who is known to you, should leave for Moscow in order to agree on conditions for bringing in some technicians (five or six people) from here for further examination of the matter on the spot. Please let me know by radio in Comrade Chicherin's secret cypher immediately upon receipt of this, whether you consider it desirable that Neumann should come now, and in general whether you think it is in our interests to carry out these plans.

                    With Communist greetings (V. Kopp)

To: Comrade Skylansky

I agree to let them in, only please inform me in good time (of the names), so that the necessary orders may be given, and please keep me *au fait* so that we may be safeguarded against surprises.

                              V. Menzhinsky

Comrade Sklyansky

Let me have a note, whether you have answered yes, as I think we should. *Return this.*

                              Lenin

6/13   LENIN: MISCELLANEOUS

(a) KRUPSKAYA'S NEPHEW*

                              16 February 1920

From: Chairman of the Council of People's Commissars of the R.S.F.S.R.

To: Comrade Sklyansky

My wife's nephew requests to be accepted for the naval commanders' courses. Be good enough to make arrangements and give orders that the answer should come to me. If there are any obstacles what are they?

                              Greetings, Lenin

* From ibid., Vol. 2, p. 44.

Soviet Naval Courses for Commander Personnel of the Navy at Petrograd (formerly Midshipmen's Classes).

Mikhail Aleksandrovich Krupsky

Gatchina: Clothing Store of the 6th Rifle Division, 6 Egerskaya Sloboda, House No. 21.

Report to Petrograd, Line 11, Vasilevsky Ostrov, House No. 8 – Naval Academy, and ask for Ignatev, or Commissar Ilinsky.

Saturday, 21 January.

(b) FLAT FOR MARKOV*

Moscow, 29 March 1920

From: The Chairman of the Council of People's Commissars of the R.S.F.S.R.

To: Comrade Trotsky

Could you make arrangements to ensure that the flat now occupied by Comrade Markov, Member of the Collegium of the People's Commissariat of Transport is reserved in his name and also that he retains the right to use a motor-car, particularly in view of the fact that he needs to see his doctor.

Chairman of the Council of People's Commissars,
V. Ulyanov (Lenin)

(c) FAST TRANSPORT FOR MARIA ILINICHNA†

(i)

9 April 1921

To: Comrade Sklyansky

My sister, Maria Ilinichna Ulyanova, has gone to the Crimea with Bukharin, his wife and a few other comrades. They have a special coach. Could you not give orders that if the passengers ask, this coach should be attached to military trains *in order to speed it up*? (There and back.)

Lenin

* From ibid., Vol. 2, p. 138.
† (i) From ibid., Vol. 2, p. 444; (ii) From ibid., Vol. 2, p. 446.

(ii)

9 April 1921

To: Comrade Sklyansky

I have just talked to Kharkov about the coach with Bukharin, my sister etc. in it. It is all arranged.
It is not worth troubling Arzhanov any more. No more orders are needed.
Thank you.

Greetings.

Lenin

(d) COMRADE NEMITS KEPT WAITING*

25 March 1921

From: The Chairman of the Council of People's Commissars of the R.S.F.S.R., Kremlin, Moscow

To: Comrade Sklyansky

It has come to my notice that Comrade Nemits was made to wait 3 and a half hours in the Defence Council, and all to no avail, since his item was not taken. I consider this incorrect, and propose that in future communication should be established by the telephonic and secretarial resources of the War Department and the Defence Council, so that Comrade Nemits should be informed a few minutes in advance and should come (in view of his illness) by car.

　　　　Chairman of the Council for Labour and Defence,
　　　　V. Ulyanov/Lenin

(e) WIRELESS†

Smolensk, 20 June 1920

To: Moscow – Council of Defence

In the latest English newspapers there is an announcement about the invention of a wireless telegraph functioning over 350 English miles. In view of the fact that such an invention is of enormous

* From ibid., Vol. 2, p. 432.
† From ibid., Vol. 2, p. 221.

interest for the work of agents and intelligence, please instruct our representative in London to acquire several sets.

> Member of the Military Revolutionary Council,
> Unshlikht

Deciphered in Secretariat of Deputy Chairman of Revvoensovet of the Republic: 22 June 1920.

In comrade Trotsky's handwriting: *telephone*, I think.

(1) *Berlin* has long been operating one *with Moscow*.
(2) Invented by us; operates over 400 ver(sts), *and a 2000 verst ordered.*

> (In Comrade Lenin's handwriting)

Precisely, I did write *of a telephone*.

(f) ON BUREAUCRACY*

6 February 1921

(i)

From: The Chairman of the Council of People's Commissars of the R.S.F.S.R., Kremlin, Moscow

To: Comrade Sklyansky

Send me the telegram of the Saratov Guberniya Military Commissariat, to which you sent me the C-in-C's 'answer' today.
The answer is stupid and illiterate in places.
It's a bureaucratic acknowledgement instead of *action*: what is needed is to wipe out banditry, not to compose acknowledgements.
Let me have twice a week *brief*, very brief, *progress reports on the struggle* against banditry.
And impress on the Field Staff that they must work, not compose acknowledgements. Who is this 'Staff Military Commissar' Ilyushin, what is his record?

> Lenin

(ii)

12 February 1921

From: The Chairman of the Council of Labour and Defence of R.S.F.S.R., Kremlin, Moscow

* (i) From ibid., Vol. 2, pp. 372, 374; (ii) From ibid., Vol. 2, p. 374.

To: Comrade Sklyansky

Unheard-of and incredible things are happening to our communications. Stalin and I are unable to *communicate with Ordzhonikidze* on *the most important matters*, or Fomin with *Smilga*.

Send an urgent telegram to Rostov-on-Don, referring to me, that they should appoint a *responsible person*, whose duty it will be to maintain communication with both of them and to give their answers (to give them all the time) to me, Stalin and Fomin (from both of them).

If this is not done, I will have those responsible here *put on trial* (or will try to have them dismissed and arrested). It is intolerable.

Lenin

P.S. This is the complete disintegration of the *top* army *command*! There are no *communications*!!! with officials like Smilga and Ordzhonikidze!!

6/14 THE PARTY

(a) VIII CONFERENCE (2–4 DECEMBER 1919): PARTY STATUTES*
The Statutes of the Russian Communist Party (Bolsheviks)

1. A member of the party is anyone who accepts the party programme, works in one of its organisations, subjects himself to the decrees of the party and pays his membership dues.

2. New members are accepted by local party committees from among candidate members and confirmed by the next general assembly of a given organisation.

Note: In exceptional circumstances, on the recommendation of two members of the party, who joined before October 1917, it is permitted to accept new members also who are not candidate members. The same exception is permitted during party week, according to the instructions of the CC.

3. Every member of one organisation when he moves into a region where another organisation works is admitted by the latter organisation with the consent of the former organisation.

* From *Kommunisticheskaya Partiya Sovetskogo Soyuza v Rezolyutsiyakh i Resheniyakh Sezdov, Konferentsii i Plenumov TsK* (Moscow 1954), Part 1, pp. 461–9.

4. The question of expelling someone from the party is decided by the general assembly of the organisation of which the person in question is a member. The decree on expulsion takes effect only when it has been confirmed by the *guberniya* committee, and moreover the person in question is removed from party work from that time till the expulsion is confirmed. The expulsion of party members is made known in the party press together with information on the reasons for expulsion.

5. All persons wishing to become members of the party are to serve a term of probation which is intended to acquaint them thoroughly with the programme and tactics of the party and to check the personal qualities of the candidate.

6. New members are admitted as candidates on the recommendation of two members of the party with six months' party membership after their recommendation has been checked by the local party committee.

7. Workers and peasants must remain candidates for not less than two months, others for not less than six months.

8. Candidate members are admitted to open general assemblies of the party organisation and have a consultative vote.

9. Candidate members pay the usual membership dues to the local party committee.

10. The guiding principle of the organisational structure of the party is democratic centralism.

11. The party is organised, on the principles of democratic centralism, on a territorial basis; an organisation serving some region or other is accounted superior to all organisations serving parts of that region.

12. All party organisations are autonomous in deciding local questions.

13. The supreme guiding organ of each organisation is the general assembly, conference or congress.

14. The general assembly, conference or congress elects the committee which is their executive organ and which guides all the current work of the local organisation...

15. The scheme of organisation of the party is as follows:
   (a) The territory of the RSFSR, the All-Russian congress, the Central Committee;
   (b) *Oblasts* and Soviet republics, within the RSFSR. *Oblast* conferences, *oblast* committees;

    (c) *Guberniyas. Guberniya* conferences, *guberniya* committees;

    (d) *Uezds. Uezd* conferences, *uezd* committees;

    (e) *Volosts. Volost* assemblies, *volost* committees;

    (f) Enterprises, villages, Red army units, institutions. General assembly of the cells, bureaux of the cells . . .

17. Special sections (national, work among women, among youth, etc.) are marked out for special forms of party work. Sections exist alongside committees and are directly subordinate to them. The procedure for organising sections is laid down in special instructions, confirmed by the Central Committee.

18. All lower organisations, right down to the *uezd* organisations, are confirmed by the *uezd* committees with the approval of the *guberniya* committee; *uezd* organisations, by the *guberniya* committee with the approval of the *oblast* committee, and where there is none, by the Central Committee; *guberniya* organisations, by the *oblast* committee with the approval of the Central Committee, and where there is no *oblast* committee, directly by the Central Committee . . .

20. The supreme organ of the party is the congress. Ordinary congresses are called annually. Extraordinary congresses are called by the Central Committee on its own initiative or at the demand of not less than one-third of the party members, present at the previous party congress. The calling of a party congress and the agenda are to be announced not later than one and a half months before the congress. Extraordinary congresses are called at two months' notice. The congress is regarded as valid if there are represented at it not less than half of all members of the party, who were represented at the previous ordinary congress.

The norms of attendance at a party congress are fixed by the CC and by the ordinary pre-congress conferences.

21. In the case of the Central Committee not calling an extraordinary congress in the period set out above, organisations which have demanded it, have the right to form an Organisational Committee, enjoying all the rights of the CC in calling a congress.

22. A congress:

    (a) Hears and confirms the reports of the CC, the revision commission and other central institutions;

    (b) Reviews and amends the party programme;

(c) Determines the tactical line of the party on current questions;

(d) Elects a CC and a revision commission, etc.

23. The Central Committee is made up of 19 members (12 candidates). In the case of absence of CC members, its numbers are made up from among the candidates elected at the congress, in the order, determined by the congress.

24. The Central Committee represents the party in its relations with other parties and institutions, organises the various institutions of the party and guides their activity, nominates the editorial board of central organs, working under its supervision, organises and manages enterprises, which have general party significance, distributes the forces and resources of the party and audits the central accounts.

The Central Committee directs the work of the central soviet and social organisations by means of party factions. The Central Committee meets, in plenary session, not less than twice per month on previously arranged days.

25. The Central Committee sets up for political work, the Political Bureau, for organisational work, the Organisational Bureau, and the Secretariat, headed by a secretary who is a member of the Organisational Bureau of the CC.

26. Once every three months, the Central Committee summons a party conference of representatives of the *guberniya* and metropolitan party committees.

27. Once a month, the Central Committee dispatches to *guberniya* and metropolitan party committees a written account of its activities.

28. The Revision Commission is formed of three persons, it audits the accounts periodically and all enterprises of the CC and presents a report to the next party congress . . .

47. The basic party organisation is the party cell. A cell is confirmed by an *uezd*, city or region committee and is composed of not less than three members . . .

50. The strictest party discipline is the primary duty of all party members and all party organisations. The decrees of party centres must be carried out quickly and precisely. At the same time within the party the discussion of all controversial questions of party life is totally free until a decision has been taken.

(b) IX CONFERENCE: RESOLUTION ON THE REGULAR TASKS
OF PARTY CONSTRUCTION*

IX All-Russian Conference of the RKP(B)
Moscow 22–25 September 1920
Resolution

On the Regular Tasks of Party Construction

The unprecedentedly difficult position of the Soviet Republic during the first years of its existence, the utter destruction and the
extreme military danger have made inevitable the emergence of
'shock' (and therefore in reality of privileged) departments and
groups of workers. This was inevitable since it was impossible to
save the devastated country without concentrating forces and
means in those departments and in those groups of workers without whom the united imperialists of the whole world would certainly have suppressed us and wouldn't even have permitted our
Soviet Republic to start the task of economic construction. These
circumstances, together with the legacy of capitalist and private
ownership habits and attitudes which are difficult to throw off,
make the necessity apparent over and over again to direct the
attention of the whole party to the struggle for the bringing into
being of greater equality, first of all, within the party, secondly,
within the proletariat, and then also within the whole toiling
masses, finally, thirdly, among the various departments and various
groups of workers, especially 'specialists' and those workers who
hold responsibilities with respect to the masses. The party in dif-
ferentiating party members only according to the degree of the
development of their consciousness, devotion, steadfastness, political maturity, their revolutionary experience, their readiness for
self-sacrifice, in doing this, the party is struggling with every kind
of attempt to differentiate among party members on some other
basis; the upper and the lower strata, intelligenty and the workers,
nationality, etc. Confirming the CC letter of the 4 September 1920
conference regards the carrying out of the following measures as
necessary:

3. It is absolutely necessary to alter the nature of the Revision
Commissions: endow them with the rights to inspect the function-

* From ibid., pp. 506–12.

ing of organisations, check the implementation of CC circulars, decrees of conferences, the rapidity of the conduct of business in party committees, the efficient working of the administrative apparatus, etc. Revision commissions are obliged to report all instances of neglect not only to the organs which elected them, but also directly to the CC of the party. Accordingly it is necessary to elect to the Revision Commissions sufficiently responsible and active comrades.

4. It is necessary to pay particularly serious attention to the organisation of party re-registration. Experience of these re-registrations has revealed more than once a too formalistic approach to the matter. If a doubtful communist, pursuing careerist goals, has produced two or three recommendations, he is enrolled as a member without further ado, while workers who for some reason did not get around to it, or who did not wish, or were not able to produce the necessary recommendation, remain outside party organisations. It is necessary to organise re-registration in such a way as to reduce to a minimum all formalities for workers and the proletarian elements in the peasantry and to raise to a maximum barriers against the entry into the party of non-proletarian elements. The use by some organisations of examinations during re-registration should be considered inappropriate.

5. Pay special attention to the organisation of effective mass propaganda, which systematically raises the level of the main mass of party members. Take all measures to regulate the running of party schools. Create, in good time, special shock schools, as for example, provisioning schools and others, and provide them with the relevant literature . . . Call regular meetings of heads of agitation and propaganda sections of *gubkoms* and when possible representatives of the party press.

6. The organisation of 'weeks' and 'days' should be strictly regulated through the relevant central organs, permitting them on an all-Russian scale only in exceptional cases according to the CC decree.

7. In order to avert the fragmentation of party work, which has come about in some places as a result of the existence of specialist organisations (political sections, etc.) and in order that the *gubkoms* should effectually take over all party work in a given territory, instruct the CC to work out a plan for the

above-mentioned unification of party work in time for the next conference or congress ...

9. In the inner life of the party it is necessary to foster a more widely based criticism both of local as well as central institutions of the party. Instruct the CC to indicate by a circular ways of broadening intra-party criticism at general meetings. Establish literary organs which are capable of offering a more systematic and wider criticism of the mistakes of the party and intra-party criticism in general (discussion leaflets etc.); for this purpose a special discussion leaflet should be established at the centre attached to 'Izvestiya of the CC'. It is desirable to establish the same type of discussion leaflets attached to 'Izvestiyas' published by *gubkoms* ...

12. .... It is necessary to enliven the activity of the plenums and congresses of Soviets, by carefully preparing them, by holding at them all-embracing discussions of the most important economic and political questions. It is especially necessary to prepare for *uezd* and *guberniya* congresses of Soviets, by drawing the attention of all the local population to them (wide pre-congress agitation, oral and written) ...

13. At the centre and at the local level it is necessary to transfer systematically responsible workers from job to job, so as to afford them the opportunity of studying work widely in the soviet and party *apparat* and to facilitate their task of struggling with routine ...

14. As regards central workers conference finds it necessary to carry out the following measures:

(a) Oblige every People's Commissar and every member of a collegium to visit at the local level at least twice a year.

(b) Alter the staff of a collegium more often by bringing in promising workers. In doing this it is necessary to take care that current work should not suffer and that accumulated experience is not lost ...

16. It is necessary to oblige all responsible communists without exception to carry out regularly party work first and foremost among the lower strata of the proletariat, the peasantry and the Red Army; for this purpose all responsible workers, irrespective of the posts they hold, should be attached to factory, works, Red Army or rural cells. They are duty bound to attend all general

meetings and to deliver reports at them of their activities . . . It is necessary to make participation in *subbotniks* absolutely obligatory for all party members, as we envisaged in the decree on *subbotniks*...

19. It is considered necessary to set up a Control Commission, side by side with the CC, which must consist of comrades who have had the longest party training and are the most experienced and must be impartial and capable of carrying out strict party control. The Control Commission, elected by the party congress, must have the right to accept all types of complaints and investigate them, in co-ordination with the CC and if necessary calling joint general meetings with it or transferring the questions to a party congress. Temporarily until the party congress, confirm as members of the Control Commission comrades Dzerzhinsky, Muranov, Preobrazhensky and one representative from the Moscow, Petrograd, Ivanovo–Voznesensk and Nizhny Novgorod organisations, who must be elected at *guberniya* conferences (until these conferences have been called, *gubkoms* together with active workers are to elect representatives) . . .

20. Bureaucratism, which prevails in many of our central boards and centres, is often painfully damaging the most legitimate interests of the popular masses and is serving as one of the most important sources of dissatisfaction with the party, on to which responsibility for the central boards and centres is being shifted.

The Central Committee of the party must adopt the most serious measures to combat this. Local organisations must aid the CC in this struggle, first and foremost, by reporting the relevant facts . . .

(c) X CONGRESS: RESOLUTION ON PARTY UNITY*

X Congress of the Russian Communist Party (Bolsheviks)
Moscow, 8–16 March 1921
Resolution

On the Unity of the Party

1. Congress draws the attention of all members of the party to the fact that the unity and cohesion of its ranks, the guarantee

* From ibid., pp. 527–30.

of complete trust between party members and work that is really harmonious, really embodies the unity of the will of the vanguard of the proletariat is especially necessary at the present time when a number of circumstances are intensifying the hesitancy of the petty bourgeois population of the country.

2. However, even before the all-party discussion about the trade unions some signs of factionalism had appeared in the party, i.e. the formation of groups with special platforms which to a certain extent aimed at closing ranks and creating their own group discipline.

It is essential that all politically-conscious workers should clearly understand the danger and impermissibility of any factionalism whatsoever which inevitably will lead in fact to the weakening of harmonious work and to the intensified and repeated attempts by enemies who have attached themselves to the ruling party to deepen the division and utilise it for counter-revolution.

The use by enemies of the proletariat of all kinds of deviation from the strictly maintained communist line was revealed with the greatest clarity in the case of the Kronstadt revolt when bourgeois counter-revolution and the White Guards in all countries of the world at once declared their willingness to accept the slogans even of the Soviet system, provided that the dictatorship of the proletariat in Russia was overturned, when SRs and in general the bourgeois counter-revolution used in Kronstadt the slogans of rebellion supposedly in the name of Soviet power against the Soviet government in Russia. Such facts fully prove that the White Guards are striving and know how to disguise themselves as communists and as those who are even further to the 'left' of them, in order to weaken and overturn the bulwark of proletarian revolution in Russia. Menshevik leaflets in Petrograd on the eve of the Kronstadt revolt prove likewise that the Mensheviks were utilising the discord inside the RKP really to urge on and support the Kronstadt mutineers, SRs and White Guards, while proclaiming themselves to be opponents of mutinies, and supporters of Soviet power only with, as it were, a few changes.

3. Propaganda about this question must consist, on the one hand, of a detailed explanation of the harmfulness and danger of factionalism, from the point of view of unity of the party and

the creation of the unity of will of the vanguard of the proletariat, as the basic condition of success of the dictatorship of the proletariat, and, on the other hand, of an explanation of the uniqueness of the latest tactical moves of the enemies of Soviet power. These enemies, convinced of the hopelessness of counter-revolution under an avowedly White flag, are now straining every nerve, utilising the discord in the RKP, to further counter-revolution in one way or another by means of a transfer of power to political groups apparently nearest to recognising Soviet power.

Propaganda must explain also the experience of previous revolutions, when counter-revolution supported the petty bourgeois grouping which were nearest to the extreme revolutionary party so as to shake and overturn the revolutionary dictatorship, opening thereby the path to the eventual complete victory of counter-revolution, capitalists and landowners.

4. It is essential that every party organisation must take the greatest care to ensure that the undoubtedly essential criticism of the shortcomings of the party, any analysis of the general line of the party or an account of its practical experience, any verification of the execution of its decisions and the ways of correcting mistakes, etc. is directed not towards the discussion of groups, adhering to some platform or other, etc. but towards the discussion of all party members. For this purpose congress has ordered the more regular publication of 'The Discussion leaflet' and special collections of articles. Anyone making criticisms must take into account the position of the party surrounded by enemies and also must strive to correct the mistakes of the party by active personal participation in soviet and party work.

5. Instructing the CC to carry out a complete elimination of all factionalism, congress declares at the same time that administrative proposals concerning questions which especially attract the attention of members of the party, i.e. a party purge of non-proletarian and unreliable elements, the struggle with bureaucratism, the development of democracy and workers' initiative etc., must be examined with the closest attention and tested in practical work. All party members must take note that on these questions the party is not carrying out all the necessary measures, encountering a series of varied obstacles and that rejecting decisively inapplicable and factious criticism, the party will tirelessly continue testing new methods, will fight bureaucratism

with every weapon, will fight for the development of democracy and of initiative, and for the discovery, unmasking and expulsion of party hangers on, etc.

6. Congress orders the immediate dispersal of all groups, without exception, which were based on some platform or other, and instructs all organisations to take the greatest care not to permit any factional speeches. Failure to execute this resolution of the congress must result in the unconditional and immediate expulsion from the party.

7. In order to establish strict discipline within the party and in all soviet work and to achieve the greatest possible unity in eliminating all factionalism, congress confers on the CC plenary powers, to apply in case(s) of a breach of discipline or the reappearance or tolerance of factionalism, all measures of party punishment up to and including expulsion from the party and in the case of members of the CC, their transfer to the status of candidates and even, as an extreme measure, expulsion from the party. A condition for applying (towards CC members, CC candidates and members of the Control Commission) such an extreme measure must be the calling of a CC plenum to which all CC candidates and all members of the Control Commission have been invited. If such a general meeting of the most responsible leaders of the party, by a two-thirds majority, considers it necessary to transfer a CC member to candidate status or to expel him from the party then such a measure must be carried out immediately.

(d) X CONGRESS: RESOLUTION ON THE SYNDICALIST AND ANARCHICAL DEVIATION IN THE PARTY*

X Congress of the Russian Communist Party (Bolsheviks)
Moscow, 8–16 March 1921
Resolution

On the syndicalist and anarchical deviation in our party

1. A syndicalist and anarchical deviation has clearly come into being these last months in the ranks of the party. It demands the most decisive measures of ideological struggle and a cleansing and a reinvigoration of the party.

* From ibid., pp. 530–3.

2. The said deviation was brought about partly by the admission into the ranks of the party of elements which have not yet fully mastered the communist *Weltanschauung*. This deviation has been brought about in the main by the influence on the proletariat and the RKP of petty bourgeois elements which is exceptionally strong in our country and which inevitably causes vacillation towards anarchism, especially at times when the situation of the masses has deteriorated sharply as a result of crop failure and the extremely destructive consequences of war and when the demobilisation of a million-strong army has released a flood of hundreds and hundreds of thousands of peasants and workers who are not immediately capable of finding employment and the means of existence.

3. The theses and other literary works of the so-called 'workers' opposition' group are one of the most consummate and most organised expressions of this deviation. The following thesis of theirs, for example, is sufficiently revealing: 'The organisation of the management of the economy is the responsibility of the all-Russian congress of producers, organised in trade union producers' unions, which elect a central organ, which manages the whole economy of the republic.'

The ideas which form the basis of this and other similar declarations are fundamentally incorrect theoretically, representing a complete break with Marxism and communism, and equally with the results of the practical experience of all semi-proletarian and the present proletarian revolutions.

Firstly, the concept 'producer' links the proletariat with the semi-proletariat and with the small goods producers, deviating, thus, fundamentally from the basic concept of class struggle and from the basic requirement to distinguish classes in a precise manner.

Secondly, the incorrect formulation of the question given in the quoted thesis about the relations between the party and the broad non-party masses, leading to the subordination of the party to non-party influences, is no less a fundamental departure from Marxism.

Marxism teaches – and this teaching was not only formally confirmed by the whole Communist International in the decision of the II congress of the Comintern (1920) on the role of the political party of the proletariat but also has been proved in practice by the whole experiences of our revolution – that only the political party of the working class, i.e. the communist party, is in a position to unite, educate, and organise a vanguard of the proletariat and all the toiling masses, which is capable of withstanding the inevitable petty bourgeois vacillations of those masses, the traditions and the inevitable recurrence of specialist narrowness and prejudices among the proletariat and to guide all aspects of the proletarian movement and this means all the toiling masses too. The dictatorship of the proletariat is inconceivable without this. An incorrect conception of the role of the communist party *vis-à-vis* the non-party working masses, on the one hand, and the equally incorrect concept of the role of the working class *vis-à-vis* the whole mass of toilers, on the other, is a fundamental theoretical departure from communism and is a deviation towards syndicalism and anarchism. Such a deviation permeates the whole outlook of the 'workers' opposition'.

4. The X congress of the RKP states that it also regards as fundamentally incorrect all attempts of the said group and individual persons to defend their incorrect views by referring to paragraph 5 of the economic part of the programme of the RKP, devoted to the role of trade unions. This paragraph states that trade unions 'must arrive at effective concentration of all management of the whole economy, as a united economic whole, in their own hands', and that they guarantee thereby the unbreakable link between central state management, the economy and the broad masses of the toilers, 'drawing' these masses 'into the immediate task of running the economy'.

The programme of the RKP in the same paragraph regards the process of 'ever greater emancipation of the trade unions from workshop narrowness' and the inclusion by them of the majority 'and gradually every single member' of the toiling masses as the pre-requisite for such a situation which the trade unions 'must arrive at'.

Finally, in the same paragraph the programme of the RKP emphasises that trade unions 'are, already, according to the laws of the RSFSR and established practice, members of all local and central organs of industrial management'.

Instead of an account of just this practical experience of participating in management, instead of the further development of this experience in strict accordance with successes achieved and

corrected mistakes, syndicalists and anarchists propose the immediate slogan of: 'congresses or a congress of producers', 'electing'
organs of economic control. The guiding, educational, organisational role of the party *vis-à-vis* the trade unions of the proletariat
and of the latter *vis-à-vis* the semi-petty-bourgeois and wholly
petty-bourgeois masses of the toilers is thus circumvented and
eliminated completely, and instead of the continuation and improvement of the practical work of construction of new forms of
the economy, already begun under Soviet power, the result is a
petty-bourgeois, anarchical destruction of this work which can
lead only to the triumph of bourgeois counter-revolution.

5. Besides the theoretical incorrectness and the fundamentally
incorrect attitude to the practical experience of economic construction begun under Soviet power, the congress of the RKP
sees in the views of the said group and analogous groups and persons
an enormous political error and an immediate political danger
to the retention of power by the proletariat.

In a country such as Russia, the very great prevalence of petty-
bourgeois influences and the inevitable destruction resulting from
the war, poverty, epidemics and failed harvests, the extreme ex-
acerbation of want and national disasters give rise to particularly
acute cases of vacillation in the mood of the petty-bourgeois and
semi-proletarian mass. These vacillations sometimes lead towards
the strengthening of the union of these masses with the proletariat
and sometimes to the restoration of the bourgeoisie. All the experience of all the revolutions of the 18th, 19th and 20th centuries
demonstrates with absolute clarity and conviction, that nothing
other than the restoration of the power and property of the capitalists and landowners can result from these vacillations – given
the slightest weakening of unity, strength and the influence of the
revolutionary vanguard of the proletariat. Therefore the views
of the 'workers' opposition' and elements similar to it are not only
theoretically incorrect, but serve, in practice, to express petty-
bourgeois and anarchical instability, and weaken, in practice, the
line on leadership held by the communist party and in reality aid
the class enemies of the proletarian revolution.

6. On the basis of all this, the congress of the RKP resolutely
rejecting the said ideas expressing syndicalist and anarchical
views resolves:

(1) to regard as indispensable the resolute and systematic struggle with these ideas;
(2) to regard the propagation of these ideas as incompatible with membership of the Russian Communist Party.

Instructing the CC of the party to put very strictly into effect these resolutions, congress points out as well that in special publications, collections of articles, etc. space can and must be allocated to a most detailed exchange of opinions among party members on all the said questions.

(e) XII CONFERENCE: ANTI-SOVIET PARTIES*

XII All-Russian Conference of the Russian Communist Party (Bolsheviks) Moscow 4–7 August 1922
Resolution

On anti-Soviet parties and trends

1. Summing up the first year of Soviet power under the New Economic Policy, the Russian Communist Party (RKP) cannot but pay the closest attention to the new groupings and regroupings which are forming in the anti-Soviet camp, the way the tactics of the anti-Soviet parties, trends, etc. are evolving and changing, in accordance with the new stage of the revolution.
2. On the whole during the past year, the beginning of a serious stratification has appeared in the anti-Soviet camp. The schism between right and left in the Kadet party and the formation, in this connection, of two separate Kadet centres abroad, the appearance of a tendency to a complete change of orientation among a certain part of the bourgeoisie, the beginnings of a deep schism in the church which is fraught with the most serious consequences, the division of the Mensheviks and SRs into a number of new groups and sub-groups ('left' SRs have split into two groups; in the camp of the right SRs, together with the former groupings, the ultra-right group of Avksentev, Kerensky, Minor, Bunakov has formed; in the camp of the Mensheviks on the right and 'Zarya' group abroad and the 'extra-party group of Social Democrats in Russia' stand out and a group criticising the Menshevik centre from the left is forming), the increased differentiation among

* From ibid., pp. 669–74.

the student body in Russia and even among the *emigré* part of the student body, the increasing differentiation among the leaders of the former White Guard generals; all this, taken together, is a symptom of the weakening of the anti-Soviet camp and an indirect confirmation of the consolidation of our positions.

3. However, the first year of the existence of Soviet power under the conditions of the New Economic Policy was accompanied by new dangerous phenomena which must be considered. Anti-Soviet parties and trends are partially changing their tactics; they are attempting to use Soviet legality in their counter-revolutionary interests and adopt a course of 'growing' into the Soviet régime, hoping gradually to change it in the spirit of bourgeois democracy. The régime, according to their calculations, is itself moving towards an inevitable bourgeois regeneration.

All the indicated processes of disintegration, decomposition and regroupings in the anti-Soviet camp are feeding on not only the long evident separation of some groups of the bourgeois intelligentsia from the old *bloc* of generals and landowners and the powerful capitalist bourgeoisie, but also on the process of the partial restoration of capitalism within the framework of the Soviet state which is encouraging the growth of elements of the so-called 'new bourgeoisie' (merchants, private lessees of land, various free professions in town and country, village, kulaks, etc.).

4. The first year of Soviet power under the conditions of the New Economic Policy, coinciding with a very grave famine, with the strengthening of the international capitalist reaction, the presentation to the Soviet state of crude demands for restoration by capitalists and the Entente governments (Genoa, The Hague), has encouraged not only the Mensheviks and the SRs to greater counter-revolutionary activity but also the scheming leaders of the supposedly non-party bourgeois intelligentsia . . .

5. The beginning of NEP temporarily aroused among Mensheviks and SRs the hope of the capitulation of the RKP and the establishment of 'democratic' coalition power. But as these hopes proved illusory, Mensheviks and SRs increasingly resorted to and are resorting to adventurism. On the one hand, Menshevik and SR leaders adopted a position of clamorous implacability and are attempting to organise a movement against Soviet power, criticising it from the point of view of the slogans and the hopes of the October revolution itself, falsely depicting their parties, as the only

organisations at the present moment ready to struggle for the actual carrying out of the demands, advanced by the masses during the years of the highest enthusiasm of the proletarian revolution . . .

6. Anti-Soviet parties and trends are attempting especially to make use of co-operatives.

The RKP can and must help with all its power the rebirth of co-operatives and the strengthening of their economic power. But the RKP must not, at the same time, for a moment close its eyes to the fact that counter-revolutionary parties and trends, neglecting the fundamental interests of co-operatives, are attempting to transform the latter into a bulwark and organisational base of counter-revolution . . .

7. . . . All the above mentioned raises the following tasks for the RKP:

(a) The party must always remember and constantly remind the whole working class and peasantry of the fact that the revolution, in the most immediate sense too, is still in danger. The outcome of the Hague conference showed this with sufficient persuasiveness. There remains one link or another, but always and invariably sufficiently close, between the international capitalist reaction and the Russian anti-Soviet parties and trends. The course and vicissitudes of the SR trial have shown that this link between internal counter-revolution and foreign capital is sufficiently strong and not at all only Platonic. Anti-Soviet parties and trends have not yet been crushed . . .

(f) At the same time one must not reject even the use of repression not only in relation to the SRs and Mensheviks, but also in relation to the intriguing leaders of the supposedly non-party, bourgeois-democratic intelligentsia who, for their own counter-revolutionary ends, are using the fundamental interests of whole corporations and for whom the genuine interests of science, tehnology, education, co-operatives, etc. are only empty words and a political screen.

Repression which inevitably does not achieve its aim since it is directed against the rising class (as for example in its time the repression of the Mensheviks and SRs against us) is dictated by revolutionary expediency when it is a matter of crushing those moribund groups which attempt to seize old positions which have been won from them by the proletariat. However, party organisations must not overestimate the role of repression and must always bear in mind that only in conjunction with all the other measures indicated above will repression achieve its aim.

(f) MEMORANDUM OF THE UKRAINIAN COMMUNIST PARTY TO THE THIRD CONGRESS OF THE COMMUNIST INTERNATIONAL (1921)*

Memorandum of the Ukrainian Communist Party to the Third Congress of the Communist International (1921)

The formation in 1905 of the Ukrainian Social Democratic Party which emerged from a social revolutionary group, the so-called 'Revolutionary Ukrainian Party' (RUP), already in existence in 1902, was simultaneously the beginning of the national and class movements of the Ukrainian proletariat. The Ukrainian Social Democratic Party participated actively in the revolution of 1905; until the revolution of 1917 it put forward as its demand the autonomy of the Ukraine as a minimal democratic programme *vis-à-vis* the national question. During the (First) World War it firmly defended the position of revolutionary struggle, was against the war and joined the Zimmerwald movement.

At that time yet another group existed in the Ukraine: the Russian Social Democratic Party which had a greater influence on the urban proletariat than the Ukrainian Social Democratic Party, the reasons for this being: the imperialist and colonialist policies of Russian and European capital in the Ukraine; the russified cities and the forcible creation of a higher stratum of qualified Russian or russified proletariat which was not linked to the masses of the Ukrainian people.

Although the workers who were Ukrainian by origin and nationality constituted the majority of the proletariat in the Ukraine, it was because of their low cultural level and their backwardness in their class development and also because they were involved primarily in agriculture, in the rural and mining

* From *Memorandum Ukrainskoi Komunistichnoi Partii Kongresovi III Komunistichnogo Internatsionalu* (Biblioteka 'Novoyi Doby', Vienna–Kiev 1920).

industries, or else filled the ranks of unqualified workers in the towns, that they were dependent on Russian elements, and were in Russian party groups and circles.

When taking into account the financial and economic exploitation of the Ukraine by the Russian metropolis and the national–political oppression of the Ukrainian people and the low cultural level of the masses connected with this, then the state of the social forces in the Ukraine from the beginning of the great eastern revolution becomes clear . . .

Prepared by the entire development of capitalism, by the Ukrainian national movement and the yoke of Russian imperialism, the Ukrainian revolution began to differentiate itself from the general course of the Russian one as a national revolution which set as its task national liberation by establishing a nation–state.

The period between February and November 1917 was a time of exceptional national enthusiasm among the masses of the Ukrainian peasantry, soldiers and workers, a period of struggle against the imperial government of the time, and the gathering together of forces to achieve national liberation which received its impulse from the October revolution in Petrograd.

The bearer of this movement became a *bloc* of the petty bourgeoisie, the peasantry and the Ukrainian part of the proletariat headed by the Central Rada. The most active and leading participant in this movement was Ukrainian Social Democracy which during the struggle against Russian imperialism defended a revolutionary national and class position which was expressed in a resolution of the Fourth Congress of the Ukrainian Social Democratic Labour Party in September 1917. Here the transitional nature of the revolution is indicated together with the toiling masses' aspirations of overthrowing capitalism and carrying out a social revolution. The resolution further raises the problem of the revolutionary dictatorship of the workers, peasants and soldiers. This period was considered as the 'Bolshevik' period of Ukrainian Social Democracy, although this 'Bolshevism' was upheld by the national struggle more than by the class struggle.

During that period Ukrainian Social Democracy gained a large influence among the Ukrainian proletarian masses and attracted into its ranks strata of workers who were tied to the spontaneous national and social movement of the popular masses. In all the industrial regions of the Ukraine, the Ukrainian Social Democratic Labour Party had its own large organisations, numbering tens of thousands of members in the party, and in some areas such as Kryvorih (Krivoi Rog) region, for example, it had the support of the majority of the proletariat. The leading role of the Ukrainian Social Democratic Labour Party, in the first stage of the Ukrainian revolution, up to November 1917, is explained by the extensive influence of the party on the Ukrainian working masses who were most closely linked to the Ukrainian peasantry.

Russian Social Democracy (Bolshevik) (today the Communist Party (Bolshevik) of the Ukraine, the regional organisation of the Russian Communist Party) did not participate in this national revolution because it considered this movement chauvinistic. As a result of this attitude the most class-conscious elements of the Russian proletariat in the Ukraine remained outside the Ukrainian revolution, regarding it as bourgeois and forgetting that it is precisely the task of the proletariat to carry the bourgeois democratic revolution to its completion.

The Bolshevik party, remaining aloof from the Ukrainian national revolution, did not take advantage of it to develop socialism. It did not take advantage of the revolutionary mood of Ukrainian Social Democracy to achieve national unification and the social liberation of the toilers, to bring about a split in the centre of the Ukrainian national *bloc*, to differentiate the Ukrainian proletariat from the bourgeoisie. Instead it remained an external force *vis-à-vis* the Ukrainian revolution and was not even united on an all-Ukrainian scale for the struggle against the Ukrainian petty bourgeoisie which, in November 1917, seized power in the Ukraine and formed the 'Ukrainian People's Republic'. The condition of the proletarian class struggle in the Ukraine worsened still with the declaration of war by the Russian Council of People's Commissars on the Central Rada which had transformed the civil war into a national war, and paralysed, or rather threw the revolutionary Ukrainian elements into the arms of the bourgeoisie . . .

The betrayal by the Central Rada, its allegiance with German imperialism, represented the defeat of the first Soviet government in the Ukraine, and Hetman rule exacerbated the class struggle, while within Ukrainian Social Democracy a split began to appear; in its midst arose a group of Independents.

At the moment of political upheaval when Hetman rule was overthrown exclusively by the indigenous national revolutionary forces of the Ukrainian people, the Communist Party (Bolshevik) of the Ukraine refused to co-operate with the Ukrainian revolutionary groups, and thus played no part in the revolution. The group of Independents was able to come forward in an organised fashion only at the VI Congress of the Ukrainian Social Democratic Labour Party in January 1919, where it formally seceded from the party and adopted a platform of Soviet government, a socialist republic, an independent Ukraine, and the name of 'Ukrainian Social Democratic Labour Party – Independents'.

The revolutionary movement against German occupation and Hetmanite reaction, initially headed by a *bloc* of national petty bourgeois parties under the leadership of the Directory, changed into a movement that was directed towards the establishment of a Soviet government. Due to the weakness of the Ukrainian proletariat and the isolation of its russified upper strata from the bulk of the working masses in the Ukraine and to the incompleteness of, and the lack of experience of the national bourgeois-democratic revolution, this movement did not produce an internal political guiding force out of itself, but was only objectively completed by an external centre – by the Pyatakov–Rakovsky government which considered the aspirations of the Ukrainian working masses for a Soviet government as a negation of their own nationality and as a denial of their desire for an independent Ukraine. Furthermore, relying on the upper strata of the Russian proletariat in the Ukraine and on Russia's military strength, the Pyatakov–Rakovsky government began consciously or unconsciously to pursue a policy of liquidating the forms of statehood which the self-determination of the Ukrainian people had assumed . . .

The All-Ukrainian Revolutionary Committee's[1] task was to seize power quickly in the main centres of the Ukraine and to proclaim an independent Ukrainian Soviet Socialist Republic, expecting in this way to forestall the seizure of the Ukraine by Petlyura, demoralise his army, and thereby attract to their side his revolutionary but nationally oriented units. On the other hand, the All-Ukrainian Revolutionary Committee aimed at forcing the Russian communists to change their attitude on the Ukrainian question, and to come to an agreement with it by the very fact of establishing a really Ukrainian Soviet government.

This struggle was an historically unprecedented occurrence, a result of the conflict between the internal and external forces of the Ukrainian revolution, a result of the imperialist heritage of old Russia in which the Communist Party (Bolshevik) of the Ukraine had no part. All this hindered a consolidation of the internal social forces of the Ukrainian revolution and hampered the maturation and the crystallisation of the Ukrainian communist proletariat . . .

Having clashed with petty bourgeois, semi-proletarian elements, the party shook off its contradictions, overcame them, and began the struggle armed with a deeper class consciousness, having adopted sharp tactics and a communist programme at its Party Congress on 22–25 January 1920. In the practice of its struggle the Ukrainian Communist Party[2] became aware of the low level of consciousness of the Ukrainian proletariat and the semi-proletariat and of the fact that the broad strata of the toiling masses in the Ukraine had not been touched by the proletarian revolution. Simultaneously, it became convinced of the incapacity of the regional organisation of the Russian Communist Party, which calls itself the Communist Party (Bolshevik) of the Ukraine, to attract the internal forces of the Ukrainian proletariat and the working peasantry towards participation in the proletarian revolution, of its inability to unite the urban proletariat with the rural semi-proletariat. This is a result of its organic absence of links with the Ukrainian revolution and its reliance on the Russian or the russified upper strata of the proletariat, on the element which is alienated from the Ukrainian people; without regard to the economic, cultural and psychological individuality of the Ukraine, it carries out the centralistic policy of past imperial Russia, and with difficulty breaks with its heritage; and finally, because that party is not strong enough to resolve correctly the tasks of the proletarian revolution in Ukrainian conditions.

The Ukrainian Communist Party decided to take upon itself all the following tasks: prepare and organise the Ukrainian proletariat to fulfil its historical role, raise its class consciousness, link its struggle to that of the entire Ukrainian working people for its social and national liberation, guide the class struggle of this proletariat not by subordinating it to another detachment of the international proletariat, but by elevating it to equal membership in the international society – the Communist International, subordinating its struggle to the interests of the general struggle of the world proletariat by means of *establishing an independent party centre, a single, real representative of the class movement of the entire proletariat of the Ukraine* – in the form of the Ukrainian Communist Party, as is resolved in our programme . . .

Experience has shown that there is no hope of healthy revolutionary thought in the Communist Party (Bolshevik) of the Ukraine gaining the upper hand by organic means because the formal leaders of the Communist Party (Bolshevik) of the Ukraine, envoys of the Russian Communist Party, do not stop short of destroying the opposition in the ranks of its party by direct physical force in order to suppress also all social life within the party. They are in fact demoralising the party itself and they have *de facto* annulled the party statutes by replacing the entire party executive, which was elected, by party officials appointed from above, just so as not to allow a spontaneously growing opposition inside their own party to seize power . . .

A fundamental break with the Communist Party (Bolshevik) of the Ukraine therefore becomes inevitable, together with the establishment of a centre which would draw together the internal proletarian forces, a centre that would be ideologically and organisationally linked to and merged with the masses, and which, while growing, would reflect the aspirations and aims of the Ukrainian proletariat and would strive to solve the tasks of the world revolution in the Ukraine.

And now the Ukrainian Communist Party is that very centre which in the process of revolution must unite all the communist forces of the Ukraine and carry out the fundamental principles of the communist programme.

This must of course necessarily happen during the present moment of our present struggle and in alliance with the Communist Party (Bolshevik) of the Ukraine against counter-revolution and world imperialism. This obliges equally the Ukrainian Communist Party and the Communist Party (Bolshevik) of the Ukraine to help each other to understand the present situation.

[1]The Ukrainian Revolutionary Committee, set up by the Ukrainian Social Democratic Labour Party – Independents, took over the leadership of the revolutionary movement and began its struggle initially against the Directory.

[2]The Ukrainian Communist Party, the so-called Ukapisty,

originated in the Ukrainian Social Democratic Labour Party, calling themselves the Independent faction of that party for a while. At first openly at war with the Bolsheviks, the Ukapisty became a legal opposition party only at the beginning of 1920. However, by that time, all the important positions in Soviet Ukrainian political life had been filled by members of the older parties: in the industrial areas by the Communist Party (Bolshevik) of the Ukraine; in the smaller towns and villages by the Borotbisty. Thus the gains of the Ukapisty among the workers were insignificant and they played a less prominent role than the Borotbisty. The Ukapisty merged eventually with the Communist Party (Bolsheviks) of the Ukraine.

6/15 THE COMINTERN

(a) CONDITIONS OF ADMISSION*

The second congress of the Communist International decrees the following conditions of adherence to the Communist International:

1. Day-to-day propaganda and agitation must be of a genuinely communist character and in conformity with the programme and decrees of the Third International. The entire party press must be run by reliable communists who have proved their devotion to the cause of the proletariat. The dictatorship of the proletariat is to be treated not simply as a current formula learnt by rote; it must be advocated in a way which makes its necessity comprehensible to every ordinary working man and woman, every soldier and peasant, from the facts of their daily life, which must be systematically noted in our press and made use of every day.

The periodical press and other publications, and all party publishing houses, must be wholly subordinated to the CC of the party, regardless of whether the party as a whole is at the given moment legal or illegal. Publishing houses must not be allowed to abuse their independence and pursue a policy which is not wholly in accordance with the policy of the party.

* From *V.I. Lenin i Kommunisticheskii Internatsional* (Moscow 1970), pp. 250–4.

In the columns of the press, at popular meetings, in the trade unions and co-operatives, wherever the adherents of the Communist International have an entry, it is necessary to denounce, systematically and unrelentingly, not only the bourgeoisie, but also their assistants, the reformists of all shades.

2. Every organisation which wishes to join the Third International must, in an orderly and planned fashion, *remove* reformists and centrists from all responsible positions in the workers' movement (party organisations, editorial boards, trade unions, parliamentary fractions, co-operatives, local government bodies) and replace them by tried communists, even if, particularly at the beginning, 'experienced' opportunists have to be replaced by ordinary rank and file workers.

3. In practically every country of Europe and America the class struggle is entering the phase of civil war. In these circumstances communists can have no confidence in bourgeois legality. They are obliged everywhere to create a parallel illegal organisation which at the decisive moment will help the party to do its duty to the revolution. In all those countries where, because of a state of siege or of emergency laws, communists are unable to do all their work legally, it is absolutely essential to combine legal and illegal work.

4. The obligation to spread communist ideas includes the special obligation to carry on systematic and energetic propaganda in the army. Where such agitation is prevented by emergency laws, it must be carried on illegally. Refusal to undertake such work would be tantamount to a dereliction of revolutionary duty and is incompatible with membership of the Communist International.

5. Systematic and well-planned agitation must be carried on in the countryside. The working class cannot consolidate its victory if it has not by its policy assured itself of the support of at least some of the agricultural labourers and the poorest peasants, and of the neutrality of part of the rest of the rural population. At the present time communist work in rural areas is acquiring great importance. It should be conducted primarily with the help of revolutionary communist urban and rural *workers* who have close connexions with the countryside. To neglect this work or to leave it in unreliable semi-reformist hands, is tantamount to renouncing the proletarian revolution.

6. Every party which wishes to join the Third International is obliged to unmask not only avowed social-patriotism, but also the insincerity and hypocrisy of social-pacifism; to bring home to the workers systematically that without the revolutionary overthrow of capitalism no international court of arbitration, no agreement to limit armaments, no 'democratic' reorganisation of the League of Nations, will be able to save mankind from new imperialist wars.

7. Parties which wish to join the Communist International are obliged to recognise the necessity for a complete and absolute break with reformism and with the policy of the 'centre', and to advocate this break as widely as possible among their members. Without this no consistent communist policy is possible.

The Communist International demands unconditionally and categorically that this break be effected as quickly as possible. The Communist International is unable to tolerate the fact that notorious opportunists, such as Turati, Kautsky, Hilferding, Hilquit, Longuet, MacDonald, Modigliani, etc., shall have the right to appear as members of the Third International. That could only lead to the Third International becoming in many respects similar to the Second International, which has collapsed.

8. A particularly explicit and clear attitude on the question of the colonies and the oppressed peoples is necessary for the parties in those countries where the bourgeoisie possesses colonies and oppresses other nations. Every party which wishes to join the Third International is obliged to expose the tricks and dodges of 'its' imperialists in the colonies, to support every colonial liberation movement not merely in words but in deeds, to demand the expulsion of their own imperialists from these colonies, to inculcate in the workers of their country a genuinely fraternal attitude to the working peoples of the colonies and the oppressed nations, and to carry on systematic agitation among the troops of their country against any oppression of the colonial peoples.

9. Every party which wishes to join the Communist International must carry on systematic and persistent communist activity inside the trade unions, the workers' organisations. Within these organisations communist cells must be organised which shall by persistent and resolute work win the trade unions, etc., for the communist cause. In their daily work the cells must everywhere expose the treachery of the social-patriots and the

instability of the 'centre'. The communist cells must be completely subordinate to the party as a whole.

10. Every party belonging to the Communist International is obliged to wage an unyielding struggle against the Amsterdam 'International' of the yellow trade unions. It must conduct the most vigorous propaganda among trade unionists for the necessity of a break with the yellow Amsterdam International. It must do all it can to support the international association of red trade unions, adhering to the Communist International, which is being formed.

11. Parties which wish to join the Third International are obliged to review the personnel of their parliamentary fractions and remove all unreliable elements, to make these fractions not only verbally but in fact subordinate to the CC of the party, requiring of each individual communist member of parliament that he subordinate his entire activity to the interests of genuinely revolutionary propaganda and agitation.

12. Parties belonging to the Communist International must be based on the principle of *democratic centralism*. In the present epoch of acute civil war the communist party will be able to fulfil its duty only if its organisation is as centralised as possible, if iron discipline prevails, and if the party centre, upheld by the conference of the party membership, has strength and authority and is equipped with the most comprehensive powers.

13. Communist parties in those countries where communists carry on their work legally must from time to time undertake purges (re-registration) of the membership of the party in order to get rid of any petty-bourgeois elements which have attached themselves to it.

14. Every party which wishes to join the Communist International is obliged to give unconditional support to any Soviet republic in its struggle against counter-revolutionary forces. Communist parties must carry on unambiguous propaganda to prevent the dispatch of military equipment to the enemies of the Soviet republics; they must also carry on propaganda by every means, legal or illegal, among the troops sent to strangle workers' republics.

15. Parties which still retain their old social-democratic programmes are obliged to revise them as quickly as possible, and to draw up, in accordance with the special conditions of their

country, a new communist programme in conformity with the decisions of the Communist International. As a rule the programme of every party belonging to the Communist International must be ratified by the regular congress of the Communist International or by the Executive Committee. Should the programme of a party not be ratified by the Executive Committee of the Communist International, the party concerned has the right to appeal to the congress of the Communist International.

16. All the decrees of the congresses of the Communist International, as well as the decrees of its Executive Committee, are binding on all parties belonging to the Communist International. The Communist International, working in conditions of acute civil war, must be far more centralised in its structure than was the Second International. Consideration must of course be given by the Communist International and its Executive Committee in all their activities to the varying conditions in which the individual parties have to fight and work, and they must take decisions of general validity only when such decisions are possible.

17. In this connexion, all parties which wish to join the Communist International must change their names. Every party which wishes to join the Communist International must be called: *Communist party* of such and such a country (section of the Third Communist International). This question of name is not merely a formal matter, but essentially a political question of great importance. The Communist International has called for a decisive struggle against the entire bourgeois world and against all yellow social-democratic parties. The difference between the communist parties and the old official 'social-democratic' or 'socialist' parties, which have betrayed the banner of the working class, must be brought home to every ordinary worker.

18. All leading party press organs in all countries are obliged to publish all important official documents of the Executive Committee of the Communist International.

19. All parties belonging to the Communist International and those which have applied for admission, are obliged to convene an extraordinary congress as soon as possible, and in any case not later than four months after the second congress of the Communist International, to examine all these conditions of admission. In this connexion Central Committees must see that the decisions of

the second congress of the Communist International are made known to all local organisations.

20. Those parties which now wish to join the Third International but which have not radically changed their former tactics, must see to it that, before entering the Communist International, not less than two-thirds of the members of their CC and of all their leading central bodies consist of comrades who publicly and unambiguously advocated the entry of their party into the Third International before its second congress. Exceptions can be made with the consent of the Executive Committee of the Third International. The Executive Committee of the Communist International also has the right to make exceptions in the case of representatives of the 'centre' mentioned in paragraph 7.

21. *Those members of the party who reject in principle the conditions and theses put forward by the Communist International are to be expelled from the party.*

This also applies to delegates to extraordinary congresses.

6 August 1920

7 The Economic and Social Revolution

Transforming a capitalist into a socialist economy can never be a simple task. Lenin and the Bolsheviks were the first to attempt it. There were no blueprints as Marx had not devoted much time to thinking about a future socialist economic structure. Given the fact that the Bolsheviks disagreed among themselves as to the form the new soviet economy was to take, Lenin counselled caution and was willing to allow industry to continue functioning, more or less, along the old lines provided management was under soviet supervision. Radicals, such as Bukharin and Preobrazhensky, wanted nationalisation on a massive scale. Workers had their own ideas and since many of them did not wish to follow the Bolsheviks, there was bound to be dissent.

Two phases can be discerned. The first covers the period up to the summer of 1918. The policies of this initial stage have been labelled as state capitalism when the state aimed at controlling industry and trade rather than implementing outright nationalisation. The second phase begins with the outbreak of the civil war in the summer of 1918 and extends to March 1921. This is the time of war communism. It was characterised by extensive nationalisation, the temporary abolition of money as a measure of value, equalisation of earnings and the direction of labour. It was a period of war, economic chaos, hunger and enormous hardship. For a period the Bolsheviks only controlled the central area of Russia and were thus faced with a desperate shortage of foodstuffs.

The Supreme Council of the National Economy was set up and given the task of organising the national economy and state finances (7/1). Banks and large scale industry were taken over and workers' control legalised (7/2 and 7/3).

War communism, which, according to Lenin, was forced on

the government as a temporary measure due to the demands of war was abandoned as soon as the war was over. By then, however, the economy had almost collapsed (7/18).

Many workers were at odds with the Bolsheviks during war communism but the major opponents of the régime were the peasants. To gain peasant support, Lenin adopted an SR land policy and legalised the peasant seizures of private land on November 8 (7/10a). Later land was socialised (7/10b). The onset of the civil war compounded the difficulties of the government. To secure food supplies for the cities, it organised committees of the poor (7/11a) and when these proved ineffectual set up food requisition detachments, containing armed workers (7/11b). Galloping inflation, a rapidly depreciating currency shortage of investment goods, forced requisitions, all contributed to the peasant sowing less. Famine reared its head. The government were in such desperate straits that Lenin decided on concessions to the peasants in March 1921. A tax in kind was to replace forced requisitions. Later a money tax was introduced. Concessions to the peasants was accompanied by concessions to small producers and private traders. The New Economic Policy helped to put Soviet Russia back on her feet.

By 1921 the old social order was no more. The depredations of the civil war period, emigration, the violence of the Cheka, the defeat of the Whites and Allied intervention resulted in the decimation of the bourgeois opponents of the régime. NEP was to see a resurgence of the entrepreneur and private trade but the 1920s were an Indian summer before the command economy was constructed at the end of the decade.

7/1   ESTABLISHMENT OF THE SUPREME COUNCIL OF THE NATIONAL ECONOMY*

14 December 1917

1. The Supreme Council of the National Economy is established and attached to the Soviet of People's Commissars.

2. The task of the Supreme Council of the National Economy is the organisation of the national economy and state finances.

* From *Resheniya Partii i Pravitelstva po Khozyaistvennym Voprosam* (Moscow 1967), Vol. 1, pp. 27–8.

As a result the Supreme Council of the National Economy will prepare general norms and plans for the regulation of the economic life of the country and co-ordinate and unify the activities of the local and central regulating organs (committees on fuel, metals, transport, food supply committee and others) that are attached to the People's Commissariats (trade and industry, food, agriculture, finance, army and navy, etc.), the All-Russian Soviet of Workers' Control, the factory committees, and the trade unions.

3. The Supreme Council of the National Economy has the power to confiscate, requisition, sequester, and amalgamate various branches of industry, commerce, and other enterprises in the field of production, distribution and state finance.

4. The Supreme Council of the National Economy is to take charge of all existing institutions for the regulation of economic life and has the right to reorganise them.

5. The Supreme Council of the National Economy is to be composed of representatives of (a) the All-Russian Soviet of Workers' Control as constituted by the decree of 27 November 1917 (b) representatives of the Commissariats and (c) experts without a vote.

6. The Supreme Council of the National Economy is divided into sections and departments (fuel, metal, demobilisation, finance, etc.). The number of the sections and departments and their respective functions are to be determined at a general meeting of the Supreme Council of the National Economy.

7. The different departments of the Supreme Council of the National Economy regulate the specific branches of the national economy and prepare measures for the respective people's commissariats.

8. The Supreme Council of the National Economy shall appoint from its own members a bureau of fifteen persons to co-ordinate the work of the different sections and departments and to solve the problems that need immediate attention.

9. All draft laws and important proposals affecting the economic life of the country as a whole are to be set before the Council of People's Commissars via the Supreme Council of the National Economy.

10. The Supreme Council of the National Economy co-ordinates and directs the work of the local economic departments

of the Soviets of Workers', Soldiers' and Peasants' Deputies, including the local organs of Workers' Control, as well as local agencies of the Commissariat of Labour, Trade and Industry, Food, etc.

If the local agencies referred to above do not yet exist, the Supreme Council of the National Economy shall organise its own. All the decisions of the Supreme Council of the National Economy are binding on the economic departments of the local soviets as agents of the Supreme Council of the National Economy.

> Chairman of the Central Executive
> Committee
> Ya. SVERDLOV
>
> Chairman of the Council of People's
> Commissars
> V. ULYANOV (LENIN)

7/2   NATIONALISATION OF THE BANKS*

27 December 1917

In the interests of a proper organisation of the national economy, a decisive eradication of banking speculation and a complete emancipation of workers, peasants and the whole toiling population from exploitation by bank capital, and in order to found a single unified State Bank for the Russian Republic which shall serve the interests of the people and the poorest classes, the Central Executive Committee decrees that:

1. Banking is declared a state monopoly.
2. All existing private joint-stock banks and banking houses are merged with the State Bank.
3. Assets and liabilities of liquidated banks will be assumed by the State Bank.
4. The manner of the amalgamation of private banks with the State Bank will be determined by a special decree.
5. The temporary management of private banks is entrusted to the Council of the State Bank.
6. The interests of small depositors will be fully protected.

* From ibid., p. 28.

7/3 WORKERS' CONTROL*

27 November 1917

1. In order to provide planned regulation of the national economy, workers' control over the manufacture, purchase, sale and storage of produce and raw materials and over the financial activity of enterprise is introduced in all industrial, commercial, banking, agricultural, co-operative and other enterprises, which employ hired labour or give work to be done at home.

2. Workers' control is exercised by all the workers of the given enterprise through their elected bodies, such as factory committees, shop stewards' councils, etc., whose members include representatives of the office employees and the technical personnel.

3. In every city, *guberniya* and industrial district a local workers' control council is set up which, being an agency of the Soviet of Workers', Soldiers' and Peasants' Deputies, is composed of representatives of trade unions, factory and office workers' committees, and workers' co-operatives.

4. Pending the convocation of the congress of workers' control councils, an All-Russia Workers' Control Council is instituted in Petrograd, with the following representation: five members from the All-Russia Central Executive Committee of the Soviet of Workers' and Soldiers' Deputies; five from the All-Russia Central Executive Committee of Peasants' Deputies; five from the All-Russia Council of Trade Unions; two from the All-Russia Workers' Co-operative Centre; five from the All-Russia Bureau of Factory Committees; five from the All-Russia Union of Engineers and Technicians; two from the All-Russia Union of Agronomists; one from every all-Russia union of workers having less than 100,000 members; two from every all-Russia union of workers having more than 100,000 members; two from the Petrograd Council of Trade Unions.

5. The supreme bodies of workers' control establish inspection commissions of specialists (technicians, bookkeepers, etc.) which are dispatched, either on the initiative of these bodies or at the insistence of lower workers' control bodies, to inspect the financial and technical activities of an enterprise.

* From Akhapkin, pp. 36–8.

6. The workers' control bodies have the right to supervise production, establish output quotas and take measures to ascertain production costs.

7. The workers' control bodies have the right of access to the entire business correspondence of an enterprise, concealment of the same by the owners is punishable by a court of law. Commercial secrecy is abolished. The owners are obliged to present to workers' control bodies all books and accounts for both the current and previous fiscal years.

8. Decisions of workers' control bodies are binding upon the owners of enterprises and may be revoked only by higher workers' control bodies.

9. The entrepreneur or the enterprise management has three days within which to appeal to a higher workers' control body against decisions of lower bodies of workers' control.

10. At all enterprises the owners and the representatives of the wage and salary earners elected to exercise workers' control are declared answerable to the state for the maintenance of the strictest order and discipline and for the protection of property. Those guilty of concealment of materials, products and orders, improper keeping of accounts and other such malpractices are held criminally responsible.

11. The district (as in Paragraph 3) workers' control councils settle all disputes and conflicts between lower control bodies, handle owners' complaints, issue instructions conformably with the specificity of production, the local conditions and the decisions and instructions of the All-Russia Workers' Control Council, and supervise the activity of the lower control bodies.

12. The All-Russia Workers' Control Council works out general plans of workers' control, issues instructions and ordinances, regulates relationships between district workers' control councils, and serves as the highest instance for all matters pertaining to workers' control.

13. The All-Russia Workers' Control Council co-ordinates the activity of workers' control bodies with that of all other institutions concerned with the organization of the national economy.

Instructions on the relationships between the All-Russia Workers' Control Council and other institutions organizing and regulating the national economy will be issued separately.

14. All laws and circulars hampering the activity of the factory

and other committees and councils of wage and salary earners are repealed.

> In the name of the Government of the
> Russian Republic, Chairman of the
> Council of People's Commissars,
> VL. ULANOV (LENIN).

7/4 ANNULMENT OF STATE LOANS*

3 February 1918

1. All state loans negotiated by the governments of the Russian landlords and the Russian bourgeoisie, enumerated in a separately published list, are annulled as from December 14, 1917. The December coupons of these loans are not subject to payments.

2. All guarantees given by the aforesaid governments to various enterprises and institutions with regard to loans are likewise annulled.

3. All foreign loans are annulled unconditionally and without exception.

4. The short-term liabilities and series of the State Treasury remain in force. No interest is paid on them, their bonds remaining in circulation on a par with bank-notes.

5. Necessitous citizens holding annulled government bonds of internal loans to a sum not exceeding 10,000 rubles (at nominal value) are issued, in exchange, registered certificates of the new loan of the Russian Socialist Federative Soviet Republic to a sum not exceeding 10,000 rubles. The terms and conditions of the loan will be determined separately.

6. State savings bank deposits and interest on them are inviolable. All bonds of the annulled loans belonging to savings banks are replaced by the book debt of the Russian Socialist Federative Soviet Republic.

7. Co-operatives, local self-government bodies and other socially useful or democratic institutions holding bonds of the annulled loans are compensated in keeping with rules being worked out by the Supreme Economic Council jointly with representatives of these institutions, provided it has been proved

* From ibid., pp. 90–1.

that these bonds were purchased prior to the publication of this decree.

NOTE. It is within the discretion of the local agencies of the Supreme Economic Council to decide which local institutions fall within the category of socially useful or democratic.

8. General guidance in the annulment of state loans is entrusted to the Supreme Economic Council.

9. All practical matters related to the annulment of loans are entrusted to the State Bank, which is instructed to commence without delay the registration of all state loan bonds held by different owners, as well as other interest bearing securities, whether subject to annulment or not.

10. The Soviets of Workers', Soldiers' and Peasants' Deputies establish, by agreement with the local national economic councils, commissions to determine what citizens belong to the category of necessitous.

These commissions have the right completely to annul savings built up from unearned income, even if these savings do not exceed 5,000 rubles.

> Chairman of the Central Executive
> Committee, YA. SVERDLOV

7/5   TRADE UNIONISTS CRITICISE THE GOVERNMENT*

29 April 1918

The trade union movement is in danger. The embattled organisations of the working class cannot develop at a time when the revolution, in which the proletariat plays such an important role, is collapsing because of national economic disorganisation and defeat from without.

The productive forces of the country are declining every day. Industry has now become a state pensioner. Most factories and works exist on treasury grants. Labour productivity is alarmingly low, the production of goods is dropping, and the printing of money is increasing rapidly. All this makes the task of the trade unions very difficult. The economic organisations of the working

* From *Novaya Zhizn*, 30 April 1918.

class have to bear the burden of running industry and introducing order into the present economic chaos. However, the economic organisations of the working class are under attack from another quarter, the Soviet government.

The Soviet government claims that it alone represents the interests of the working class and that, therefore, all other organisations can exist only if they support, without complaint, the internal and external policies of the Council of People's Commissars. Since the October revolution we have seen endless examples of how big, small or even pigmy commissars have employed every kind of oppression, including bayonets, in their dealings with stubborn proletarian organisations.

Here are a few examples: the Soviet government closed the offices of the Union of Employees of Credit Institutions, arrested its board of directors several times, shut the co-operative shop which was used by the employees' families so as to force the starving employees to recognise the Soviet government formally. In Rybinsk the executive committee ordered an 'inspection' of the local councils of trade unions. New trade unions which support the Soviet government have been set up to counteract the opposition of certain trade unions. The government then decides which union really represents the interests of the working class.

Besides the persecution of implacable trade unions, other trade unions are being forced into submission and are being transformed into instruments of Soviet power. A scheme for putting the different branches of national industry under the management of trade unions is being worked out. This will lead to greater confusion and to the disintegration of the political life of the country.

7/6 MARTIAL LAW IN URAL COAL MINES*

Ekaterinburg, 17 February 1920

To: Moscow – for the C.C.

I consider it essential to proclaim martial law in the Ural coalmines. At the Chelyabinsk mines out of three thousand five hundred fewer than two thousand are turning up for work. The effort

* From Meijer, Vol. 2, p. 49.

they put into the work is negligible. At other mines the situation is about the same. On this question the opposition of local 'trade-unionists', and indeed of those at the centre too, must be overcome. When agitational and organisational preparations have been made, I shall apply to the Council of Defence for official approval.

Trotsky

7/7   USE OF THE ARMY FOR ECONOMIC PURPOSES*

30 May 1921

From: Chairman of the Council of People's Commissars, Kremlin, Moscow

To: Comrade Sklyansky

On the question of using the army for economic purposes.
This must not be forgotten for a minute.
We must conceive, prepare, and elaborate a systematic plan for such a use of the army and put it into effect precisely.
Two aspects of this question deserve special attention:

(1) The current and most urgent economic tasks (guarding and mining salt; fuel work, etc.);

(2) Work on the putting into effect of the general state economic plan, over a period of years. The electrification plan, which is calculated to take ten years (first phase of the work), will require 370 million working days. Per year per man in the army this comes to $(37 : 1.6) = 24$ working days, i.e. *two days a month*.

Of course the location of the army, transport to places of work, etc. will create a multitude of difficulties, but all the same the army can and must (with the aid of the Universal Military Training Organisation) provide enormous assistance to the goal of electrification. We must link the army to this great cause – ideologically, organisationally and economically – and must work systematically on it.

Please submit this question to the Military Revolutionary

* From ibid., Vol. 2, pp. 458, 460.

Council of the Republic after circulating this letter. I shall be glad to hear the views of the members of the Military Revolutionary Council of the Republic, or to have brief comments at least from them on this question.

Chairman of the Council of Labour
and Defence, V. ULYANOV (LENIN)

7/8 CONSUMERS' CO-OPERATIVES*

10 April 1918

1. Consumers' co-operatives shall serve all the population of a given district.

All commercial enterprises providing the population with consumer goods are subject to a tax of 5 per cent on their turnover. Members of consumers' societies are exempt from the tax, if they receive from their co-operatives 5 per cent of the sum expended by them, on the basis of annual accounts.

2. Persons, who are not well to do, who wish to become members of a consumers' society shall pay the minimum dues (not more than 50 kopecks). Membership shares for these persons can be made up by a deduction from the 5 per cent tax on purchased goods.

3. Every district or locality shall be served by a separate consumers' society and its branches.

4. No more than two consumers' co-operatives, general and workers', may operate within the confines of a given locality or territorial area.

5. Norms laid down by the central or local organs of soviet power and in particular by the organs of supply concerning the distribution of products, etc. are obligatory for private commercial enterprises as well as for co-operative organisations.

6. Representatives of unions of consumers' societies shall take part in the work of state, central and local organs of supply, regulating private, commercial enterprises and shall have the right to place them under state management.

* From *Resheniya Partii i Pravitelstva po Khozyaistvennym Voprosam* (Mosstvacow 1967), Vol. 1, pp. 48–50.

7. Owners and heads of commercial and industrial enterprises of a private, capitalist nature are not allowed to be members of the management of consumers' societies.

8. All co-operative organisations which provide for the whole community in their locality will be granted tax concessions, which will be specially determined.

9. Ways of putting into practice existing regulations are to be determined by co-operative organisations under the supervision of the state organs of supply.

10. Providing co-operatives with products must be linked to the introduction of coupons providing the working population, as well as wages, with evidence of their right to receive a fixed amount of consumers' goods from co-operatives.

11. The People's Commissariat of Supply, in agreement with the Supreme Council of the National Economy, decrees the form and the periods of the accounts of co-operative societies, as well as the forms of supervision and inspection of co-operatives and private commercial enterprises, in particular the paying by them of a 5 per cent turnover tax to the state treasury.

12. Consumers' societies shall render all round assistance to soviet power so that all capital in the form of money and the working means of private persons and institutions be deposited in the State Bank and shall implement this measure as it affects their capital and working means and immediately agree, jointly with the People's Commissariat of Finance, the necessary guarantees and benefits securing them full power over the means which belong to them.

13. The organs of soviet power involve the unions of consumers' societies, as the technical and economic apparatus develops, in purchasing, procuring, processing and producing products on the instructions of the state organs of supply and the Supreme Council of the National Economy, with their assistance and under their control.

Chairman of the Council of People's
Commissars, V. ULYANOV (LENIN)

7/9   TRADE CONCESSIONS*

5 April 1921

To: Ordzhonikidze

Your answer is incomplete and unclear, please find out from the Georgian Revolutionary Committee the following details:

(i) Has the Soviet Government of Georgia confirmed the Italians' concession for the Tkvarcheli mines, when and on what conditions?
Reply briefly by telegram and in more detail by letter.

(ii) About the Chiatury manganese mines – have the German owners been turned into lessees or concessionaries, when and on what conditions? It is extremely important that there should be the quickest possible decisions on these and similar questions, it is of enormous significance both for Georgia and for Russia, for concessions are absolutely essential, especially with Italy and Germany, as also is goods exchange on a large scale with these countries in return for oil and later with others too. Please inform me of the measures taken by the Georgian Revolutionary Committee.

Lenin

7/10   THE LAND

(a) THE LAND DECREE†

8 November 1917

(1) Landed proprietorship is abolished forthwith without any compensation.

(2) The landed estates, as also all crown, monastery, and church lands, with all their livestock, implements, buildings and everything pertaining thereto, shall be placed at the disposal of the *volost* land committees and the *uezd* Soviets of Peasants' Deputies pending the convocation of the Constituent Assembly.

* From Lenin, *Polnoe Sobranie Sochinenii*, Vol. 52 (Moscow 1965), pp. 126–7.
† From Akhapkin, pp. 23–5.

(3) All damage to confiscated property, which henceforth belongs to the whole people, is proclaimed a grave crime to be punished by the revolutionary courts. The *uezd* Soviets of Peasants' Deputies shall take all necessary measures to assure the observance of the strictest order during the confiscation of the landed estates, to determine the size of estates, and the particular estates subject to confiscation, to draw up exact inventories of all property confiscated and to protect in the strictest revolutionary way all agricultural enterprises transferred to the people, with all buildings, implements, livestock, stocks of produce, etc.

(4) The following peasant Mandate, compiled by the newspaper *Izvestiya Vserossiiskogo Soveta Krestyanskikh Deputatov* from 242 local peasant mandates and published in No. 88 of that paper (Petrograd, No. 88, August 19, 1917), shall serve everywhere to guide the implementation of the great land reforms until a final decision on the latter is taken by the Constituent Assembly.

ON LAND

'The land question in its full scope can be settled only by the popular Constituent Assembly.

'The most equitable settlement of the land question is to be as follows:

'(1) Private ownership of land shall be abolished for ever; land shall not be sold, purchased, leased, mortgaged, or otherwise alienated.

'All land, whether State, crown, monastery, church, factory, entailed, private, public, peasant, etc., shall be confiscated without compensation and become property of the whole people, and pass into the use of all those who cultivate it.

'Persons who suffer by this property revolution shall be deemed to be entitled to public support only for the period necessary for adaptation to the new conditions of life.

'(2) All mineral wealth – ore, oil, coal, salt, etc. and also all forests and waters of state importance, shall pass into the exclusive use of the State. All the small streams, lakes, woods, etc., shall pass into the use of the communes, to be administered by the local self-government bodies.

'(3) Lands on which high-level scientific farming is practised – orchards, plantations, seed plots, nurseries, hot-houses, etc. – shall not be divided up, but shall be converted into model farms, to be turned over for exclusive use to the state or to the communes, depending on the size and importance of such lands.

'Household land in towns and villages, with orchards and vegetable gardens, shall be reserved for the use of their present owners, the size of the holdings, and the size of tax levied for the use thereof, to be determined by law.

'(4) Stud farms, government and private pedigree stock and poultry farms, etc., shall be confiscated and become the property of the whole people, and pass into the exclusive use of the State or a commune, depending on the size and importance of such farms.

'The question of compensation shall be examined by the Constituent Assembly.

'(5) All livestock and farm implements of the confiscated estates shall pass into the exclusive use of the State or a commune, depending on their size and importance, and no compensation shall be paid for this.

'The farm implements of peasants with little land shall not be subject to confiscation.

'(6) The right to use the land shall be accorded to all citizens of the Russian State (without distinction of sex) desiring to cultivate it by their own labour, with the help of their families, or in partnership, but only as long as they are able to cultivate it. The employment of hired labour is not permitted.

'In the event of the temporary physical disability of any member of a village commune for a period of up to two years, the village commune shall be obliged to assist him for this period by collectively cultivating his land until he is again able to work.

'Peasants who, owing to old age or ill health, are permanently disabled and unable to cultivate the land personally, shall lose their right to the use of it but, in return, shall receive a pension from the State.

'(7) Land tenure shall be on an equality basis, i.e. the land shall be distributed among the working people in conformity with a labour standard or a subsistence standard, depending on local conditions.

'There shall be absolutely no restriction on the forms of land tenure – household, farm, communal, or co-operative, as shall be decided in each individual village and settlement.

'(8) All land, when alienated, shall become part of the national land fund. Its distribution among the peasants shall be in charge of the local and central self-government bodies, from democratically organized village and city communes, in which there are no distinctions of social rank, to central regional government bodies.

'The land fund shall be subject to periodical redistribution, depending on the growth of population and the increase in the productivity and the scientific level of farming.

'When the boundaries of allotments are altered, the original nucleus of the allotment shall be left intact.

'The land of the members who leave the commune shall revert to the land fund; preferential right to such land shall be given to the near relatives of the members who have left, or to persons designated by the latter.

'The cost of fertilizers and improvements put into the land, to the extent that they have not been fully used up to the time the allotment is returned to the land fund, shall be compensated.

(b) SOCIALISATION OF THE LAND*

Adopted by the Central Executive Committee

9 February 1918

Article 1. All private ownership of land, minerals, waters, forests, and natural resources within the boundaries of the Russian Federated Soviet Republic is abolished for ever.

Article 2. Henceforth, the land is handed over without compensation (open or secret) to the entire toiling population for their use.

Article 3. The right to use the land belongs to those who cultivate it with their own labour, except in cases specially stipulated in the present law.

Article 4. The right to use the land cannot be limited on account of sex, religion, nationality, or citizenship.

Article 5. Minerals, forests, waters, and natural resources, depending on their importance, are placed at the disposition of the *uezd*,

* From S. Pollard and C. Holmes, *The End of Old Europe 1914–9391* (London 1973), pp. 98–100.

guberniya, regional and federal soviets, under the control of the latter. The method of use and disposition of the minerals, forests, waters, and natural resources will be determined by a special law.

Article 6. All privately owned livestock and agricultural implements of estates that are worked by hired labour shall be handed over, depending on their importance, to the disposition of the land departments of the *uezd*, *guberniya*, regional and federal soviets without compensation.

Article 7. All buildings of estates referred to in Article 6, together with agricultural enterprises attached to them, shall be handed over, depending on their importance, to the *uezd*, *guberniya*, regional and federal soviets without compensation.

Article 8. Pending the promulgation of a general law on the insurance of citizens unable to work, all such persons who are completely deprived of a means of livelihood because of the present law on the alienation of lands and forests and also of livestock and so forth found on these pieces of property, can, upon certification of the local courts and land departments of the soviets, enjoy the right of receiving a pension (until death or the coming of age) equivalent to the existing soldiers' pension.

Article 9. The distribution of lands of agricultural value among the toilers shall be in the hands of the village, volost, *uezd*, *guberniya*, regional, main and federal land departments of soviets, depending on the importance of these lands.

Article 10. The reserve land fund in each republic shall be in the hands of the main land departments [of the republics] and the federal soviet.

Article 11. Besides effecting a just distribution of lands of agricultural value among the toiling agricultural population and effecting the most productive use of national resources, the land departments of the local and central soviet authority have the following tasks in the distribution of the land: (a) creating conditions favourable to the development of the productive forces of the country by increasing the productivity of the land, improving agricultural techniques, and finally, raising the level of agricultural knowledge in the toiling masses of the agricultural population; (b) creating a reserve fund of agricultural land; (c) developing agricultural enterprises such as horticulture, apiculture, market-gardening, stock raising, dairying, etc.; (d) hastening in certain regions the transition from a less productive to a more productive system of land cultivation through an even settling of toiling farmers in new places; (e) developing the collective farm in agriculture at the expense of individual homesteads, the former being more profitable in saving labour and materials, with a view to passing on to a socialist economy.

Article 12. The distribution of land between toilers should proceed on labour-equalizing bases, so that the consumption–labour norm, adapted in a given area to the historically established system of land tenure, should not exceed the labour capacity of the available work force of each individual household, but should, at the same time, provide the family of the farmer with the opportunity of a comfortable existence.

Article 13. The general and basic source of the right to use agricultural land is personal labour. In addition, in order to raise agricultural standards (through the organization of model farms or experimental and demonstration fields), the organs of the Soviet Government are permitted to secure certain portions of land from the reserve land fund (formerly belonging to monasteries, the State, the Imperial family, the Tsar, and *pomeshchiks*) and to work them with labour paid by the State. Such labour is subject to the general regulations of workers' control.

Article 14. All citizens engaged in agriculture are to be insured at the expense of the State against loss of life and incapacitating old age, sickness or injuries.

Article 15. All incapacitated farmers and members of their families who are unable to work are to be supported at the expense of the organs of the Soviet Government.

Article 16. Every toiler's farm is to be insured against fire, livestock epidemics, poor crops, drought, hail and other natural calamities through mutual soviet insurance.

Article 17. Surplus income derived from the natural fertility of the best pieces of land or from nearness to markets is to be turned over to the organs of the Soviet Government for the benefit of social needs.

Article 18. The organs of the Soviet Government have a monopoly of trade in agricultural machinery and seeds.
Article 19. The grain trade, both foreign and domestic, is to be a State monopoly.

7/11 GRAIN REQUISITION

(a) *Kombedy* SET UP*

11 June 1918

1. *Volost* and village committees of the rural poor, organised by the local Soviets of Workers' and Peasants' Deputies with the participation of the food organs, which is absolutely essential, and under the general control of the People's Commissariat of Food and the Central Executive Committee, shall be set up everywhere. The present decree must be put into effect immediately by all Soviets of Workers' and Peasants' Deputies. *Guberniya* and *uezd* Soviets of Workers' and Peasants' Deputies must play an active role in the organisation of committes of the poor . . .

2. Both local and newly arrived inhabitants of villages and rural areas may elect and be elected to *volost* and village committees of the poor, without any restriction whatsoever, with the exception of notorious *kulaks*, rich people and owners who have a surplus of grain or other food products, and owners of commercial and industrial enterprises, employing farm labourers or hired labour, etc.

Note: Peasants employing hired labour on farms not exceeding the consumption norm may elect and be elected to committees of the poor.

3. *Volost* and village committees of the poor are responsible for the following:

(a) The distribution of grain, goods of prime necessity and agricultural implements.
(b) Assisting local food organs to extract grain surpluses from *kulaks* and rich people.

4. *Volost* and village committees of the poor shall decide the

* From *Resheniya Partii i Pravitelstva po Khozyaistvennym Voprosam* (Moscow 1967), Vol. 1, pp. 91–4.

persons whom they are to provide with grain, goods of prime necessity and agricultural implements . . .

7. The distribution of grain, goods of prime necessity and agricultural implements shall be according to norms worked out by *guberniya* food organs, in strict accordance with the special supply plans of the People's Commissariat of Food and norms decreed by *guberniya* food organs.

Note: Depending on the degree of need for grain in consuming districts and the success in extracting grain from the *kulaks* and rich people, the size of the grain share handed over to the poor may vary during the various periods of distribution by the *guberniya* food organs.

8. Temporarily and until a special instruction is issued by the People's Commissariat of Food, the following rules for the distribution of grain shall apply:

(a) The distribution of grain to the rural poor according to the norms decreed shall be free and at the expense of the state until 15 July of this year. The grain shall come from the surpluses, on the instructions of the Soviets of Workers' and Peasants' Deputies and the corresponding food organisations, taken exclusively from *kulaks* and rich people and added to state grain reserves.

(b) The distribution of grain to the rural poor according to the norms decreed shall be paid for at a price 50 per cent less than the fixed price after 15 July and not later than 15 August of this year. The grain shall come from the surpluses extracted from the *kulaks* and rich people.

(c) The distribution of grain to the rural poor according to the norms decreed shall be paid for at a price 20 per cent less than the fixed price, during the second half of August. The grain shall come from the surpluses extracted from *kulaks* . . .

10. Complex agricultural implements are to be handed out according to the instructions of the *volost* committees of the poor so as to organise the social working of the fields and the bringing in of the harvest of the rural poor; no charge will be made for the use of such machinery in areas where the *volost* and village committees of the poor actively aid food organs to extract surpluses from *kuluks* and rich people.

11. The money, necessary to implement this decree by the

People's Commissariat of Food, will be provided by the Council of
People's Commissars.

Chairman of the Central Executive Committee
Ya SVERDLOV

Chairman of the Council of People's Commissars
V. ULYANOV (LENIN)

(b) HARVESTING AND GRAIN REQUISITION DETACHMENTS*

4 August 1918

1. All *guberniya* and *uezd* Soviets of Workers' and Peasants'
Deputies, all committees of the poor, all trade union organisations
of workers, together with the local organs of the People's Commissariats of Food and Agriculture are to form immediately
harvesting and grain requisition detachments. Detachments of
workers and peasants from starving *guberniyas*, sent to requisition
grain, are to help in bringing in the new harvest. Form immediately
new detachments from among local peasants and workers to carry
out these tasks.

2. The tasks of the above-mentioned detachments are:

(a) Harvest winter grain in former landlord owned estates;
(b) Harvest grain in front line areas;
(c) Harvest grain on the land of notorious *kulaks* and rich people;
(d) Help in harvesting grain in good time everywhere and in the
    transfer of all surpluses to state storehouses.

3. All grain, collected by harvesting and grain requisition
detachments, is to be distributed on the following basis: firstly,
of course, the necessary amount of grain to satisfy the need for
food of the poorest strata of the local population is to be distributed. This part of the grain collected is not to be removed but
to remain at the local level. All other grain is to be immediately
and unconditionally delivered to grain collection centres. The distribution of this grain is to be carried out by the *guberniya* food
committees on the instructions of the People's Commissariat of
Food.

4. Members of harvesting and food requisition detachments,
if they are not being rewarded according to previously published

* From *Dekrety Sovetskoi Vlasti* (Moscow 1964), Vol. 3, pp. 168–9.

decrees (e.g. the decree on the maintenance of volunteer workers, going to the front and in food detachments, their localities and average earnings) are to be rewarded, firstly, by an allowance *in natura*; secondly, by payment in cash according to local conditions and; thirdly, by special bonuses for successful and rapid fulfilment of harvesting work and the transfer of grain to storage centres. The extent of rewards and bonuses are to be determined by *guberniya* food committees on the basis of instructions from the Commissariat of Food.

Chairman of the Council of People's Commissars
V. ULYANOV (LENIN)

People's Commissar of Food
TSYURUPA

(c) INSTRUCTIONS FOR REQUISITIONING GRAIN*

20 August 1918

1. Every food requisition detachment is to consist of not less than 75 men and two or three machine guns.

2. A commander is to head each detachment. He is to be appointed by the chief commissar responsible for the organisation of food armies and a political commissar appointed by the Comsariat of Food.

The commander is to control purely military and economic activities. The political commissar's duties are (a) to organise local committees of the rural poor (b) to ensure that the detachment carries out its duties and is full of revolutionary enthusiasm and discipline.

3. *Guberniya* and *uezd* military commanders are to be in charge of all food requisition detachments operating in a given *guberniya* or *uezd*.

4. Plans for grain requisition in a *uezd* are to be drawn up by the head of the requisition department appointed by the *guberniya* food committee.

5. Food requisition detachments are to be subject only to the orders of their commanders...

7. The food requisition detachments shall be deployed in such

* From *Sistematicheskii Sbornik Dekretov i Rasporyazhenii Pravitelstva po Prodovolstvennomu Delu* (Nizhny Novgorod 1919), Vol. 1, pp. 106–7.

a manner as to allow two or three detachments to link up quickly. Continuous cavalry communication shall be maintained between the various food requisition detachments.

People's Commissar of Food
A. TSYURUPA

7/12   LOCAL DIFFICULTIES

(a) CONCEALMENT OF GRAIN*

Every day the post brings information concerning the concealment of grain and other foodstuffs, and the difficulties encountered by the registration commissions in their work in the villages. All this shows the want of consciousness among the masses, who do not realise what chaos such tactics introduce into the general life of the country.

No one can eat more than the human organism can absorb; the ration – and that not at all a 'famine' one – is fixed. Everyone is provided for. And yet there is concealment, concealment everywhere, in the hopes of selling grain to town speculators at fabulous prices.

How much is being concealed, and what fortunes are being made by profiteers, may be seen from the following example. The Goretsky Extraordinary Commission has fined Irina Ivashkevich, a citizen of Lapinsky village, for burying 25,000 rubles' worth of grain in a hole in her backyard.

Citizeness Irina Ivashkevich has much money, but little understanding of what she is doing.

(b) DIFFICUTIES IN THE DISTRIBUTION OF LAND†

The acute food crisis in the towns has occasioned a great influx into the villages of peasants who have long since given up agriculture and followed some other trade. Formerly these peasants either rented their land to others or simply abandoned it. Now they have reappeared in the villages and are asserting their rights to this

* From *Derevenskaya Kommuna*, October 1919.
† From ibid., 28 December 1919.

land, thereby creating a great deal of misunderstanding and discontent. The local Soviets are taking part in all these quarrels,
being still influenced by old customs, and are allowing the land to
change hands freely. This should not take place. All peasant new-
comers to the village should remember that according to the law
of the socialisation of land they can only receive plots available
from the land fund if such exist, but they have no right to any
claim on their former plots.

7/13   LENIN AND VLADIMIROV ON THE FOOD
       SITUATION

(a)*

1 February 1920

From: The Chairman of the Council of Workers' and Peasants'
Defence of the R.S.F.S.R., Kremlin, Moscow

To: Moscow – Comrade Trotsky

The situation concerning railway transport is really catastrophic.
Grain supplies are no longer getting through. Extraordinary
emergency measures are required to save the situation. For a period
of two months (February–March) measures of the following kind
must be adopted (as well as conceiving other measures too of a
comparable kind):

1. The individual bread ration *is to be reduced* for those not
    engaged on transport work, and *increased* for those engaged
    on it.
    Thousands more may perish but the country will be saved.
2. Three-quarters of the senior party workers from all depart-
    ments, except the Commissariats of Supply and of Military
    Affairs, are to be transferred to railway transport and mainten-
    ance work for these two months.
    The work of the other Commissariats is to stop (or to be
    reduced by 90 per cent) during these two months.
3. Within a 30–50 verst wide stretch along each of the railway
    lines martial law is to be introduced so as to conscript labour
    for clearing the tracks; and three-quarters of the senior party

* From Meijer, Vol. 2, p. 22.

workers from the *volost* and *uezd* executive committees of the corresponding regions are to be transferred to the *volosts* in this area.

> Chairman of the Council of Defence
> V. ULYANOV (LENIN)

(b)*

2 March 1921

To: Moscow, The Kremlin – Tsyurupa

Conditions of work are becoming such as to wreck all plans. After the complete destruction of the whole food supply system in the Aleksandrovsk and Berdyansk *uezds*, which was accompanied by mass murders of food supply workers, Makhno is destroying the system in the Kherson *uezd*. We have just received information that Makhno's band has got across the Dnepr from the Dneprovsk *uezd* and killed the district supply commissar and forty-two supply workers in the Bolshe–Aleksandrovsk district food supply committee. Work on loading grain and delivering it to stations on the Merefa–Kherson line has been slowed down. I should add that there is over a million puds on the Merefa–Kherson line, and grain was being urgently loaded for the Donets Basin. Its further progress threatens to lead to even greater complications. In such conditions ensuring supplies for the Donets Basin and the Red Army becomes an almost insoluble problem.

> The People's Commissar for Food Supply
> Vladimirov.

(c)†

29 March 1921

To: Ordzhonikidze

We have had a desperate telegram from Narimanov, Buniatzade and Serebrovsky correctly pointing out that it is completely impossible to return the Eleventh Army to starving and plundered Azerbaidzhan. Take energetic measures to leave this army in Georgia and at all costs speed up the import of grain from abroad

* From ibid., Vol. 2, pp. 386, 388.
† From ibid., Vol. 2, p. 436.

in return for concessions in Georgia – manganese and so forth. Answer quickly.

On the instructions of the Politburo, Lenin.

7/14   BREAD PRICES IN PETROGRAD*

Here are the prices on the Petrograd market last week. Bread 450 rubles per lb.; flour 500–700 rubles per lb.; meat 550–660 rubles per lb.; pork 720 rubles per lb.; salt 300 rubles per lb.; butter 2,600–3,200 rubles; groats 500–700 rubles per lb.; makhorka 5,000–6,000 rubles per lb.; matches from 75–100 rubles per box; cigarettes 11–13 rubles each; yellow soap 700–800 rubles per lb. A single fare on a tram costs 6 rubles. In spite of these prices salaries are comparatively low. A woman typist get 3,200 rubles per month, without food. A nurse receives 2,600 rubles per month and a soldier's one day ration.

7/15   TOMSKY ON LABOUR SHORTAGE†

In his report Tomsky, President of the Central Trade Union Council, also dwelt upon the labour crisis:

Where have the working forces of the industrial proletariat vanished to? Whereas in capitalist countries the shortage of labour is a consequence of intensified industrial production, in Russia we are faced with conditions hitherto unknown under the capitalist social order. Only part of our industry is working, yet, nevertheless, in all towns and industrial centres we are faced with a dearth of labour. The hundreds of skilled work-men needed to assure a minimum production have dispersed and gone either to the villages, to labour communes, to Soviet farms, or to societies of producers. Many of them are to be found in the army. But, to our great regret and disgrace, the proletariat is also engaged in profiteering and barter. This fact is to be observed everywhere, and can neither be overlooked nor denied.

* From *Rossiya*, 4 March 1920.
† From *Novaya Russkaya Zhizn*, 28 March 1920.

7/16 STALIN ON NEP*
A YEAR OF GREAT CHANGE
On the Occasion of the 12th Anniversary of the October Revolution

The past year was a year of great *change* on all fronts of socialist construction. This change was marked by and continues to be marked by the decisive offensive of socialism against capitalist elements in town and countryside. The characteristic feature of this offensive is that it has already brought us a number of successes in the basic sectors of the socialist reconstruction of our economy.

It follows from this that the party has succeeded in using our withdrawal during the first stages of the New Economic Policy expediently so as to organise a *change* and to launch a *successful offensive* against capitalist elements in its subsequent stages.

Lenin said when NEP was introduced:

We are now retreating, going back as it were, but we are doing this so as to retreat first and then run and leap forward more vigorously. We retreated on this one condition alone when we introduced our New Economic Policy . . . so as to begin a most determined offensive after the retreat. (Lenin, Vol. 27 pp. 361, 162.)

7/17 THE NEW CALENDAR†

6 February 1918

In order to establish the system of time-reckoning used by almost all cultured nations, the Council of People's Commissars resolves to introduce into civil life, after the expiry of the month of January of this year, a new calendar. In virtue of this:

(1) The first day after January 31, this year, shall be reckoned, not as February 1, but as February 14; the second day, as 15, and so on.

* From I. V. Stalin, *Sochineniya* (Moscow 1953), Vol. 12, p. 118.
† From Akhapkin, pp. 93–4.

(2) The terms of all obligations, both contractual and under law, that would have fallen due, under the previous calendar, between February 1 and 14 of this year, shall be regarded as due between February 14 and 27, by adding 13 days to every respective date.

(3) The terms of all obligations that would have fallen due, under the previous calendar, between February 14 and July 1, this year, shall be regarded as due, given the agreement of both sides, 13 days later.

(4) The terms of all obligations that would have fallen due, under the previous calendar, beginning with July 1, this year, shall be regarded as due on the same dates also under the new calendar.

(5) In reckoning, on the first day after February 14 under the new calendar, the date of payment of interest on all state and private loans, dividend warrants, bank deposits and current accounts, 13 days shall be dropped from the time that has elapsed since the last payment of interest.

(6) Persons whose wages or salaries are paid at the end of every month shall receive, on February 28 of this year, their monthly pay minus thirteen thirtieths of it.

(7) Persons whose wages or salaries are paid on the 15th and 30th of every month shall receive no pay on February 15 but shall receive, on February 20 of this year, their monthly pay minus thirteen thirtieths of it.

(8) Persons whose wages or salaries are paid on the 20th of every month shall receive, on February 20 of this year, their monthly pay minus thirteen thirtieths of it.

(9) After January 31 of this year, the dates of payment of pensions and special allowances fixed in the relevant rules shall be reckoned as coming 13 days later.

(10) Until July 1 of this year, the date according to the heretofore effective calendar shall be indicated in brackets after the date according to the new calendar.

Chairman of the Council of People's Commissars,
V. ULYANOV (LENIN)

7/18   THE ECONOMY IN 1913 AND IN 1921*

	1913	1921
Gross output of all industry (index)	100	31
Large-scale industry (index)	100	21
Coal (million tons)	29	9
Oil (million tons)	9.2	3.8
Electricity (milliard Kwhs)	2039	520
Pig iron (million tons)	4.2	0.1
Steel (million tons)	4.3	0.2
Bricks (millions)	2.1	0.01
Sugar (million tons)	1.3	0.05
Railway tonnage carried (millions)	132.4	39.4
Agricultural production (index)	100	60
Imports ('1913' rubles)	1374	208
Exports ('1913' rubles)	1520	20

* From A. Nove, *An Economic History of the U.S.S.R.* (London 1969), p. 68.

8 Culture

The years immediately following the October revolution were marked by great innovations in the cultural field. Artists of the stature of Malevich, Gabo, Chagall, Kandinsky and El Lissitzky were all active in Soviet Russia. In the theatre Meyerhold, in literature Mayakovsky, in the cinema, Vertov, to name only a few, were in full flow in their various spheres. Some wanted to dismiss the cultural achievements of the pre-1917 era since they were almost entirely the work of bourgeois writers and artists. The Proletarian Culture movement sought to promote culture among the workers and encourage them to express themselves in art, drama, poetry, literature, etc. The Proletcult theatre was very significant. Propaganda, promoting the new order, was put on wheels. An agit-train travelled around providing workers, peasants and soldiers with new sensations. The advent of a Soviet Russia meant the beginning of a new era and how better to drive this home than to provide **entertainment based on the marvels of the machine age.**

8/1 MALEVICH

(a) ON NEW SYSTEMS IN ART*

> *I follow*
> *u-el-el-ul-el-te-ka*
> *my new path.*

Let rejection of the old world of art be traced on the palms of your hands.

Standing on the economic Suprematist surface of the square as the absolute expression of modernity, I leave it to serve as the basis for the economic extension of life's action.

* From K. S. Malevich, *Essays on Art 1915–1933* (London 1969), Vol. 1, pp. 83–5.

I declare Economy to be the new fifth dimension which evaluates and defines the Modernity of the Arts and Creative Works. All the creative systems of engineering, machinery and construction come under its control, as do those of the arts of painting, music and poetry, for they are systems of expressing that inner movement which is an illusion in the tangible world.

K. MALEVICH.

No *utilitarian* form is created without the help of aesthetic action, which sees everything except the utilitarian as pictorial. The aesthetic, the pictorial, takes part in the construction of the whole world. In foliage, every leaf is ornamentally engraved and set in place, and a whole branch is put together. A flower is drawn with the accuracy of compasses and coloured. We are ecstatic about it, and nature, and the whole starry heaven. We are enraptured because nature forms the interaction of harmony and discord, which we have named aesthetics. Aesthetics exist in the world, therefore we are one with it. The creative act is in notion, and from its achievements and their contradictions harmony emerges in the form of the aesthetic. Thus one can assume that the creation of signs is inseparably linked with the co-ordination of several elements, which when combined give rise to the unity of a form with its scattered units. Both in nature and in man's creation there exists the urge to embellish the created form whether it is utilitarian or not, to give it an artistic appearance and lend it beauty, even though the latter is relative, for the new object contains a new beauty. This tendency arises from the aesthetic movement, which is set alight by the emergence of creative thought and the new form. Thus in nature leaves may be ornamentally shaped and flowers formed, birds receive their decoration and the whole world its colours; each stone and metal burns with colour, all the different elements merge in a general community and form a picture. It would seem that this aesthetic unity should embrace everything and that all our endeavours at creation should lead towards this unity, for it has the highest aim, that of beauty to which everything aspires and which all men revere. But another question arises, the economic question which is probably the primary source of all activity, which affirms that every activity is the result of bodily energy, but that all bodies attempt to preserve their energy;

therefore all my actions must be the result of economic method. This is the way in which nature, and bodies, and the whole of man's creation move. For a long time human creative thought has been trying to escape from weaving confused, if beautiful, patterns and designs to the simple *economic expression* of the action of energy, so that all forms of this action are composed not of *aesthetic*, but of *economic necessity*.

The *latest* movements in art – *Cubism, Futurism, Suprematism* – are based on this action.

Aesthetic action is not static, but in perpetual motion, and takes part in the construction of new forms.

We exclaim: 'Nature is beautiful!' – but why is she beautiful? Would a flower be beautiful if there were no other form beside it, if there were no diversity of structure in the flower itself? No, it would not be. Beauty excites us because nature consists of various signs. We say: 'A wonderful landscape', we say it because we can see the horizon in the far distance, wrapped in blue, beyond which there are mountains, woods and further distances. We say it because there is a river running among the meadows below and boats and vessels are sailing on it; because there are people clothed in bright colours who are walking in the meadow; because we are standing on the mountain and looking at the horizons and depths and the visible picture excites the action of the aesthetic and we exclaim: 'How fine, how beautiful.'

But what does the painter see in the landscape described above? He sees the painterly masses in motion and at rest; he sees the composition of nature, the unity of various painterly forms, he sees the symmetry and harmony of contradictory elements in the unity of nature's picture. He stands and exults in the flow of forces and their harmony. Thus nature formed her landscape, her great comprehensive picture, whose technical pattern is contradictory to human form. She embraces fields, mountains, rivers and seas, and in man's likeness she reduces the link between animals and insects to dust, making a gradation of forms on her creative surface. Just such a creative surface confronts the *artist–creator* – on canvas *on which he builds the world of his intuitions* and where he regulates the flowing forces of colour and painterly energy in various forms, lines, and surfaces. He also creates forms, and separate elements of their symbols, and achieves a contradiction on the surface of his picture. Thus the creation of contrasts between forms leads to a single correspondence in the body of the construction; without which creation would be inconceivable.

15 July 1919
NEMCHINOVKA

(b) REVOLUTION 'A' IN ART*

1. A fifth measurement is set up. (Economy.)
2. All creative discoveries, their building, construction and system should be developed on the basis of the fifth measurement.
3. All discoveries developing the movements of elements in painting, colour, music, poetry and constructions (sculpture) are evaluated from the viewpoint of the fifth measurement.
4. The perfection and contemporaneity of discoveries (works of art) is assessed by the fifth measurement.
5. Aesthetic control is rejected as being a reactionary measure.
6. To link all the arts – painting, colour, music, constructions – as 'Technical creativity'.
7. To reject the spiritual power of content as belonging to the earthly world of flesh and bone.
8. To temporarily recognise dynamism as the power that brings form into action.
9. To recognise light as well as colour of metallic origin, and the discovery of beams as an equivalent of the economic development of the town.
10. To relate the sun as a bonfire of illumination to the system of our earth of flesh and bone.
11. To free time from the hands of the state and to turn it to the benefit of inventors.
12. To recognise labour to be a left-over from the old world of violence, since the contemporary world stands on creation.
13. To recognise in every man the ability to make discoveries, and to announce that unlimited amounts of material will be found, both in and above the earth, to bring them to fruition.

* From ibid., pp. 117–18.

14. To recognise life as an auxiliary path to what for us is the most important thing: movement.
15. All forms of heavenly bliss are rejected, as are those on this earth of kingdoms, and as are also all their representations by art workers: they are a lie concealing reality.
16. To commit to social care all the workers of academic arts, as invalids and the *arrière-garde* of the economic movement.
17. Cubism and Futurism are defined as the economic perfection of 1910 and their constructions and systems must be defined as the classicism of the first decade of the century.
18. To convoke an economic council (of the fifth measurement) to liquidate all the arts of the old world.

K. MALEVICH.
VITEBSK, 15 NOVEMBER, 1919.

(c) THE SUPREMATIST MIRROR*

Amongst all the changing phenomena the essence of nature is invariable.

A.1

| The World as human distinctions | God The Soul The Spirit Life Religion Technology Art Science The Intellect Weltanschauung Labour Movement Space Time | = O |

1. Science and art have no boundaries because what is comprehended infinitely is innumerable and infinity and innumerability are equal to nothing.
2. If the world's creations are God's paths and if 'His ways are inscrutable', then both He and His paths are equal to nothing.
3. If the world is the creation of science, knowledge and labour, and if their creation is infinite then it is equal to nothing.

* From ibid., pp. 224–5.

4. If religion has comprehended God, it has comprehended nothing.

5. If science has comprehended nature, it has comprehended nothing.

6. If art has comprehended harmony, rhythm and beauty, it has comprehended nothing.

7. If anyone has comprehended the absolute he has comprehended nothing.

8. There is no existence either within or outside me; nothing can change anything, since nothing exists that could change itself or be changed.

A.2

The essence of distinctions.

The world as non-objectivity.

8/2 EL LISSITZKY

(a) PROUNS*

Not world visions, BUT – world reality, 1920

Proun is the name we gave to the stage on the road to neoplasticism, which is rising on the ground fertilized by the dead bodies of pictures and their painters. The picture crashed together with the church and its god, whom it served as a proclamation; with the palace and its king, whom it served as a throne; with the sofa and its philistine, whose icon of happiness it was. And as the picture fell, so did its painter. The expressionistic turning of the clear world of things upside down by the artists of 'imitative art' will not save the picture nor the painter: it remains an occupation for caricaturists. Nor will 'pure painting' with its lack of subject matter preserve the pre-eminence of the picture, but here at least the artist is beginning his own transformation. The artist is turning from an imitator into a constructor of the new world of objects. This world will not be built in competition with technology. The paths of art and science have not yet crossed.

Proun is the creation of form (control of space) by means of the economic construction of material to which a new value is assigned.

* From El Lissitzky, *Life Letters Texts* (London 1968), p. 343.

The path of the Proun does not run through the narrow maze of scattered individual scientific systems. These are all centralized by the constructor in the knowledge gained from his experiments.

Creation of form outside of space $= 0$
Creation of form outside of material $= 0$

$$\frac{\text{Creation of form}}{\text{Material}} = \frac{\text{Mass}}{\text{Force}}$$

Material receives form through construction. Modern demand and economy of means require each other.

We inspected the first stages of the two-dimensional space of our structure, and found it to be as firm and resistant as the earth itself. We are building here in the same way as in three-dimensional space and therefore the first need here, too, is to effect a balance between the tensions of the forces of the individual parts. Combining the effects of the various forces produces a new kind of result in the Proun. We saw that the surface of the Proun ceases to be a picture and turns into a structure round which we must circle, looking at it from all sides, peering down from above, investigating from below. The result is that the one axis of the picture which stood at right angles to the horizontal was destroyed. Circling round it, we screw ourselves into the space. We have set the Proun in motion and so we obtain a number of axes of projection; we stand between them and push them apart. Standing on this scaffolding in the space we must begin to mark it out. Emptiness, chaos, the unnatural, become space, that is: order, certainty, plastic form, when we introduce markers of a specific kind and in a specific relationship to each other. The structure and the scale of the group of markers give the space a specific tension. By changing the markers we alter the tension of the space, which is formed from one and the same emptiness.

(b) THE BOOK*

Topography of typography 1923

(1) The words on the printed sheet are learnt by sight, not by hearing.

(2) Ideas are communicated through conventional words, the idea should be given form through the letters.

* From ibid., p. 355.

(3) Economy of expression – optics instead of phonetics.

(4) The designing of the book-space through the material of the type, according to the laws of typographical mechanics, must correspond to the strains and stresses of the content.

(5) The design of the book-space through the material of the illustrative process blocks, which give reality to the new optics. The supernaturalistic reality of the perfected eye.

(6) The continuous page-sequence – the bioscopic book.

(7) The new book demands the new writer. Ink-stand and goose-quill are dead.

(8) The printed sheet transcends space and time. The printed sheet, the infinity of the book, must be transcended.

THE ELECTRO-LIBRARY.

(c) WHEEL – PROPELLER AND WHAT FOLLOWS, 1923*

Our creation of form – our systems of motion

First state
The human being walks, he strides. The movement is discontinuous, from point to point—
The whole sole must touch the ground.
The moving force—
the organic energy of the human body.
The moving apparatus—
the system of bones and muscles.

The Egyptian Pyramid: so that a point at a height of 150 metres could be reached, a stone mountain was piled up on top of a colossal foundation.

THAT IS THE FORMING OF THE WALKING HUMAN BEING.

Second state
The first invention – the WHEEL. The discontinuous walking changes into continuous rolling, the wheel touches the ground in one spot.
The moving force—
as in State 1, or steam, exploding gas, electricity.
The moving apparatus—
as in State 1, or the system of connecting-rod, cylinder, etc. of the machine.

* From ibid., p. 345.

Now systems of construction are being invented – not the piling up of material, but the arranging of it into supporting and seperating agents. The Pantheon, the aqueducts, the great halls, the skyscrapers, the Eiffel Tower.

While buildings rise up and new energies are exploited, the speed of the rolling wheel increases and a new shape originates – MOVABLE ARCHITECTURE – the Pullman car, dining-car, ocean liner. The train – a rolling, collective dwelling.

THAT IS THE FORMING OF THE TRAVELLING HUMAN BEING.

Third state
The second invention – SCREW, PROPELLER. The continuous rolling changes into continuous gliding.

NAUEN. Here the 250-metre aerial masts stand in one spot.

The Egyptian Pyramid is obsolete,

The flying human is at the frontier – at the frontier of the old conceptions. A new energy must be released, which provides us with a new system of movement (for example, a movement which is not based on friction, which offers the possibility of floating in space and remaining at rest). The new design must supersede the old machine, which is only an imitation of the human hand. Only inventions will move us forward. Only inventions will determine design. Even for revolutions new forms must be invented.

(d) ARCHITECTURE, 1925*

Modern Architecture in Russia?
There is no such thing. What one does find is a fight for modern architecture, as there is everywhere in the world today. Still nowhere is there a new architectonic CULTURE. Any isolated really new buildings were designed to meet the need of the moment, and only by some anonymous character, some engineer, over the head of the artist with a diploma. At the same time, modern architects in various countries have been fighting for some decades to establish a new tectonics. The main watchwords remain the same: *expedient, in suitable material, constructive.* Every generation puts a different meaning into the same ideas. For many this process is not developing rapidly enough. There is

* From ibid., pp. 367–8.

certainly no lack of forces. The trouble lies in the economic abnormality of the present time and the utter confusion of their intentions.

In the world of today, Russia is moving at record speed. This is manifested ever in the name of the country: – Russia RSFSR, SSSR. Art also advanced at the same tempo. There the revolution in art began by giving form to the elements of time, of space, of tempo and rhythm, of movement. Before the war the cubists in France and the futurists in Italy advanced new theses in art. These re-echoed loudly in Russia; but from the early years of our isolation we went our own way and put forward antitheses.

The European thesis was: THE FINE ARTS (BEAUX-ARTS) FOREVER. Thus the arts were made to become a completely private, subjective-aesthetic concern. The antithesis was: ANYTHING BUT THE FINE ARTS. Let us have something universal, something clear and simple. Thus a square is simple, or a glass cylinder. Out with the painting of pictures! 'The future belongs to those who have a remarkable lack of talent for the fine arts.' Organic growth is a simple thing – so is building, architecture.

These are the bare outlines of one component part. Then in the second place: according to the old law in Russia only architects with their diploma, civil servants, had the right to build, which made this fraternity into a living corpse. These two circumstances were the cause; the effect was the first offensive from the front of the painters and sculptors.

In the years 1917–18, some young architects (Ladovsky, Krinsky and others), painters (such as Rodchenko, Shevchenko), sculptors (Korolev and so on) organized themselves into a group, which sought to achieve a synthesis on these lines:

$$\begin{array}{l} \text{ARCHITECTURE} \\ + \quad \text{SCULPTURE} \\ + \qquad \text{PAINTING} \\ = \quad \text{SYNTHESIS} \end{array}$$

However, as with every approach to a synthesis, the first results were destructive. The several elements of design were already finding expression here, only they were disconnected and without a function. One was still caught in the trap. To this period belongs the design for a telephone kiosk by Rodchenko (1919).

Then came the Revolution and the belief that now everything

would immediately become reality. Tatlin created his tower. His preparatory school was the training of hand and eye acquired from working with technical materials. He had no schooling in engineering, no knowledge of technical mechanics or of iron constructions. His starting-points were the incorporation of a new form – the spiral – and the revelation of the glories of iron and glass. The strength of the antithesis, the 'remarkable lack of talent' for the fine arts, preserved him from the pitfall of aesthetic ventures. In this glorification of mechanical technology, this revelation of the possibilities of well-known materials, there is more of value than just a powerful reaction against the old aesthetics. The reaction merely provides the impetus, the action must be based on deeper foundations. The aim was to make effective in architecture the entire energy which was crystallised in the new painting – not using the newly-introduced forms (the square, for example) but the forces which had been liberated for the building of the new body. Least of all should one let oneself be enticed by the primary element of painting, namely colour. Fulfilment depends on the arrangement of space by means of lines, planes, volumes. No self-contained, individual bodies, but relations and proportions. The unconfined, bodies which originate from movement, from communication and in communication. New constructions. Taking into consideration the fifth view (from above). A demand for new materials, but not material-fetishism. Under the controlling influence of a single idea: function.

8/3   LENIN ON PROLETARIAN CULTURE*

8 October 1920

We see from *Izvestiya* of October 8 that, in his address to the Proletcult Congress, Comrade Lunacharsky said things that were *diametrically opposite* to what he and I had agreed upon yesterday.

It is necessary that a draft resolution (of the Proletcult Congress) should be drawn up with the utmost urgency, and that it should be endorsed by the Central Committee, in time to have it put to the vote *at this very* session of the Proletcult. On behalf

* From Lenin, *Selected Works,* Vol. 3 (Moscow 1971), pp. 484–5.

of the Central Committee it should be submitted not later than today, for endorsement both by the Collegium of the People's Commissariat of Education and by the Proletcult Congress, because the Congress is closing today.

DRAFT RESOLUTION

(1) All educational work in the Soviet Republic of workers and peasants, in the field of political education in general and in the field of art in particular, should be imbued with the spirit of the class struggle being waged by the proletariat for the successful achievement of the aims of its dictatorship, i.e., the overthrow of the bourgeoisie, the abolition of classes, and the elimination of all forms of exploitation of man by man.

(2) Hence, the proletariat, both through its vanguard – the Communist Party – and through the many types of proletarian organisations in general, should display the utmost activity and play the leading part in all the work of public education.

(3) All the experience of modern history and, particularly, the more than half-century-old revolutionary struggle of the proletariat of all countries since the appearance of the *Communist Manifesto* has unquestionably demonstrated that the Marxist world outlook is the only true expression of the interests, the viewpoint, and the culture of the revolutionary proletariat.

(4) Marxism has won its historic significance as the ideology of the revolutionary proletariat because, far from rejecting the most valuable achievements of the bourgeois epoch, it has, on the contrary, assimilated and refashioned everything of value in the more than two thousand years of the development of human thought and culture. Only further work on this basis and in this direction, inspired by the practical experience of the proletarian dictatorship as the final stage in the struggle against every form of exploitation, can be recognised as the development of a genuine proletarian culture.

(5) Adhering unswervingly to this stand of principle, the All-Russian Proletcult Congress rejects in the most resolute manner, as theoretically unsound and practically harmful, all attempts to invent one's own particular brand of culture, to remain isolated in self-contained organisations, to draw a line dividing the field of work of the People's Commissariat of Education and the

Proletcult, or to set up a Proletcult 'autonomy' within establishments under the People's Commissariat of Education and so forth.
On the contrary, the Congress enjoins all Proletcult organisations
to fully consider themselves in duty bound to act as auxiliary
bodies of the network of establishments under the People's Commissariat of Education, and to accomplish their tasks under the
general guidance of the Soviet authorities (specifically, of the
People's Commissariat of Education) and of the Russian Communist Party, as part of the tasks of the proletarian dictatorship.

* * *

Comrade Lunacharsky says that his words have been distorted.
In that case this resolution is needed *all the more* urgently.

8/4   THE PROLETCULT THEATRE*

. . . I next come to the section of the Left Group theatre under the
direction of the workers themselves, who seek self-expression and
are excluding professionalism in favour of voluntaryism. At the
head of this division is the Proletcult theatre. This theatre is second
in importance to the Meyerhold theatre, from which it derives a
great deal. As its name implies, it belongs to the proletarian culture
movement which sprang up after the Revolution. This movement
was designed to promote culture among the workers, and to
encourage gifted young men and women from the common people,
largely factory workers, to express themselves freely in art, drama,
poetry, literature, etc. It was the culture of a class striving for self-
explanation and self-publication. The founders rightly assumed
that the Russian people are naturally gifted, and the common
people have a rich store of natural abilities and apparently inex-
haustible physical health.

At the head of the Moscow organization is V. F. Pletnev,
a gifted working-man author and organizer. He has written
plays and essays, and has closely concerned himself with the
cultural problems of a class to which he belongs who struggle
to free themselves from the tyranny of the monied classes, and

* From H. Carter, *The New Theatre and Cinema of Soviet Russia* (London
1924), pp. 81–3.

seeks to make institutions, including a theatre, for their own use.

The Proletcult theatre was then conceived of as a theatre for the special use of the working-class and for promoting working-class culture. It was organised by representatives of the workers, to be controlled and directed by workers, and to admit certain instructors drawn from the old anarchist intelligentsia and the Right theatre. Its methods were designed to superimpose the modern industrial 'will' upon the traditional 'will' of the theatre, and thus to make the theatre, as far as possible, a party instrument and a State and a national one; to make the workers understand that their destiny was in their own hands, and they must no longer support the ruling and subjecting of their own lives by others; and to develop them as citizens and defenders of their country. According to the latter purpose acting was based on a system of physical drill, and at one time the Proletcult theatre was largely a recruiting ground for the army. This attempt to drill the workers through the theatre into 'cannon fodder' and to use the drilled for every passing war whim of the military governors has died down. Physical drill still forms the basis of the method of acting followed by the workers, because it is necessary to the expression of the spirit of a vital life.

Viewed historically, the Proletcult theatrical movement started in 1918, as a part of a general working-class cultural movement. It attracted the support of many able thinkers and workers, theorists and practitioners, who ever since have continued to speak and write on the ideas, ideals and methods to be pursued. Morever, they have urged on every possible occasion that the utmost encouragement should be given, and every facility offered to the workers to express themselves, whether in literature, art, drama, or any other high form. The columns of the Press were to be thrown open to them, publication made easy, and paths of communication of all sorts opened up. They recognised the urgent need of self-explanation and self-publication by the working-class. We have only to turn to the Proletcult Bulletins published since 1917 to see the amount of time, trouble and thought expended in this endeavour to express and propagate proletarian cultural ideas. Among the many theorists one notes A. Lunacharsky, with his workers' aesthetic; P. Kergentseff, with his encouraging ideas on the self-expression of the working-class in new forms of theatre and plays, and emphasis on the importance of the Socialist Mass theatre and plays; and V. Smyschlaiev, with his carefully elaborated system for training the worker–actor. The object before all three writers was the common one of the workers themselves in building their theatre. They saw (1) that the workers were conscious of a new life; (2) that a new culture was needed; (3) that new conditions of life were likely to determine its form; and (4) that a new social synthesis must, inevitably follow.

8/5 LENIN ON YOUTH*

2 October 1920

(*The Congress greets Lenin with a tremendous ovation.*) Comrades, today I would like to talk on the fundamental tasks of the Young Communist League and, in this connection, on what the youth organisations in a socialist republic should be like in general.

It is all the more necessary to dwell on this question because in a certain sense it may be said that it is the youth that will be faced with the actual task of creating a communist society. For it is clear that the generation of working people brought up in capitalist society can, at best, accomplish the task of destroying the foundations of the old, the capitalist way of life, which was built on exploitation. At best it will be able to accomplish the tasks of creating a social system that will help the proletariat and the working classes retain power and lay a firm foundation, which can be built on only by a generation that is starting to work under the new conditions, in a situation in which relations based on the exploitation of man by man no longer exist.

And so, in dealing from this angle with the tasks confronting the youth, I must say that the tasks of the youth in general, and of the Young Communist Leagues and all other organisations in particular, might be summed up in a single word: learn.

Of course, this is only a 'single word'. It does not reply to the principal and most essential questions: what to learn, and how to learn? And the whole point here is that, with the transformation of the old, capitalist society, the upbringing, training and education of the new generations that will create the communist society cannot be conducted on the old lines. The teaching, train-

* From Lenin, *Selected Works*, Vol. 3 (Moscow 1971), pp. 470–83.

ing and education of the youth must proceed from the material that has been left to us by the old society. We can build communism only on the basis of the totality of knowledge, organisations and institutions, only by using the stock of human forces and means that have been left to us by the old society. Only by radically remoulding the teaching, organisation and training of the youth shall we be able to ensure that the efforts of the younger generation will result in the creation of a society that will be unlike the old society, i.e., in the creation of a communist society. That is why we must deal in detail with the question of what we should teach the youth and how the youth should learn if it really wants to justify the name of communist youth, and how it should be trained so as to be able to complete and consummate what we have started.

I must say that the first and most natural reply would seem to be that the Youth League, and the youth in general, who want to advance to communism, should learn communism . . .

Naturally, the first thought that enters one's mind is that learning communism means assimilating the sum of knowledge that is contained in communist manuals, pamphlets and books. But such a definition of the study of communism would be too crude and inadequate. If the study of communism consisted solely in assimilating what is contained in communist books and pamphlets, we might all too easily obtain communist text-jugglers or braggarts, and this would very often do us harm, because such people, after learning by rote what is set forth in communist books and pamphlets, would prove incapable of combining the various branches of knowledge, and would be unable to act in the way communism really demands . . .

That is why it would be most mistaken merely to assimilate book knowledge about communism. No longer do our speeches and articles merely reiterate what used to be said about communism, because our speeches and articles are connected with our daily work in all fields. Without work and without struggle, book knowledge of communism obtained from communist pamphlets and works is absolutely worthless, for it would continue the old separation of theory and practice, the old rift which was the most pernicious feature of the old, bourgeois society.

It would be still more dangerous to set about assimilating only communist slogans. Had we not realised this danger in time, and had we not directed all our efforts to averting this danger, the half million or million young men and women who would have called themselves Communists after studying communism in this way would only greatly prejudice the cause of communism. . . .

I first of all shall deal here with the question of communist ethics.

You must train yourselves to be Communists. It is the task of the Youth League to organise its practical activities in such a way that, by learning, organising, uniting and fighting, its members shall train both themselves and all those who look to it for leadership; it should train Communists. The entire purpose of training, educating and teaching the youth of today should be to imbue them with communist ethics.

But is there such a thing as communist ethics? Is there such a thing as communist morality? Of course, there is. It is often suggested that we have no ethics of our own; very often the bourgeoisie accuse us Communists of rejecting all morality. This is a method of confusing the issue, of throwing dust in the eyes of the workers and peasants.

In what sense do we reject ethics, reject morality?

In the sense given to it by the bourgeoisie, who based ethics on God's commandments. On this point we, of course, say that we do not believe in God, and that we know perfectly well that the clergy, the landowners and the bourgeoisie invoked the name of God so as to further their own interests as exploiters. Or, instead of basing ethics on the commandments of morality, on the commandments of God, they based it on idealist or semi-idealist phrases, which always amounted to something very similar to God's commandments.

We reject any morality based on extra-human and extra-class concepts. We say that this is deception, dupery, stultification of the workers and peasants in the interests of the landowners and capitalists.

We say that our morality is entirely subordinated to the interests of the proletariat's class struggle. Our morality stems from the interests of the class struggle of the proletariat.

The old society was based on the oppression of all the workers and peasants by the landowners and capitalists. We had to destroy all that, and overthrow them but to do that we had to create unity. That is something that God cannot create . . .

The members of the League should use every spare hour to improve the vegetable gardens, or to organise the education of young people at some factory, and so on. We want to transform Russia from a poverty-stricken and wretched country into one that is wealthy. The Young Communist League must combine its education, learning and training with the labour of the workers and peasants, so as not to confine itself to schools or to reading communist books and pamphlets. Only by working side by side with the workers and peasants can one become a genuine Communist. It has to be generally realised that all members of the Youth League are literate people and at the same time are keen at their jobs. When everyone sees that we have ousted the old drill-ground methods from the old schools and have replaced them with conscious discipline, that all young men and women take part in subbotniks, and utilise every suburban farm to help the population – people will cease to regard labour in the old way.

It is the task of the Young Communist League to organise assistance everywhere, in village or city block, in such matters as – and I shall take a small example – public hygiene or the distribution of food. How was this done in the old, capitalist society? Everybody worked only for himself and nobody cared a straw for the aged and the sick, or whether housework was the concern only of the women, who, in consequence, were in a condition of oppression and servitude. Whose business is it to combat this? It is the business of the Youth Leagues, which must say: we shall change all this; we shall organise detachments of young people who will help to assure public hygiene or distribute food, who will conduct systematic house-to-house inspections, and work in an organised way for the benefit of the whole of society, distributing their forces properly and demonstrating that labour must be organised.

9 The Eye Witness

Revolutions are about people. They can radically alter the lives of millions of people. The October Revolution, one of the most important, turned Russian society upside down. One can hardly expect those who suffered as a result of it to be very charitable about its advent. Document 9/1 is a graphic account of conditions in Petrograd as viewed by British refugees returning to London in the summer of 1918.

H. G. Wells visited St Petersburg and Moscow in January 1914. He was invited to revisit the two capitals in September–October 1920 and eagerly seized the opportunity of assessing the impact of the revolution. He had no special regard for Marx before he visited Soviet Russia. His stay seems to have confirmed his dislike of Marxist socialism (9/2).

Carl Lindhagen was a well-known Swedish Left Social Democrat and a pacifist who visited Petrograd in January 1918. He attended the opening session of the Constituent Assembly in January 1918 and has written a vivid account of the scene (9/3).

Karl Idman was a member of the Finnish government and accompanied the state secretary Carl Enckell to Petrograd on 28 December 1917 to ask the Bolshevik government to grant Finland independence. (It was granted on 31 December 1917.) He met Lenin and has drawn a very interesting pen portrait of him (9/4).

9/1 CONDITIONS IN PETROGRAD*

These people are unanimous in describing conditions prevailing in Russia as unbearable, owing to the rule of terror of the Bolsheviks, as well as to the appalling economic conditions brought about by Lenin's régime. Eighty-five per cent of the members of the soviets and commissariats are Jews, many of whom have lived in America.

* From Sir B. Pares, Private Papers.

Those men, like their leaders Lenin and Trotsky, have as their programme the total destruction of all organisations of civilisation, and their hatred is especially directed against the bourgeoisie, the British and against religion.

The bourgeoisie is being systematically exterminated. No one is safe – of whatever nationality, age or sex. People are arbitrarily made prisoners – for no reason whatever they are executed, and every night one hears the sound of firing. The bourgeoisie is compelled to work under the threat of death. Engineers, technical experts, etc. are forced to remain at their posts in factories, or be shot. Even the workmen are kept from striking by the threat of death. For instance, the English manager of a certain factory was taken prisoner, whereupon the factory hands who loved him, threatened to strike unless their chief was released, when the Bolshevik commissar threatened to turn machine-guns upon them and kill every man; naturally work was resumed.

In Moscow the same conditions of terror prevail – There is, however, one difference. The Bolshevik members of the soviets and the commissariats are at loggerheads, mutually threatening to shoot each other if their commands are not carried out. In the other towns of the empire, conditions vary according to whether the Red Guards are in the majority or the minority. In the latter case, life is more secure.

The Russian nation is groaning under the tyranny of the Bolsheviks and is suffering from general dislocation of ordinary life brought about by Bolshevik rule; but as with the exception of the Red Guards no one has any weapons, a rising of the people is not possible; for unarmed people cannot stand against machine-guns, and at present it is these which keep the people in abject submission.

There is no doubt in the minds of all those who have returned from Russia that Lenin and Co. are obeying German orders, and the following fact is of interest. Lectures against the British are publicly advertised to be held in halls and private houses, and the English are described as the enemies of liberty. Also large placards are displayed on the walls in German and in Russian calling upon the people to fight against those 'traitorous' English, the enemies of Russian freedom. German soldiers in Russia consider themselves masters. In Moscow they walk about in full uniform, which they also did at one time in Petrograd. The following incident is illustrative of the situation:

When asked by a lady in the Anglo–Russian hospital the name of his native town, a soldier boldly replied 'Berlin'. 'We do not receive patients here who come from Berlin,' she said. 'Put my name down immediately, I tell you,' the soldier arrogantly retorted. 'We Germans are masters here and the Bolsheviks do as we command.'

FAMINE

Famine is rife in Petrograd, and it is a common occurrence when a horse falls down in the street for the people to rush out of the houses to cut off the flesh of the animal the moment it has breathed its last. My informant has also seen lying in the street the carcass of a horse, the head and shoulders of which had been cut off for food. The peasants refuse to sell food for money, but are ready to barter it for clothes, boots, furniture; the shops are all empty . . .

Money is paid out at the banks in an absolutely arbitrary way to those who have deposits, but by heavy bribes it is possible to get out larger sums. Until quite recently people sold their possessions: *objets d'art,* jewellery, pictures, furniture – either privately or deposited them in commission shops where they were bought by wealthy Jews, rich speculators and affluent working people. Now, however, no furniture may be sold as it has been declared the common property of the nation, just as all house property has been nationalised, the rents being paid to the Bolshevik Government. People are no longer permitted to take any furniture with them if they leave their flats, and they are often compelled to leave their homes because these have been commandeered by the Bolsheviks; and on nearly every family Red Guards have been quartered. At one time blankets were requisitioned, and every bourgeois family was compelled to hand over one good woollen blanket, ostensibly for the Red Guards, but it was common knowledge that they were being sold to the Germans.

Unless people had about 1000 rubles (£100) a month per person, they had to starve, and even these favoured ones had to satisfy their hunger with the following food: a certain kind of dried fish, which had to be soaked for 24 hours before it could be boiled; flour, buckwheat and other cereals at 30/- a pound; potatoes, five twice a week, at 6/6 or 7/- a lb. The peel of the potatoes is minced, mixed with breadcrumbs and made into rissoles. In order to buy these vegetables one has to go in the early hours of the morning to a certain market. Another way of getting food was by buying it at exorbitant prices from members of the Red Guards who are well-fed. Many people, who are not Bolsheviks, have joined the Red Guards for the sake of the food given them. Lenin and his colleagues are living in affluence.

1 October 1918.

9/2   EVERYDAY LIFE IN PETROGRAD*

The electric street cars are still running and busy – until six o'clock. They are the only means of locomotion for ordinary people remaining in town – the last legacy of capitalist enterprise. They became free while we were in Petersburg. Previously there had been a charge of two or three rubles – the hundreth part of the price of an egg. Freeing them made little difference in their extreme congestion during the homegoing hours. Every one scrambles on the tramcar. If there is no room inside you cluster outside. In the busy hours festoons of people hang outside by any handhold; people are frequently pushed off, and accidents are frequent. We saw a crowd collected round a child cut in half by a tramcar, and two people in the little circle in which we moved in Petersburg had broken their legs in tramway accidents.

The roads along which these tramcars run are in a frightful condition. They have not been repaired for three or four years; they are full of holes like shell-holes, often two or three feet deep. Frost has eaten out great cavities, drains have collapsed, and people have torn up the wood pavement for fires. Only once did we see any attempt to repair the streets in Petrograd. In a side street some mysterious agency had collected a load of wood blocks and two barrels of tar. Most of our longer journeys about the town were done in official motor-cars – left over from the former times. A drive is an affair of tremendous swerves and concussions. These

* From H. G. Wells, *Russia in the Shadows* (London n.d.), pp. 15–19.

surviving motor-cars are running now on kerosene. They disengage clouds of pale blue smoke, and start up with a noise like a machine-gun battle. Every wooden house was demolished for firing last winter, and such masonry as there was in those houses remains in ruinous gaps, between the houses of stone.

Every one is shabby; every one seems to be carrying bundles in both Petersburg and Moscow. To walk into some side street in the twilight and see nothing but ill-clad figures, all hurrying, all carrying loads, gives one an impression as though the entire population was setting out in flight. That impression is not altogether misleading. The Bolshevik statistics I have seen are perfectly frank and honest in the matter. The population of Petersburg has fallen from 1,200,000 (before 1919) to a little over 700,000, and it is still falling. Many people have returned to peasant life in the country, many have gone abroad, but hardship has taken an enormous toll of this city. The death-rate in Petersburg is over 81 per 1,000; formerly it was high among European cities at 22. The birth-rate of the underfed and profoundly depressed population is about 15. It was formerly about 30.

These bundles that every one carries are partly the rations of food that are doled out by the Soviet organisation, partly they are the material and results of illicit trade ...

There is also much underground trade between buyers and sellers who know each other. Every one who can supplements his public rations in this way. And every railway station at which one stops is an open market.

9/3   THE CONSTITUENT ASSEMBLY*

By a stroke of fortune, the so-called Constituent, the legislative assembly for Russia, was at last about to have its first session shortly before I had to leave Petrograd.

It was an event attended by much excitement ... the inhabitants of the city were ordered by the authorities to stay indoors on the day prior to and the actual day of the assembly, for safety reasons. A number of searches took place in the hotel after a rumour had gone about that the followers of Kaledin and other counter-revolutionaries had arrived to provoke disturbances . . . A couple of

* From C. Lindhagen, *I Revolutionsland* (Stockholm 1918), pp. 98–107.

hours before the time announced for the opening of the session
I took myself to the Tauride Palace . . . Demonstrations in favour
of the Constituent Assembly could already be seen here and there
on the broad boulevards. They were preceded by red flags, since
all parties with pretensions to importance called themselves socialist. This was the demonstration of the first revolution against the
second.

At last the hall began to fill up with the deputies . . . They
arranged themselves according to parties like a fan, grouped around
the presidential tribunal. The Bolsheviks sat on the left, followed
by the left-SRs. Then came the right-wing SRs, separated from
the former by a small group, which we were told were Ukrainians.
Finally, on the right were the seats of the representatives of the
different nationalities, although these groups tended to blend in
with the right SRs during the debates, at least as far as I could
see.

To the right and left of the president's seat sat the commissars
and a number of departmental civil servants . . . The roomy
benches which stretched around the whole of the four-cornered
assembly hall were crowded. In one of the corridors leading from
the hall, a detachment of armed sailors could be glimpsed, occupying the palace.

All the deputies on the right wore the social democratic First
of May red rose in their buttonholes, the Bolsheviks and left SRs
on the other hand bore no marks of recognition . . .

I was informed that several of the deputies as well as the commissars and other civil servants were armed. I asked at random
a member of the commissariat if this was true. 'Of course,' he
replied and showed me the butt of a revolver in his trouser-pocket.
Someone told me that it was not known whether they would start
shooting at each other or not. A second person told me that for the
sake of impartiality entry to the public galleries had been opened
to adherents of all parties, even of the Black Hundreds. No one
knew, my informant told me, what the latter might get up to, and
it dawned on me that the possibility of a bomb thrown from the
public galleries was not to be excluded. If Lenin showed himself
in the hall, a third thought, an attempt on his life from the gallery
or the hall is not to be ruled out. Nothing like this happened, but
the fears aroused uneasiness in all . . .

The chairman elected by the assembly delivered a long speech

... First he praised socialism, peace and the fight against imperialism endlessly. The right loudly applauded all the most beautiful expressions about peace, humanity and democracy; the left remained silent. But finally the speaker had to deal with more day-to-day matters and then roars of approval and interruptions raged on both sides. When he announced that the civil war should now cease, the left shouted: Kaledin! Kaledin! When he spoke of the victims of revolution and the sacrifices of the troops, the left broke into a real uproar. In particular, the Bolshevik deputies who were dressed in military uniform rose from their seats and uttered threats, shook their fists . . . It was a further outburst of the hatred of the soldiers against the coalition of ministers which had ordered the famous offensive, reintroduced the death penalty and shot soldiers for refusing to go on the offensive....

Whilst Chernov was speaking, Lenin had returned, or perhaps he had been in the hall the whole time. I saw him lying on a small staircase which led from the presidium up to a higher section of the semicircle of seats above. He lay uncomfortably on the step itself, on his left side with his hand over his eyes. In front of him was the balustrade of the staircase which effectively concealed him from the hall. What was he thinking of at this moment, whilst his triumphant opponent in the Constituent Assembly was making his chairman's speech?

9/4   LENIN: A PEN PORTRAIT*

Smolny

We were taken into an anteroom, where a soldier was standing at the door on the far side . . . After we had stepped through the door into the room, V. I. Lenin stood there before us. I felt somewhat surprised that a person who – irrespective of one's views of his ideology – had had such a far-reaching influence on the fate of his huge fatherland should make such a modest impression. Of average size, bald-headed, with slightly reddish hair at the sides, a short, scanty and reddish beard. His eyes were sharp and wise and left the impression that the man possessed firmness of will.

* From K. G. Idman, *Maame itsenäistymisen vuosilta* (Porvoo–Helsinki 1953), p. 216.

His speech was very simple and unforced, as was his manner. If one did not know him, one could never have been able to comprehend the strength that he must have possessed. It was said of Kerensky that he only talked, but this could never be said of his conqueror. Lenin received us cordially, apologising for keeping us waiting. The room in which we found ourselves was divided into two by a board partition. In the front part, two people were sitting at a table. Lenin asked us to come to the other side of the partition, which seemingly was the 'holy of holies'. The room was in no way different from any of the other rooms in Smolny. It was as simple as all the rest. The walls were painted white, there was a wooden table and a few chairs.

10 The Verdict

A revolution sets in motion a train of events. The eventual outcome of these events cannot be predicted with certainty. Lenin argued before the seizure of power that the socialist revolution in the advanced countries would provide the support and expertise necessary to transform Russia into a modern industrial society. Soviet Russia, as it turned out, had to go it alone. This meant that the dictatorship of the proletariat, as it developed in Soviet Russia, was faced with a mammoth task. The party found itself in a minority and had to use violence to stay in power.

One of the most percipient critics of the Bolshevik Revolution was Rosa Luxemburg. She saw the land policy as the precursor of a mighty struggle with the peasants. She objected to the Bolshevik view that the October revolution could serve as a model for future revolutions elsewhere (10/1).

Trotsky's disillusionment with the Soviet Union came later when he found Stalin and his bureaucracy too formidable to overcome. In the passage chosen, he is full of optimism and waves aside all criticism (10/2).

Lenin's thoughts on the progress of the revolution are very interesting. He foresaw the split between Trotsky and Stalin and was troubled by Great Russian chauvinism in nationalities' policy. He felt he had great tasks ahead of him but, for better or for worse, he was not to live to influence personally any solutions adopted (10/3).

10/1   ROSA LUXEMBURG*

Fundamental Significance of the Russian Revolution

The Russian Revolution is the mightiest event of the World War. . . .

* From M.–A. Waters, ed., *Rosa Luxemburg Speaks* (New York 1970), pp. 367, 374, 375, 393–5.

The party of Lenin was the only one which grasped the mandate and duty of a truly revolutionary party and which, by the slogan – 'All power in the hands of the proletariat and peasantry' – insured the continued development of the revolution. . . .

Whatever a party could offer of courage, revolutionary farsightedness and consistency in an historic hour, Lenin, Trotsky and the other comrades have given in good measure. All the revolutionary honour and capacity which western social democracy lacked were represented by the Bolsheviks. Their October uprising was not only the actual salvation of the Russian Revolution; it was also the salvation of the honor of international socialism. . . .

The Bolshevik Land Policy

. . . Surely the solution of the problem by the direct, immediate seizure and distribution of the land by the peasants was the shortest, simplest, most clear-cut formula to achieve two diverse things: to break down large landownership, and immediately to bind the peasants to the revolutionary government. As a political measure to fortify the proletarian socialist government, it was an excellent tactical move. Unfortunately, however, it had two sides to it; and the reverse side consisted in the fact that the direct seizure of the land by the peasants has in general nothing at all in common with socialist economy . . .

Now the slogan launched by the Bolsheviks, immediate seizure and distribution of the land by the peasants, necessarily tended in the opposite direction. Not only is it not a socialist measure; it even cuts off the way to such measures; it piles up insurmountable obstacles to the socialist transformation of agrarian relations . . .

The Leninist agrarian reform has created a new and powerful layer of popular enemies of socialism in the countryside, enemies whose resistance will be much more dangerous and stubborn than that of the noble large landowners.

Democracy and Dictatorship

The basic error of the Lenin–Trotsky theory is that they too, just like Kautsky, oppose dictatorship to democracy. 'Dictatorship or democracy' is the way the question is put by Bolsheviks and Kautsky alike. The latter naturally decides in favour of 'democracy', that is, of bourgeois democracy, precisely because he opposes it to the alternative of the socialist revolution. Lenin and Trotsky, on the other hand, decide in favour of dictatorship in contradistinction to democracy, and thereby, in favour of the dictatorship of a handful of persons, that is, in favour of dictatorship on the bourgeois model. They are two opposite poles, both alike being far removed from a genuine socialist policy. The proletariat, when it seizes power, can never follow the good advice of Kautsky, given on the pretext of the 'unripeness of the country', the advice being to renounce the socialist revolution and devote itself to democracy. It cannot follow this advice without betraying thereby itself, the International, and the revolution. It should and must at once undertake socialist measures in the most energetic, unyielding and unhesitant fashion, in other words, exercise a dictatorship, but a dictatorship of the *class*, not of a party or of a clique—dictatorship of the class, that means in the broadest public form on the basis of the most active, unlimited participation of the mass of the people, of unlimited democracy. 'As Marxists,' writes Trotsky, 'we have never been idol worshippers of formal democracy.' Surely, we have never been idol worshippers of formal democracy. Nor have we ever been idol worshippers of socialism or Marxism either. Does it follow from this that we may also throw socialism on the scrap-heap, *à la* Cunow, Lensch and Parvus, if it becomes uncomfortable for us? Trotsky and Lenin are the living refutation of this answer.

'We have never been idol worshippers of formal democracy.' All that really means is: We have always distinguished the social kernel from the political form of *bourgeois* democracy; we have always revealed the hard kernel of social inequality and lack of freedom hidden under the sweet shell of formal equality and freedom – not in order to reject the latter but to spur the working class into not being satisfied with the shell, but rather, by conquering political power, to create a socialist democracy to replace bourgeois democracy – not to eliminate democracy altogether.

But socialist democracy is not something which begins only in the promised land after the foundations of socialist economy are created; it does not come as some sort of Christmas present for the worthy people who, in the interim, have loyally supported a handful of socialist dictators. Socialist democracy begins simultaneously with the beginnings of the destruction of class rule and of the construction of socialism. It begins at the very moment of the seizure of power by the socialist party. It is the same thing as the dictatorship of the proletariat.

Yes, dictatorship! But this dictatorship consists in the *manner of applying democracy*, not in its *elimination*, in energetic, resolute attacks upon the well-entrenched rights and economic relationships of bourgeois society, without which a socialist transformation cannot be accomplished. But this dictatorship must be the work of the *class* and not of a little leading minority in the name of the class – that is, it must proceed step by step out of the active participation of the masses; it must be under their direct influence, subjected to the control of complete public activity; it must arise out of the growing political training of the mass of the people.

Doubtless the Bolsheviks would have proceeded in this very way were it not that they suffered under the frightful compulsion of the World War, the German occupation and all the abnormal difficulties connected therewith, things which were inevitably bound to distort any socialist policy, however imbued it might be with the best intentions and the finest principles.

A crude proof of this is provided by the use of terror to so wide an extent by the Soviet government, especially in the most recent period just before the collapse of German imperialism, and just after the attempt on the life of the German ambassador. The commonplace to the effect that revolutions are not beds of roses is in itself pretty inadequate.

Everything that happens in Russia is comprehensible and represents an inevitable chain of causes and effects, the starting point and end term of which are: the failure of the German proletariat and the occupation of Russia by German imperialism. It would be demanding something superhuman from Lenin and his comrades if we should expect of them that under such circumstances they should conjure forth the finest democracy, the most exemplary dictatorship of the proletariat and a flourishing socialist economy. By their determined revolutionary stand, their exemplary strength in action, and their unbreakable loyalty to international socialism, they have contributed whatever could possibly be contributed under such devilishly hard conditions. The danger begins only when they make a virtue of necessity forced upon them by these fatal circumstances, and want to recommend them to the international proletariat as a model of socialist tactics. When they get in their own light in this way, and hide this genuine, unquestionable historical service under the bushel of false steps forced upon them by necessity, they render a poor service to international socialism for the sake of which they have fought and suffered; for they want to place in its storehouse as new discoveries all the distortions prescribed in Russia by necessity and compulsion – in the last analysis only by-products of the bankruptcy of international socialism in the present world war.

Let the German government socialists cry that the rule of the Bolsheviks in Russia is a distorted expression of the dictatorship of the proletariat. If it was or is such, that is only because it is a product of the behaviour of the German proletariat, in itself a distorted expression of the socialist class struggle. All of us are subject to the laws of history, and it is only internationally that the socialist order of society can be realized. The Bolsheviks have shown that they are capable of everything that a genuine revolutionary party can contribute within the limits of the historical possibilities. They are not supposed to perform miracles. For a model and faultless proletarian revolution in an isolated land, exhausted by world war, strangled by imperialism, betrayed by the international proletariat, would be a miracle.

What is in order is to distinguish the essential from the nonessential, the kernel from the accidental excrescences in the policies of the Bolsheviks. In the present period, when we face decisive final struggles in all the world, the most important problem of socialism was and is the burning question of our time. It is not a matter of this or that secondary question of tactics, but of the capacity for action of the proletariat, the strength to act, the will to power of socialism as such. In this, Lenin and Trotsky and their friends were the *first*, those who went ahead as an example to the proletariat of the world; they are still the *only ones* up to now who can cry with Hutten: 'I have dared!'

This is the essential and *enduring* in Bolshevik policy. In *this* sense theirs is the immortal historical service of having marched at the head of the international proletariat with the conquest of political power and the practical placing of the problem of the realization of socialism, and of having advanced mightily the settlement of the score between capital and labour in the entire world. In Russia the problem could only be posed. It could not be solved in Russia. And in *this* sense, the future everywhere belongs to 'bolshevism.'

10/2   LEON TROTSKY*

What questions does the October Revolution raise in the mind of a thinking man?

1. Why and how did this revolution take place? More concretely, why did the proletarian revolution conquer in one of the most backward countries of Europe?
2. What have been the results of the October Revolution? and finally,
3. Has the October Revolution stood the test?

The first question, as to the causes, can now be answered more or less exhaustively. I have attempted to do this in great detail in my *History of the Russian Revolution.* Here I can formulate only the most important conclusions.

The fact that the proletariat reached power for the first time in such a backward country as the former tsarist Russia seems mysterious only at first glance; in reality, it is fully in accord with historical law. It could have been predicted and it was predicted. Still more, on the basis of the prediction of this fact the revolutionary Marxists built up their strategy long before the decisive events.

The first and most general explanation is: Russia is a backward country, but only a part of world economy, only an element of the capitalist world system. In this sense Lenin exhausted the riddle of the Russian Revolution with the lapidary formula, 'The chain broke at its weakest link.'

A crude illustration: the Great War, the result of the contradictions of world imperialism, drew into its maelstrom countries of *different* stages of development, but made the *same claims* on all the participants. It is clear that the burdens of the war had to be particularly intolerable for the most backward countries. Russia was the first to be compelled to leave the field. But to tear itself away from the war, the Russian people had to overthrow the ruling classes. In this way the chain of war broke at its weakest link.

Still, war is not a catastrophe coming from outside, like an earthquake, but as old Clausewitz said, the continuation of politics by other means. In the last war, the main tendencies of the

* From S. Lovell, ed., *Leon Trotsky Speaks* (New York 1972), pp. 249, 250, 253–5.

imperialist system of 'peacetime' only expressed themselves more crudely. The higher the general forces of production, the tenser the competition on the world markets, the sharper the antagonisms, and the madder the race for armaments, in that measure the more difficult it became for the weaker participants. For precisely this reason the backward countries assumed the first places in the succession of collapses. The chain of world capitalism always tends to break at its weakest link . . .

The subsoil of the revolution was the agrarian question . . .

Had the bourgeoisie courageously solved the agrarian question, the proletariat of Russia would not, obviously, have been able to take the power in 1917 . . .

Without the armed insurrection of 7 November 1917, the Soviet state would not be in existence. But the insurrection itself did not drop from heaven. A series of historical prerequisites was necessary for the October Revolution.

1. The rotting away of the old ruling classes – the nobility, the monarchy, the bureaucracy.
2. The political weakness of the bourgeoisie, which had no roots in the masses of the people.
3. The revolutionary character of the peasant question.
4. The revolutionary character of the problem of the oppressed nations.
5. The significant social weight of the proletariat.

To these organic preconditions we must add certain conjunctural conditions of the highest importance:

6. The revolution of 1905 was the great school, or in Lenin's words, the 'dress rehearsal' of the revolution of 1917. The soviets, as the irreplaceable organizational form of the proletarian united front in the revolution, were created for the first time in the year 1905.
7. The imperialist war sharpened all the contradictions, tore the backward masses out of their immobility and thereby prepared the grandiose scale of the catastrophe.

But all these conditions, which fullly sufficed for the *outbreak of the revolution*, were insufficient to assure the *victory of the proletariat* in the revolution. For this victory one condition more was needed:

8. The Bolshevik Party.

10/3   LENIN

(a) OUR REVOLUTION*

OUR REVOLUTION

(APROPOS OF N. SUKHANOV'S NOTES)

I

I have lately been glancing through Sukhanov's notes on the revolution. What strikes one most is the pedantry of all our petty-bourgeois democrats and of all the heroes of the Second International. Apart from the fact that they are all extremely faint-hearted, that when it comes to the minutest deviation from the German model even the best of them fortify themselves with reservations – apart from this characteristic, which is common to all petty-bourgeois democrats and has been abundantly manifested by them throughout the revolution, what strikes one is their slavish imitation of the past.

They all call themselves Marxists, but their conception of Marxism is impossibly pedantic. They have completely failed to understand what is decisive in Marxism, namely, its revolutionary dialectics. They have even absolutely failed to understand Marx's plain statements that in times of revolution the utmost flexibility is demanded, and have even failed to notice, for instance, the statements Marx made in his letters – I think it was in 1856 – expressing the hope of combining a peasant war in Germany, which might create a revolutionary situation, with the working-class movement – they avoid even this plain statement and walk round and about it like a cat around a bowl of hot porridge.

Their conduct betrays them as cowardly reformists who are afraid to deviate from the bourgeoisie, let alone break with it, and at the same time they disguise their cowardice with the wildest rhetoric and braggartry. But what strikes one in all of them even from the purely theoretical point of view is their utter inability to grasp the following Marxist considerations: up to now they have seen capitalism and bourgeois democracy in Western Europe follow a definite path of development, and cannot conceive that

* From Lenin, *Selected Works*, Vol. 3 (Moscow 1971), pp. 767–70.

this path can be taken as a model only *mutatis mutandis,* only with certain amendments (quite insignificant from the standpoint of the general development of world history).

Firstly – the revolution connected with the first imperialist world war. Such a revolution was bound to reveal new features, or variations, resulting from the war itself, for the world has never seen such a war in such a situation. We find that since the war the bourgeoisie of the wealthiest countries have to this day been unable to restore 'normal' bourgeois relations. Yet our reformists – petty bourgeois who make a show of being revolutionaries – believed, and still believe, that normal bourgeois relations are the limit (thus far shalt thou go and no farther). And even their conception of 'normal' is extremely stereotyped and narrow.

Secondly, they are complete strangers to the idea that while the development of world history as a whole follows general laws it is by no means precluded, but, on the contrary, presumed, that certain periods of development may display peculiarities in either the form or the sequence of this development. For instance, it does not even occur to them that because Russia stands on the border-line between the civilised countries and the countries which this war has for the first time definitely brought into the orbit of civilisation – all the Oriental, non-European countries – she could and was, indeed, bound to reveal certain distinguishing features; although these, of course, are in keeping with the general line of world development, they distinguish her revolution from those which took place in the West-European countries and introduce certain partial innovations as the revolution moves on to the countries of the East.

Infinitely stereotyped, for instance, is the argument they learned by rote during the development of West-European Social-Democracy, namely, that we are not yet ripe for socialism, that, as certain 'learned' gentlemen among them put it, the objective economic premises for socialism do not exist in our country. It does not occur to any of them to ask: but what about a people that found itself in a revolutionary situation such as that created during the first imperialist war? Might it not, influenced by the hopelessness of its situation, fling itself into a struggle that would offer it at least some chance of securing conditions for the further development of civilisation that were somewhat unusual?

'The development of the productive forces of Russia has not

attained the level that makes socialism possible.' All the heroes of the Second International, including, of course, Sukhanov, beat the drums about this proposition. They keep harping on this incontrovertible proposition in a thousand different keys, and think that it is the decisive criterion of our revolution.

But what if the situation, which drew Russia into the imperialist world war that involved ever more or less influential West-European country and made her a witness of the eve of the revolutions maturing or partly already begun in the East, gave rise to circumstances that put Russia and her development in a position which enabled us to achieve precisely that combination of a 'peasant war' with the working-class movement suggested in 1856 by no less a Marxist than Marx himself as a possible prospect for Prussia?

What if the complete hopelessness of the situation, by stimulating the efforts of the workers and peasants tenfold, offered us the opportunity to create the fundamental requisites of civilisation in a different way from that of the West-European countries? Has that altered the general line of development of world history? Has that altered the basic relations between the basic classes of all the countries that are being, or have been, drawn into the general course of world history?

If a definite level of culture is required for the building of socialism (although nobody can say just what that definite 'level of culture' is, for it differs in every West-European country), why cannot we begin by first achieving the prerequisites for that definite level of culture in a revolutionary way, and *then,* with the aid of the workers' and peasants' government and the Soviet system, proceed to overtake the other nations?

16 January 1923

II

You say that civilisation is necessary for the building of socialism. Very good. But why could we not first create such prerequisites of civilisation in our country as the expulsion of the landowners and the Russian capitalists, and then start moving towards socialism? Where, in what books, have you read that such variations of the customary historical sequence of events are impermissible or impossible?

Napoleon, I think, wrote: *'On s'engage et puis . . . on voit.'*
Rendered freely this means: 'First engage in a serious battle and
then see what happens.' Well, we did first engage in a serious
battle in October 1917, and then saw such details of development
(from the standpoint of world history they were certainly details)
as the Brest peace, the New Economic Policy, and so forth. And
now there can be no doubt that in the main we have been
victorious.

Our Sukhanovs, not to mention Social-Democrats still farther
to the right, never even dream that revolutions cannot be made
in any other way. Our European philistines never even dream
that subsequent revolutions in Oriental countries, which possess
much vaster populations and a much vaster diversity of social
conditions, will undoubtedly display even greater distinctions than
the Russian revolution.

It need hardly be said that a textbook written on Kautskian
lines was a very useful thing in its day. But it is time, for all that,
to abandon the idea that it foresaw all the forms of development
of subsequent world history. It would be timely to say that those
who think so are simply fools.

17 January 1923

(b) LENIN'S 'TESTAMENT'*

24/25 December 1922

By stability of the Central Committee, of which I spoke above, I
mean measures against a split, as far as such measures can be
taken. For, of course, the White Guard writer in *Russkaya Mysl*
(it seems it was S. F. Oldenburg) was right when, in the first place,
in their game against Soviet Russia, he banked on a split in our
party, and, when, secondly, he banked on really grave differences
in our party to cause that split.

Our party relies on two classes and therefore its instability
would be possible and its fall inevitable if these two classes were
not able to come to an agreement. In that case adopting this or
that measure and all discussion generally about the stability of
our Central Committee would be a waste of time. No measures in

* From Lenin, *Polnoe Sobranie Sochinenii*, Vol. 45 (Moscow 1964),
pp. 334–8, 356–62.

such a case would be efficacious in preventing a split. But I hope that this is too remote a future and too improbable an event to be discussed.

I have in mind stability as a guarantee against a split in the near future and I intend to deal with a number of considerations of a purely personal nature.

I think that basic to the question of stability from this point of view are members of the Central Committee, such as Stalin and Trotsky. I think that relations between them account for the greater part of the danger of a split, which could be avoided and I think this could be served, among other things, by increasing the number of Central Committee members to 50 or 100.

Comrade Stalin, having become Secretary General, has concentrated *unlimited authority* in his hands and I am not certain *whether he will always be capable of using that authority with sufficient caution.* On the other hand, Comrade Trotsky, as his struggle with the CC on the question of the People's Commissariat of Transport and Communications has already shown, is distinguished not only by *outstanding abilities.* As a person, he is probably *the most capable man on the CC at present,* but he has revealed excessive self-assurance and shown excessive preoccupation with the purely administrative side of the work.

These two qualities of the *two outstanding leaders of the present CC* can inadvertently lead to a split, and if our party does not take steps to stop this, the split may occur unexpectedly.

I shall not make any further appraisals of the personal qualities of other members of the CC. I shall just recall that the October episode of Kamenev and Zinoviev, was of course, not an accident but neither can the blame be placed on them personally, any more than Trotsky can be called a non-Bolshevik.

Speaking of the young CC members, I wish to say a few words about Bukharin and Pyatakov. They are, I think, the most outstanding representatives (among the youngest ones) and the following should be taken into consideration: Bukharin is not only the most valuable and most powerful theorist in the party, he is already rightly considered the darling of the whole party, but his theoretical views can be regarded as fully Marxist only with great reserve, for there is something scholastic about him (he has never studied and I think has never fully understood the dialectic).

As for Pyatakov, he is undoubtedly a man of great willpower and outstanding ability, but is too attracted to administration and the administrative side of work to be relied upon in a serious political question.

Of course, remarks about both of these are made only for the present, on the assumption that both these outstanding and devoted party workers will not find an opportunity of supplementing their knowledge and remedying their one-sidedness.

Lenin

4 January 1923

Stalin is too rude and this defect, although quite tolerable in our midst and in relations among us Communists, becomes intolerable in the post of Secretary General. That is why I suggest that comrades think of a way of removing Stalin from that post and appointing another man to replace him who in all other respects differs from Comrade Stalin in having only one advantage, namely, that of being tolerant, more loyal, more polite and more considerate to his comrades, less capricious, etc. This circumstance may seem an insignificant detail. But I think that from the point of view of safeguarding against a split and from the standpoint of what I wrote about the relationship between Stalin and Trotsky it is not a detail, or else it is a detail which could acquire decisive significance.

26 December 1922

The increase in the number of CC members to 50 or even 100 must, in my opinion, serve a double or even a treble purpose: the more members there are in the CC, the more men will be trained in CC work and the less danger there will be of a split due to some indiscretion. The addition of many workers to the CC will help the workers to improve our apparatus which is pretty bad. We inherited it, in effect, from the old régime, for it was absolutely impossible to reorganise it in such a short time, especially in conditions of war, famine, etc. That is why those 'critics' who point to the defects of our apparatus out of mockery or malice may be calmly answered that they do not in the least understand the conditions of the revolution today. It is altogether impossible in five years to reorganise the apparatus adequately, especially in the conditions in which our revolution took place. It is enough that in five years we have created a new type of state in which the workers are leading the peasants against the bourgeoisie; and in a hostile international environment this in itself is a gigantic achievement. But knowledge of this must on no account blind us to the fact that, in effect, we took over the old state apparatus from the tsar and the bourgeoisie and that now, with the onset of peace and the satisfaction of the minimum requirements against famine, all our work must be directed towards improving the administration.

I think that a few dozen workers, being members of the CC, can deal better than anybody else with checking, improving and remodelling our apparatus. The Workers' and Peasants' Inspection on whom this function devolved at the beginning proved unable to cope with it and can be used only as an 'appendage' or, on certain conditions, as an assistant to these members of the CC. In my opinion, the workers admitted to the Central Committee should come preferably not from among those who have had long service in Soviet bodies (in this part of my letter the term workers everywhere includes peasants), because those workers have already acquired the very traditions and the very prejudices which it is desirable to combat.

The working-class members of the CC must be mainly workers of a lower stratum than those promoted in the last five years to work in Soviet bodies; they must be people closer to being rank-and-file workers and peasants, who, however, do not fall into the category of direct or indirect exploiters. I think that by attending all sittings of the CC and all sittings of the Political Bureau, and by reading all the documents of the CC, such workers can form a staff of devoted supporters of the Soviet system, able, first, to give stability to the CC itself, and second, to work effectively on the renewal and improvement of the state apparatus.

Lenin

30 December 1922

On the Question of Nationalities or 'Autonomisation'

I suppose I have been very guilty *vis-à-vis* the workers of Russia for not having intervened energetically and decisively enough in the notorious question of autonomisation, which, it appears, is officially called the question of the union of Soviet socialist republics.

When this question arose last summer, I was ill; and then in autumn I relied too much on my recovery and on the October and December plenary meetings giving me an opportunity of intervening in this question. However, I did not manage to attend the October plenary meeting (when this question came up) or the one in December, and so the question passed me by almost completely.

I have only had time for a talk with Comrade Dzerzhinsky, who came from the Caucasus and told me how this matter stood in Georgia. I have also managed to exchange a few words with Comrade Zinoviev and express my apprehension on this matter. From what I was told by Comrade Dzerzhinsky, who was at the Georgian incident, I could only draw the gravest conclusions. If matters had come to such a pass that Ordzhonikidze could go to the extreme of applying physical violence, as Comrade Dzerzhinsky informed me, we can imagine what a mess we have got ourselves into. Obviously the whole business of 'autonomisation' was radically wrong and ill timed.

It is said that a united apparatus was needed. Where did that assurance come from? Did it not come from that same Russian apparatus which, as I pointed out in one of the preceding sections of my diary, we took over from tsarism and slightly anointed with Soviet oil?

There is no doubt that that measure should have been delayed somewhat until we could say that we vouched for our apparatus as our own. But now, we must, in all conscience, admit the contrary; the apparatus we call ours is, in fact, still quite alien to us; it is a bourgeois and tsarist hotch-potch and there has been no possibility of getting rid of it in the course of the past five years without the help of other countries and because we have been 'busy' most of the time with military engagements and the fight against famine.

It is quite natural that in such circumstances the 'freedom to secede from the union' by which we justify ourselves will be a mere scrap of paper, unable to defend the non-Russians from the onslaught of that really Russian man, the Great-Russian chauvinist, in substance a rascal and a tyrant, such as the typical Russian bureaucrat is. There is no doubt that the minute percentage of Soviet and sovietised workers will drown in that tide of chauvinistic Great-Russian riffraff like a fly in milk.

It is said in defence of this measure that the People's Commissariats directly concerned with national psychology and national education were set up as separate bodies. But there the question arises: can these People's Commissariats be made quite independent? And secondly: were we careful enough to take measures to provide the non-Russians with a real safeguard against the truly Russian bully? I do not think we took such measures although we could and should have done so.

I think that Stalin's haste and his infatuation with pure administration, together with his spite against the notorious 'socialist-nationalism', played a fatal role here. In politics spite generally plays the basest of roles.

I also fear that Comrade Dzerzhinsky, who went to the Caucasus to investigate the 'crime' of those 'socialist-nationalists', distinguished himself there by his truly Russian frame of mind (it is common knowledge that people of other nationalities who have become Russified overdo this Russian frame of mind) and that the impartiality of his whole commission was typified well enough by Ordzhonikidze's 'physical violence'. I think that no provocation or even insult can justify such Russian physical violence and that Comrade Dzerzhinsky was inexcusably guilty in adopting a light-hearted attitude towards it.

For all the citizens in the Caucasus Ordzhonikidze was the authority. Ordzhonikidze had no right to display that irritability to which he and Dzerzhinsky referred. On the contrary, Ordzhonikidze should have behaved with a restraint which cannot be demanded of any ordinary citizen, still less of a man accused of a 'political' crime. And, to tell the truth, those socialist–nationalists were citizens who were accused of a political crime, and the terms of the accusation were such that it could not be described otherwise.

Here we have an important question of principle: how is internationalism to be understood?

Lenin

Appendix I

artel	Russian artisans' or farm co-operative
bednyak	Poor peasant, owning some land but usually not enough to support a family
billion	Thousand million
Bolsheviks	The 'majority' group of the Russian Social Democratic Labour Party
CC	Central Committee of the Communist Party
CEC	Central Executive Committee of the Soviet
Cheka	The Extraordinary Commission to Fight Counter-Revolution, Sabotage and Speculation
desyatina	Measure of land, 2·7 acres or 1·09 hectares
Duma	The Russian Parliament during the period 1905–17
guberniya	Administrative province
Gubkom	*Guberniya* committee of the Communist Party
hectare	2·47 acres
kolkhoz	Collective Farm
kommuna	Commune. The most complete collective farm in which there was no private property; all land was worked collectively and its produce shared. Sometimes included collective eating and living
kulak	Rich peasant, employing labourers
Mensheviks	The 'minority' group of the Russian Social Democratic Labour Party
NEP	New Economic Policy
oblast	Administrative area
obshchestvo	Society or commune; also company as in joint-stock company
okrug	Administrative area, subdivided into *oblasts* and further into *raions*
pomeshchik	Landowner
pud	36·1 lb. or 16·38 kilograms

raion	Administrative area
Revvoensovet	Revolutionary Military Council
RKP(B)	Russian Communist Party (Bolsheviks)
RSDRP	Russian Social Democratic Labour Party. Founded in 1898, it split into Bolshevik and Menshevik factions in 1903
	Middle or 'average' peasant. Self-sufficient and did not hire labour
soviet	Council
Sovnarkom	The Council of People's Commissars
SRs	Socialist Revolutionaries. Peasant Party. Founded in 1900. It split in 1917 into right and left factions. The left SRs supported the Bolsheviks until March 1918
subbotnik	Working for a day in the interests of society without pay
toz	The loosest form of collective farm. Each peasant retained his animals, implements, etc. but the land was worked in common
ty	The familiar form of address; second person singular; thou
uezd	Administrative area, comparable to the *okrug*
verst	0·7 mile
volost	Administrative area, comparable to the *raion*
VSNKh	The All-Russian Council of the National Economy
zemstvo	Pre-revolutionary *uezd* and *guberniya* assembly

Appendix II

ANTONOV-OVSEENKO, Vladimir Aleksandrovich (1884–1938). Joined the RSDRP in 1902. He was active in the 1905 revolution and was arrested. During the First World War he was founder of and collaborator in the periodicals *Golos* and *Nashe Slovo*. On his return to Russia he joined the Bolsheviks and took part in the capture of the Winter Palace. Was C-in-C for a short period. Was C-in-C in the Ukraine from December 1918 to June 1919. Held government posts 1920–2.

BUBNOV, Andrei Sergeevich (1883–1940). A Bolshevik from 1903. A professional revolutionary. A member of the Petrograd Military Revolutionary Committee during the October Revolution and after it a member of the Collegium of the Commissariat of Transport. In 1918 he went to the Ukraine and became a member of the Ukrainian CC and of the Ukrainian government of January 1919.

BUKHARIN, Nikolai Ivanovich (1888–1938). Joined the Bolsheviks in 1906 and became a member of their Moscow Committee in 1908. Played active part in October Revolution and was editor of Moscow *Izvestiya*. Was editor of *Pravda* from December 1917 to 1929. A Left Communist at the time of the Brest negotiations and a co-editor of their journal, *Kommunist*.

CHERNOV, Viktor Mikhailovich (1876–1952). An SR leader and theorist. Took part in the Zimmerwald and Kienthal conferences. Became Minister of Agriculture in the Provisional Government and in January 1918, Chairman of the Constituent Assembly. Emigrated in 1921.

CHICHERIN, Georgy Vasilevich (1872–1936). Employed in the Ministry of Foreign Affairs from 1896 onwards. Returned to Russia in January 1918 and was soon appointed deputy People's Commissar for Foreign Affairs. Joined the Bolshevik party. Served as People's Commissar for Foreign Affairs from 30 May 1918 to 1930.

DYBENKO, Pavel Efimovich (1889–1938). Joined Bolsheviks in 1912. A naval rating in the Baltic Fleet from 1911. Elected head of the CC of the Baltic Fleet after the February Revolution. Played a prominent role in the October Revolution and was a member of the military collegium of the first *Sovnarkom* in November 1917. During the Civil War held various commands, including that of the first Ukrainian army in January 1919.

DZERZHINSKY, Feliks Edmundovich (1877–1926). Elected to the Party CC at its VI Congress. Head of Cheka from its foundation on 20 December 1917 until his death (except for a short time in August 1918). Chairman first of the Cheka, then of OGPU. From 1921 People's Commissar for Transport.

FRUMKIN, Moisei Ilich (1878–1938). Joined RSDRP in 1898. In 1906 a member of Bolshevik Military Organisation in Petrograd. After the February Revolution he was a member of the Regional Party Committee and the Executive Committee in Krasnoyarsk and later in Omsk. Member of Collegium of the People's Commissariat of Food, 1918–22.

FRUNZE, Mikhail Vasilevich (1885–1925). A Bolshevik from 1904. Took part in the October Revolution in Moscow. In 1918 he was appointed Military Commissar of the Yaroslavl Military District and in December 1918 given command of the Fourth Army. In April 1919 he became commander of the Southern Army Group of the Eastern Front, in July 1919 Commander of the Eastern Front and in September 1920 of the Southern Front. At the end of 1920 he became C-in-C of the newly created Southern Front against Wrangel and a member of the Ukrainian CC. In 1921–2 on a mission to Turkey.

GUSEV (DRABKIN), Sergei Ivanovich (Yakov Davydovich) (1874–1933). Became a Bolshevik in 1903. A professional revolutionary. He was secretary of the Petrograd Military Revolutionary Committee. During the Civil War he was a member of the Revolutionary Military Council of, successively, the Fifth Army, the Second Army, the Eastern Front, the Southeastern Front and the Southern Front. Appointed head of the Army Political Administration in the spring of 1921.

IOFFE, Adolf Abramovich (1883–1927). Joined the Bolshevik Party in 1917. He served on the Brest–Litovsk peace delegation and opposed signing the peace treaty. Appointed ambassador to Berlin on 6 April 1918.

KALININ, Mikhail Ivanovich (1875–1946). A worker. Member of the SD party from 1898. Active in both revolutions in 1917. After the October Revolution was head of the City of Petrograd. In March 1919 succeeded Sverdlov as Chairman of the CEC. Travelled widely in a propaganda train during the Civil War.

KAMENEV (ROZENFELD), Lev Borisovich (1883–1936). Joined the RSDRP in 1901. Expelled from Moscow University in 1902 and went abroad. A Bolshevik from 1903. In 1914 editor of *Pravda*. In 1915 exiled to Siberia. In 1917 returned to Petrograd and resumed editorship of *Pravda*. Criticised Lenin's April Theses and was opposed to the seizure of power in October 1917. Headed the Moscow Party Committee 1918–26.

KERENSKY, Aleksandr Fedorovich (1881–1971). Lawyer. An SR member of the Duma from 1912. Became Minister of Justice in first Provisional Government. Later Prime Minister. After the Kornilov revolt he took over as C-in-C as well.

KOLCHAK, Aleksandr Vasilevich (1873–1920). At Naval Academy 1888–94. Afterwards served in the Baltic and Pacific Fleets. Taken prisoner during the Russo–Japanese war. Served in the Baltic Fleet during the First World War. Appointed Commander of the Black Sea Fleet in 1916 with the rank of Rear Admiral. Resigned his command in July 1917. Appointed Minister of Defence by Ufa Directorate. Staged military *coup* in November 1918 and assumed title of Supreme Ruler. Detained by Czechs in Irkutsk and handed over to the local Revolutionary Committee which tried him and had him shot.

KRASIN, Leonid Borisovich (1870–1926). A Marxist since the end of the 1880s. On SD work since the 1890s. A first class engineer, he worked as such during emigration from 1908 to 1917. After the October Revolution he was engaged on diplomatic work. In August 1918 he became head of a commission providing the Red Army with supplies. In November 1918 he became People's Commissar of Trade and Industry. Later he was People's Commissar for Transport. From 1919 he was mainly engaged in diplomatic work. Played important part in arranging Anglo–Soviet trade agreement in 1921.

KRESTINSKY, Nikolai Nikolaevich (1883–1938). Joined RSDRP in 1903. After the October Revolution worked on the Petrograd Commune. He was People's Commissar for Finance from August 1918 to 1921 as well as being a CC secretary, 1919–21. Lost secretaryship at X Party Congress. From October 1921 Soviet diplomatic representative in Berlin.

KRYLENKO, Nikolai Vasilevich (1885–1940). Joined the RSDRP in 1904. Together with Antonov-Ovseenko and P. E. Dybenko he was made a member of the Collegium for Military and Naval Affairs of the *Sovnarkom* on 8 November. Made C-in-C on 22 November when Dukhonin refused to negotiate an armistice. Relieved of his post when it was abolished on 13 March 1918. Appointed Public Prosecutor on 3 April 1918.

LENIN (ULYANOV), Vladimir Ilich (1870–1924). Leader of Bolsheviks at II Congress in 1903. Leader and dominant influence in Bolshevik party until his death. After October Revolution appointed Chairman of Council of People's Commissars. (*Sovnarkom.*)

MOLOTOV (SKRYABIN), Vyacheslav Mikhailovich (1890–   ). Worked for Bolshevik organisations and newspapers before 1914. Active in the October Revolution. Held several government and Party posts before being elected Party Secretary at the X Congress in 1921.

ORDZHONIKIDZE, Grigory Konstantinovich (1886–1937). Joined the RSDRP in 1903. Took part in the October Revolution. In January 1918 made plenipotentiary for the Ukraine. In April sent to the Caucasus as an extraordinary Commissar with the Southern Front. After the reverse there he worked on other fronts. From 1921 a member of the Party CC, posted to the Caucasus.

OSINSKY (OBOLENSKY), Valerian Valerianovich (1887–1938). A Bolshevik from 1907. After the February Revolution member of the editorial board of the Moscow *Sotsial-Demokrat*. During the October Revolution member of the Military Revolutionary Committee in Kharkov. Then Director of the State Bank in Moscow Chairman of VSNKh until February 1918. At that time a Left

Communist. Chairman of the Executive Committee of the Tula Region, 1919–20. In 1920 worked in the People's Commissariat of Food. In People's Commissariat of Agriculture, 1921–3.

PETLYURA, Simon Vasilevich (1877–1926). A right-wing SD and active as such before the revolution. In June 1917 he became Secretary General for Military Affairs in the Rada Government and was at that time a member of the Directorate. He acquired notoriety for the pogroms carried out by his troops. In the summer of 1919 he captured Kiev. When he failed to come to an understanding with Denikin he allied himself with Poland and took part in the Polish–Soviet war of 1920.

PODVOISKY, Nikolai Ilich (1880–1948). Joined the RSDRP in 1901. Served in the Petrograd Military Organisation in 1917. During the October Revolution he was Chairman of the Petrograd Military Revolutionary Committee. He was the first People's Commissar for Military Affairs. Replaced by Trotsky on 13 March 1918. In 1919 he was People's Commissar for Military Affairs of the Ukraine.

RADEK, Karl Bengardovich (1885–1939). Took part in the Zimmerwald and Kienthal Conferences. After the October Revolution moved to Petrograd. Belonged to Bolshevik left wing. Appointed head of the Central European Department of the People's Commissariat of Foreign Affairs in April 1918. Went to Germany in November 1918. Arrested there in February 1919. Released in December 1919 and returned to Russia and worked in Comintern.

RAKOVSKY, Christian Georgevich (1873–1941). After the October Revolution he served in the People's Commissariat of Foreign Affairs. Headed commission on Russo–Rumanian affairs, January–April 1918. Leader of Soviet peace delegation in Kiev, May–September 1918. Head of Ukrainian Soviet government in 1919.

RYKOV, Aleksei Ivanovich (1881–1938). Joined the RSDRP in 1900. Elected to the Bolshevik CC at the III Party Congress. After October Revolution appointed first People's Commissar for Internal Affairs but left his post in November together with Milyutin and others. Chairman of VSNKh in February 1918. Replaced Lenin as Chairman of *Sovnarkom* in 1921 and after Lenin's death appointed to succeed him permanently in this post.

SEREBRYAKOV, Leonid Petrovich (1888 or 1890–1937). A worker. After the October Revolution was a member of the Presidium of the Moscow Soviet and later of the Presidium of the CEC. In military work in 1919–20. Appointed deputy Commissar for Transport in 1922.

SHLAPNIKOV, Aleksandr Gavrilovich (1884–1943). An industrial worker. He was active in working class revolutionary circles from 1900 onwards before joining the RSDRP in 1903. He took part in the 1905 revolution and was arrested. Between 1908 and 1914 he was in emigration abroad. In April 1917 he became Chairman of the Metal Workers' Trade Union, and after the October Revolution was appointed the first People's Commissar of Labour. He served in the army during the Civil War. From 1919 to 1922 he was chairman of the Metal Workers' Trade Union. In 1919–21 he was leader of the 'Workers' Opposition' and afterwards was often under fire for his oppositional views.

SKLYANSKY, Efraim Markovich (1892–1925). Doctor. Joined RSDRP in 1913. After the October Revolution he became chairman of the Army committee of the Fifth Army in Dvinsk. Appointed Supreme Commissar at GHQ on 25 November, two days after being appointed deputy People's Commissar for Military Affairs. Elected to the Constituent Assembly on 28 November as a delegate for the Northern Front. Throughout the Civil War he was Trotsky's most trusted supporter and deputy.

SOKOLNIKOV, Grigory Yakovlevich (1888–1939). Lawyer and economist. Became a Bolshevik in 1905 when he took part in the Moscow uprising. Member of the Moscow Party Committee in April 1917. After the October revolution he organised the nationalisation of the banks. One of the signatories of the Brest treaty in March 1918. Between 1918 and 1920 he served on the Revolutionary Military Councils of, successively, the Second, Ninth, Thirteenth and Eighth Armies. From August 1920 he was in charge of the Turkestan committee of the CEC and organised the Bolshevik takeover in Bukhara. In 1921 Deputy People's Commissar of Finance.

SPIRIDONOVA, Maria Aleksandrovna (1889–1941). Member of the SR party. In 1906 assassinated the Vice Governor of Tambov in retaliation for his persecution of the peasants. Sent to Siberia to do forced labour; remained until February Revolution. Became a left SR and a member of their CC. Disagreed with the Bolsheviks over the Brest Peace Treaty and helped to organise the left SR uprising in July 1918. Arrested and sent to sanatorium.

STALIN (DZHUGASHVILI), Iosef Vissarionovich (1879–1953). Joined the RSDRP in 1898. Returned to Petrograd in March 1917. Played active role in October Revolution. People's Commissar for Nationalities' Affairs, November 1917 to July 1923. Head of Commissariat of Workers' and Peasants' Inspection, February 1920 to April 1922.

SVERDLOV, Yakov Mikhailovich (1885–1919). Became a Bolshevik in 1903. Member of the Bolshevik CC since 1913. Played leading role in the October Revolution and became Chairman of the Central Executive Committee of the Soviets and was one of the most able Bolshevik administrators.

TOMSKY, Mikhail Pavlovich (1880–1936 or 1937). Joined the RSDRP in 1904. Member of the Petrograd Executive Committee after the February Revolution. Chairman of the Central Council of Trade Unions, 1919–28.

TROTSKY (BRONSTEIN), Lev Davydovich (1879–1940). Arrested 1898 and exiled to Siberia in 1901 for four years. Escaped and arrived in London in 1902. Sided with Mensheviks at II Congress in 1903. Played leading role in St Petersburg Soviet in 1905. Arrested and deported to Siberia for life in 1906. Escaped *en route*. Returned to Petrograd in May 1917 and led a group called the *Mezhraiontsy*. Joined the Bolsheviks in July 1917. Chairman of the Petrograd Soviet and of its Military Revolutionary Committee in September 1917. Played important role in October Revolution. People's Commissar for Foreign Affairs, November 1917–February 1918. Founder of the Red Army. People's Commissar for Military Affairs, February 1918–December 1922.

TSYURUPA, Aleksandr Dmitrevich (1870–1928). Joined RSDRP in 1898. During the October Revolution was a member of the Military Revolutionary Committee in Ufa. Appointed deputy People's Commissar for Food on 13 December 1917. Later became Commissar and held post until 1921.

TUKHACHEVSKY, Mikhail Nikolaevich (1893–1937). Officer in 1914 and taken prisoner in 1915. Escaped and returned in October 1917 and elected a company commander. Joined the Bolshevik Party in August 1918 and became one of the commissars of the Moscow Military District. Worked in the Military Department of the CEC until appointed to command the First Army. In 1921 he organised and directed military operations against the Kronstadt mutineers.

VACETIS, Ioakim Ioakimovich (1873–1938). Colonel in First World War, went over to Red Army. He suppressed the SR revolt in Moscow on 6 and 7 July 1918. On 10 July was appointed commander of the Eastern Front and Commander of the Fifth Army. C-in-C of the Red Army from 4 September 1918 to 8 July 1919.

ZINOVIEV (RADOMYSLSKY), Grigory Evseevich (1883–1936). Joined the RSDRP in 1901, a Bolshevik from 1903. Returned to Russia with Lenin. Opposed him on April Theses at first; also opposed to taking power in October at first as well as opposing the Brest–Litovsk peace. Appointed Chairman of the Northern Commune when government moved to Moscow. Chairman of the Comintern from its foundation until 1926.

Index